P9-BII-763

Cremation

in America

Cremation

in America

Fred Rosen

 Prometheus Books

59 John Glenn Drive
Amherst, New York 14228-2197

Published 2004 by Prometheus Books

Inquiries should be addressed to
Prometheus Books
59 John Glenn Drive
Amherst, New York 14228-2197
VOICE: 716-691-0133, ext. 207
FAX: 716-564-2711
WWW.PROMETHEUSBOOKS.COM

08 07 06 05 04   5 4 3 2 1

Library of Congress Cataloging-in-Publication Data

Rosen, Fred.
     Cremation in America / By Fred Rosen.
         p. cm.
     Includes bibliographical references.
     ISBN 1-59102-136-7
     1. Cremation—United States—History. 2. Undertaking and undertaking—
United States—History. 3. United States—Social life and customs. I. Title.

GT3331.U6R67 2004
363.7'5'0973—dc22

2003023764

Printed in the United States on acid-free paper

For my cousin Amy
who found peace in the retort

"*I wish to be cremated. One tenth of my ashes shall be given to my agent, as written in our contract.*"

Groucho Marx

Acknowledgments

My editor, Linda Regan, has been the most patient editor possible. I thank her for her kindness and support and all the pros at Prometheus Books.

Lori Perkins said to me, "It's writing about history." She knew I'd snap at that bait. I thank her for letting me use "Mr. Peabody's Way Back Machine" once again.

Jim Tipton, "Head Honcho" at findagrave.com provided database support for the appendixes, which I really appreciate; Jim DeFelice, who thought it a good idea; Carolyn Hayek, former executive director of Seattle's People's Memorial Association; Dean Vanden-Biesen at LifeGem; and my family for their love and support always.

Contents

Introduction

A popular history of cremation in the United States has never been written. There are quite a few good academic texts about cremation (see the endnotes section of this book). But as far as looking at the practice of cremation from a popular point of view; that is, how it fits into the culture of the moment, nothing has been written.

By 2010, 40 percent of the people who die in this country will be cremated. That's millions of people who are now *alive* who upon death wish their bodies cremated into ashes. Why cremation rather than earth burial? Where did the whole idea of burning a body upon death come from anyway? How is it done? Why was it illegal in the United States until the 1870s? How much does it cost? The answers to these questions form the heart of this book. Some names have been changed to protect the privacy of the individuals involved.

Along the way, from Stone Age times to the present, the adventure of getting cremation accepted into the culture is explored. There are heroes—the brilliant and courageous British surgeon Sir Henry Thompson and his American counterpart Dr. Julius LeMoyne. There is the illustrious Baron De Palm, the first person cremated in North America since preantiquity. And there are natural disasters, including the Galveston hurricane and the San Francisco earth-quake. There is the contemporary figure of the cremation move-ment, John F. Kennedy Jr.

I think it says a lot about a person how they wish their remains to be treated after death. That's why I've included appendixes of famous people who've been cremated. For those who would like to be cremated or are thinking about it, I've also included examples of forms for various types of cremations.

But any story of adventure needs a man fit for adventure. Like Robin Hood, Zorro, or . . .

Prologue
1971
James Bond's Cremation

*J*ames Bond was about to be cremated. I squirmed in my faux leather seat in the Oceana Theater on Brighton Beach Avenue in Brooklyn. As I looked up at the screen, my palms started getting wet. The whole idea of being stuck inside a coffin with fire licking up through every part of it, burning my flesh . . . hell, that's what it was, pure hell.

Now this was Sean Connery I'm talking about, the *real* James Bond. Not that walking caricature Roger Moore or Pierce Brosnan's bland persona. Connery always injected vulnerability into Bond. Whether he had a tarantula crawling over his body in *Dr. No* or Odd Job trying to slice his head off with that deadly hat in *Goldfinger,* Connery made you *believe* Bond could be killed.

To the withdrawn, pale, slight seventeen-year-old I was, Connery *was* James Bond. When Bond found himself in that crematory chamber in *Diamonds Are Forever,* it struck a primal chord. I knew that if Bond didn't find a way to get out fast, he was burnt toast. Well, of course he did get out; I wasn't *that* naive. But as I walked out of the movie theater into the bright sunshine, I couldn't help shivering every time I thought of that crematory chamber.

Not once did I think that such a chamber was designed for *dead* people. I walked past the pushcarts and under the elevated train tracks over which the "D" and "QB" trains rumbled. Crossing Coney Island Avenue, I passed Mrs. Stahl's Knishes. On the other side was Brighton Beach Baths, the last of the great Coney Island bathhouses.

The bathhouses were the country clubs of the lower-middle-class Jews who had settled in Brooklyn throughout the twentieth century. They lined the Coney Island boardwalk. Jewish families like mine went there to socialize with their friends and families. Inside the bathhouses were handball courts, steam baths—which the old-timers called *schvitzes*—and at Brighton Beach Baths, the greatest bathhouse of all, there was a huge outdoor pool. By the early 1970s, all the bathhouses had closed except for "the Baths," where my parents were still members.

It was just after a game of paddleball that my father told me the story. We were toweling off, and my father looked at me and reminded me that I looked a lot like my grandmother, whom I'd never met. She had died a month before I was born.

"Did I ever tell you the story about what happened when we went to bury your grandmother?"

"Nope."

My father nodded his head, his bald pate glistening from sweat under the hot summer sun.

"I helped dig her grave."

My grandmother Fanny died in February 1953. She was to be buried at Mount Hebron Cemetery on the Brooklyn-Queens border. The problem was there was nobody to dig the grave. My grandmother had had the misfortune to die when the grave-diggers were on strike.

The only thing I knew about grave-diggers related to a ballplayer named Richie Hebner. He was a third baseman who spent eighteen years in "the show," eight of those as Pittsburgh's third baseman from 1968 to 1976. Despite the fact that he had a respectable life-time batting average of .276, every time he came to bat, New York

Mets announcer Ralph Kiner insisted on identifying him as "the grave-digger." That was Hebner's off-season job—in those days, ballplayers didn't make enough money to last them a full year.

With Hebner's New York buddies on strike, bodies began piling up in the refrigerators of the city's funeral homes. This was a particularly acute problem for the Orthodox Jewish families of the city. Orthodox Jewish custom demands that the body be placed in the ground within twenty-four hours after death. And so, my father and my uncles Nat and Irving got into Nat's '51 Caddy and tooled out to the cemetery. In their trunk was an assortment of shovels.

When they got there, they spied the family plot, got out of the car, and started digging. Problem was it was *February*. The ground was frozen solid. So Nat went trudging back up to the equipment building since he was the biggest and strongest. He came back with a couple of pickaxes with which all three of them took turns. After a couple of hours, they had finally gotten the grave dug. Nat sat down on the side, thoroughly exhausted.

After my father finished telling me the story I said, "Dad, a few years after that Nat had a massive coronary."

My father nodded.

"Could he have injured his heart digging Grandma's grave?"

Was it really worth the risk of heart attack to obey that religious custom? Wouldn't it have made a helluvalot more sense to cremate her?

I remembered James Bond's cremation and started sweating.

Part One

Chapter One

February 2002

The Tri-State Crematory Scandal

On Sunday, February 17, 2002, the *New York Times* published its first story on the Tri-State Crematory scandal in Noble, Georgia. The *Times* said that a woman walking a poodle "stumbled over a skull," leading cops to discover "at least 120 rotting corpses in sheds and on the ground near the crematory."[1] It was a story about death and cremation, or, rather, the lack of cremation. How could I not pass it up? It was a chance for me and Bond to connect again. Besides, I doubted what the *Times* reported.

I've been investigating murder cases for the past decade, and I've yet to come across one where a dog walker suddenly has the bad fortune to discover "at least 120 rotting corpses." It usually takes lots of things to discover death en masse—search warrants, cadaver dogs, forensic criminalists—unless of course someone just happens to leave a human skull in the middle of the street.

I couldn't get the image of that woman walking the poodle out of my mind. It reminded me of the bumbling Aunt Clara character on the TV show *Bewitched* suddenly discovering a skull in the street and lapsing into Hamlet's soliloquy. But as I checked with sources, the story's details, sans the lady and the poodle, were confirmed. I couldn't help feeling for the families of those whose bodies had not been properly treated.

Some bodies lay out in the open, the sun bleaching their bones. Others among the 314 were stacked up like kindling in sheds, the flesh rotting off their bodies, right down to their toe tags.

They had been waiting, some of them, five years or more to be cremated. In November 2001, they were still waiting in the forest behind the crematorium when someone made an anonymous call to the Environmental Protection Agency (EPA) in Atlanta, Georgia.

"I really don't know why we got the call," Carl Terry told me. "I mean, we're the EPA. The call should have gone to the sheriff. We still can't figure it out."[2]

Terry is the press officer for EPA Region 4. In a private interview, he said that after they got the anonymous call reporting body parts behind the Tri-State Crematory in Noble, the EPA immediately notified Walker County sheriff Steve Wilson.[3]

Noble is a small, unincorporated town of fifteen hundred people that sits in the isolated northwestern corner of Georgia that borders Alabama and Tennessee. Tri-State Crematory had profited over its twenty-plus years of operation. Pulling in customers from the tristate region, the crematory was an annual multimillion-dollar business.

A weathered black sign that juts a bit over a sparse country road marks Tri-State Crematory. The sheriff's deputies followed the sign several hundred yards back on Center Point Road, past a Baptist church, a block more and then, before they got to Veeker Road, there it was. Confronting them was a thirty-six-square-acre property filled with densely wooded old-growth trees and a pond deep in the interior. The crematory was located down a driveway that went one square city block deep into the property.

The deputies knew that without a warrant they could go no farther than the crematory's entrance. They saw nothing out of the ordinary and, more importantly, smelled nothing strange. The latter would become an issue three months later, in February 2002, when the Tri-State Crematory scandal would dominate national headlines and people would ask, "Didn't *anyone* smell anything out of the ordinary?"

No, they didn't. And with good reason. Contrary to common belief, it takes only two weeks in hot weather and a month in the cold weather for bodies to decompose to the point that they stop smelling. Even if the crematory had just a few bodies in that active state of "decomp," the smell would have been no worse than that of a dead animal you might drive past. And so, the dead in Georgia waited to be discovered and given their due.

Out in California, the dead were faring no better. In Riverside, crematory and mortuary owner Michael Brown was arrested and indicted on charges that he sold human remains that he had been paid to cremate or bury. On February 12, 2002, Brown, forty-two, was booked on suspicion of 154 counts of embezzlement and mutilation of human remains and two counts of falsifying death certificates. Authorities alleged that Brown earned more than $400,000 from the sale of human remains and body parts bound for the crematory and the grave.[4]

The dead don't have the law on their side. Regulation of the death industry is shoddy and spotty, with crematories low on the list of priorities. It wasn't until 1998, for example, that Ohio passed a law requiring crematories to be licensed and inspected.

Connecticut has a law requiring yearly inspections of funeral homes. But as of 2001, the state hadn't done annual inspections since 1989, when its part-time inspector retired. On June 27, 2001, a New Haven police report begins, "At approximately 4:00 PM, investigators received information that there were two bodies stored in a garage area of the funeral home that appeared to be inappropriately prepared for burial/cremation and interment."[5] Those to be buried, like those to be cremated, had been treated with less than considerate care.

"As the result of the information provided, detectives went to the location to conduct an investigation. In the process of their investigation, police discovered a total of five bodies in the garage area which had not been interred in a timely fashion. It has not yet been determined how long the bodies were kept at the location. The remains have been sent to the State Medical Examiner's Office."[6]

The corpses were found stacked up in the Wade Funeral Home's garage in New Haven on June 26, 2001. State legislators' "surprise" at the revelation seemed disingenuous. They knew inspections were virtually nonexistent.[7]

In Virginia, the law doesn't even require that crematories be inspected. Farther north in Maryland, the state senate is only now reconsidering legislation that would subject crematories to regulations and inspections, this after legislation to accomplish what was killed in committee two years earlier. As for Colorado, all state regulation of the funeral industry was eliminated twenty years ago. That goes for burial and cremation as well.

These are not isolated cases. The multibillion-dollar funeral business is subject to little supervision, with laws varying inconsistently from state to state. Cremation in particular remains largely unregulated. As the EPA's Carl Terry told me, "We have no jurisdiction over the burning of bodies."[8] This despite the fact that cremation is going through a boom time.

According to the Cremation Association of North America (CANA), cremation is now used in 25 percent of deaths, up from 5 percent thirty years ago, for a net gain of 500 percent.[9] With the rising cost of interment, cremation's popularity continues its ascendancy. As for the clientele, they were generally looked upon as detritus by the living. In their grief, the living are not too inclined to closely inspect the details of their loved one's disposal. That makes the burial and crematory business easy pickings for scam artists.

Until 1990, Georgia didn't even license crematories. Anyone could own one. Even after the law was passed, crematoriums regularly operated without a license. But by 1994, the Georgia Board of Funeral Service had started to crack down on abuses, and high on their list was Tri-State. Tommy Ray Marsh, the owner of Tri-State Crematory, knew the state was closing in.

Two years earlier, in 1992, Rep. Mike Snow (D-GA) introduced a bill on the Georgia House floor that would have ensured that Tri-State, located in his legislative district, receive a pass and never be inspected. The bill died, but Snow got an amendment passed on the House floor that gave Tri-State's owners a two-year reprieve from getting licensed.[10] The feeling among members of Georgia's Funeral Services Board was that Marsh would get tired of the business and close up, because he was approaching retirement age.[11]

Marsh proved resilient, however. In 1997, he turned the business over to his son, Ray Brent Marsh, who allegedly stacked up the bodies, dumped them in the woods, and collected fees for cremations that never took place. On February 14, 2002, the EPA received its second anonymous call about Tri-State. This time, the agency dispatched its own investigators.

"The Federal Open Field Laws allowed our investigators to enter the sixteen-acre grounds of Tri-State and begin a search," explained the EPA's Carl Terry.[12]

When one of those investigators stumbled upon a bleached skull in the grass behind the crematory, the EPA knew things were amiss. By the time the case broke the next day, February 15, 2002, and became national news, "only" thirty-six bodies had been found. But over the next week, the body total mounted.

While the Georgia police investigated Marsh and looked for answers, I decided to take a closer look at what I had been so afraid of since *Diamonds Are Forever*. *What exactly happens when a person's body is cremated?* I wondered.

Among the country's crematories, it is hard to find one that actually admits that cremation is burning a human body until there's nothing left but ashes. Since we live in politically correct times, more often than not the description offered is that cremation is the "extreme dehydration" of the human body. Of course, that is correct too.

Since a human being is 70 percent water, if you boil out the water, you ain't gonna have a helluvalot left. But the words "dehydration" and "boiling" don't do justice to what's *really* happening. Here's how it actually works.

The body is placed in an enclosed, rigid container simply for the purpose of temporary storage. The container can be anything from a cardboard box made especially for this purpose up to and including beautifully handcrafted mahogany, maple, and oak caskets. The only requirement is that the material the container is made out of must be easily combustible because it is going to be subjected to 1800 Fahrenheit degrees of heat.

Unfortunately, dead people are increasingly going out with a loud "bang" that threatens to damage the equipment and crematory workers. Pacemakers and other medical devices are supposed to be removed from the body prior to cremation because batteries explode under the intense heat. If the next of kin fails to inform the crematory operator of the existence of such devices, the danger of an explosion is very real. In Sweden, for example, a growing number of explosions have occurred during cremation due to this problem.

Then there's the problem of well-meaning relatives. At an open casket service prior to cremation, friends and family sometimes drop mementos into the coffin, including such disparate items as bottles of alcohol, fireworks, and ammunition cartridges. These, too, will explode when subjected to high temperature, thus damaging the crematorium equipment, not to mention staff members.[13] Bodies, therefore, have to be stripped of any special mementos, even jewelry, because most if not all of it will be consumed by the heat.

The container holding the body is placed in the cremation chamber, known in the trade as the retort. While laws vary from state to state, it is common for only one casket or container to be cremated at a time. The crematory operator raises the dial to approximately 1600 to 1800 degrees. Soon, flames fill the retort.

Over the next two to two-and-a-half hours, the container will quickly burn up, and then the heat and flames will go to work on the body. As it begins burning down, the unmistakable stench of burning flesh—a smell so primal that all humans, regardless of their backgrounds, recognize it immediately—fills the air.

As the flesh burns, all of the liquid in the body evaporates. All skin, hair, muscle, tissue, nails eventually vaporize. In the end, after two-and-a-half hours of constant flame and heat, the only thing left is ash and small bone fragments, collectively referred to as cremated remains.

The bone fragments and body metal—bridgework, artificial joints, etc.—are swept into the back of the cremation chamber into a cooling pan made out of stainless steel. Through visual inspection and then the use of powerful magnets, the crematory operator separates metal from bone. The remaining bone fragments are then put into a grinder, where they are processed into coarse-grain sand that is whitish/light grainy gray in color.

Once composing the physical essence of a human being, these particles are now placed in a receptacle provided by the crematorium or in an urn purchased by relatives. The remains of an average-sized adult usually weigh between four and six pounds. Throughout the cremation process, a carefully controlled labeling system ensures correct identification.

But unlike burial, where the body can actually be retrieved years later and, in the case of an embalmed body, offer some clues to how death occurred, cremation is an obviously irreversible process. The process itself eliminates any ability to determine the exact cause of death. Therefore, many states require that each cremation be authorized by a coroner or medical examiner. Some states even have specific minimum time limits that must elapse before cremation may take place.

Because of the waiting period, the body needs to be refrigerated or embalmed to retard what cops call decomp, the actual decomposition of body tissue that naturally occurs after death and that, also in the first two weeks of the process, produces the other kind of primal stench that humans can't tolerate.

Because of my religion, cremation would not be an option for disposal of my body. I was raised as a Conservative Jew. Like the Orthodox Jews, Conservatives believe that the body must be returned to the ground from whence it came within twenty-four hours of death. Cremation is banned. This belief stems from the first of the five books of Moses that make up the Old Testament: Gen. 3:19: "For dust you are and to dust you shall return."

For Jews, this is the most ancient proscription against cremation. The natural decomposition of the body, sans embalming fluid, is of utmost importance in Jewish law. Biblical scholars and rabbis interpret Gen. 3:19 to mean that the casket must not be made of a material that slows down the body's natural return to the elements. Metal caskets are therefore not permitted. Wood is the only material allowed; several holes are opened at the bottom to hasten the body's return to the earth.

The Orthodox believe that when a person dies, the soul, or *neshama*, hovers around the body. The soul is the essence of the person, the thing that made this individual totally unique from every other that ever lived. The body was its vessel. But the *neshama* refuses to leave until the body is buried.

In effect, the totality of the person who died continues to exist for a while in the vicinity of the body. A Jewish funeral is therefore concerned with the feelings of the deceased as well as the feelings of the mourners. How the body is treated and how people behave around the body must reflect how they would act around the person if he or she were still alive.

At an Orthodox Jewish burial, the body is supposed to be kept company by a *shomer*, or guard, before being prepared for burial. "The *neshama* . . . waits for the body's burial and its ascent to the Eternal World."[14] The body has to leave the world in exactly the same way it entered. As a newborn is cleaned and washed, so is the body.

Just as in biblical times, members of the Jewish Burial Society, the Chevra Kadisha, clean and dress the body in accordance with Jewish law and custom. Prayers asking for the forgiveness of the deceased and the soul's eternal peace are offered. During this phase of the burial process called *Tahara*, embalming, cosmetizing, or any other attempts to create a lifelike appearance through artificial means are contrary to strict Jewish law.

Since the *neshama* is about to face Judgment Day, clothes are negligible, good deeds everything. An Orthodox Jew should be dressed in a simple white linen shroud. The shrouds have no pockets to accentuate the fact that no worldly belongings accompany the soul. Prior to the introduction of the rabbinate after the time of Jesus, the Jewish people were led by high priests. The shrouds worn by the Jewish dead even today are modeled after the white uniform that was worn by the high priest in the Holy Temple on Yom Kippur. The high priest would go into the Temple, later destroyed by the Romans, and plead with God to inscribe the names of all the Jewish people in God's Book of Life. These shrouds are therefore especially appropriate because each and every *neshama* is supposed to ask for the needs of his or her family to be taken care of by God on the final judgment day.

The *neshama*'s return to heaven—where all souls come from—is dependent upon the body's return to the ground. This is what is meant by Eccles. 12:7: "The dust returns to the earth. . . . And the spirit returns to God who gave it." With family members and friends helping to fill the grave, the body is deposited in the ground in its simple casket to undergo natural decomposition.

When I die, it seems my choices are to be buried in a box and have the worms get at me or to violate my religion's beliefs and combust. Why, I wondered, is my choice so dependent on things that happened in the past? Why are those beliefs and customs so strong that they reached out across centuries to affect my decision today?

Was the answer simply "Tradition," as Tevye sings? As always, I had to examine the past for answers.

Chapter Two

Preantiquity through the Eleventh Century

From the cartoon character Fred Flintstone in his leopard-skin suit and tie to Raquel Welch in her formfitting sarong in the movie *One Million Years B.C.*, popular culture has long defined the Stone Age as something that it is not. In fact, Raquel's real-life counterpart, a female living during one million years BCE, would have looked more like an ape than a screen goddess because modern humans had not yet evolved. As late as 35,000 BCE, Neanderthals existed in Europe and the Near East.

Most archaeologists define the Stone Age as beginning around 35,000 BCE and divide it into three distinct periods: the Old Stone Age or Paleolithic period, 35,000 to 10,000 BCE; the Middle Stone Age or Mesolithic period, from 10,000 to 6000 BCE; and the New Stone Age or Neolithic period, from 6000 to 3000 BCE. During these 32,000 years of history, humans evolved from primitive into sophisticated beings. Nowhere was this reflected more clearly than in their burial habits.

Stone Age man gradually developed a belief in life after death, evidenced by the fact that the dead were buried with provisions for the afterlife. For example, a body found in a shallow grave in a cave in South Wales, buried there twenty thousand years ago during the Old Stone Age, was surrounded by a rich assemblage of grave goods, including a shell necklace, ivory beads, and bracelets.

The Middle Stone Age cemetery discovered at Bøgebakken in Denmark contains seventeen graves of hunters and their families dating from 6,500 years ago. Grave number ten contains the body of a man, five feet, six inches tall, suffering from the first stages of arthritis. He lies on two red deer antlers and has two flint blades near the stomach. Red ochre is scattered around his head. Archaeologists believe the relics reflect "a sense of communion with the rest of the natural world which was undoubtedly replaced by something else entirely when Neolithic peoples started building massive barrow cemeteries and filling graves with finely worked goods."[1]

And yet, even during this period when graves were dug by hand with stone implements, some of our ancestors dared to think there might be an easier way. It would take the indigenous peoples of what is now Canada, during the early days of the New Stone Age, to blaze the way into the future.

In 3900 BCE, there was no United States, no Canada. Throughout the North American continent, indigenous peoples, who would later be described as Indians and currently as Native Americans, roamed the land.

In the far north and west of what would today be called the Canadian province of Manitoba, there lived a group of bison hunters. They followed game across the prairie into the newly formed grasslands, beside a beautiful lake that would later be named Caribou.

Little is known about the social organization of the Native Americans in what today is called the Caribou Lake Complex. They were probably organized into small groups. Modern excavations indicate that they settled down, that is, inhabited the area during all four seasons. Thus they could take advantage of the abundant natural resources while moving from site to site as the seasons changed.

The Caribou Lake Complex was inhabited by these indigenous peoples who lived there for centuries. They raised their families and cremated them when they died. They left behind a cremation pit, fragments of skeletons, and the remains of tooth enamel that, using carbon-14 dating methods, are from around 3900 BCE.[2]

At the same time, across the ocean, the practice of cremation began to spread across northern Europe. Decorative pottery urns circa 3900 BCE found in western Russia contain the ashes and bone fragments of human beings. By the Bronze Age, an era that stretched from 2500 to 1000 BCE, the practice of cremation appears to have moved west to the British Isles and what is now Spain and Portugal.[3]

Back then, the cremation process involved burning the body over a funeral pyre. Rarely was enough heat achieved to complete the process, so large bones usually had to be buried. Cremation cemeteries sprang up in Hungary and northern Italy, where the bones and ashes were interred.

Cremation became the preferred method of body disposal in the ancient world of what is now the Middle East, except in Judea, where bodies were buried in sepulchers, and in Egypt, where bodies were embalmed.

Even in death, the Egyptian belief in polytheism determined the way the body was handled. Like many ancient peoples, the Egyptians had gods for just about everything, including Hathor, the god of fertility; Thoth, the god for scribes; Hapy, god of the Nile; Bes, god of home and hearth; and Re, the king of gods. After death, Egyptians were protected by Anubis, god of mummies. Egyptians had a strong belief in the afterlife, but life after death was not possible unless the body did not decay. That's why Egyptians preserved their bodies as mummies.

The first step in preserving a dead body was removing the brain and most of the internal organs. While the brain held no intrinsic value, the other organs did. They were saved in canopic jars, special pots constructed to contain particular organs. Each jar was carved to look like an animal that Egyptians believed corresponded to a particular organ. For instance, the stomach was preserved in a jar that looked like a jackal, the lungs in a jar that represented a baboon, and intestines in a jar with a falcon's image. The liver was kept in a jar with a human face.

With the organs preserved it was time to get to the body. It was packed with a drying salt to stop rotting of flesh. Then, after the salt was removed, the body was wrapped in long strips of linen. Amulets or magic charms were placed among the wrappings to protect the mummy in the afterlife. Among these were ankhs that represented the breath of life, the eye of hours for protection, and scarabs that represented rebirth. Once the mummy was completely wrapped, a beautiful mask was placed over its face. Finally, the mummy was placed in a case ready for entombment.

Clearly, for an Egyptian, cremation was absolutely blasphemous. But in Greece during this same era, cremation was accepted, and only suicides, unteethed children, and persons struck by lightning were denied the right to be burned.

Socrates, the great Greek philosopher, was born in 469 BCE and died seventy years later in 399 BCE, when he was forced to commit suicide by ingesting poison. In 1658, English philosopher and writer Sir Thomas Browne wrote in his discourse on urn burial titled *Hydriotaphia*, "Thus Socrates was content that his friends should bury his body, so they would not think they buried Socrates; and, regarding only his immortal part, was indifferent to be burnt or buried."[4]

Socrates was murdered. That he was murdered by the state made it no less of a crime. If his body were cremated, the evidence of his poisoning literally would have gone up in smoke, but because of his stature, stories would abound. However, Browne contends that because Socrates believed in an immortal soul, whatever happened to his dead body was meaningless.

Modern scholars generally agree that Jesus was born sometime between 6 BCE and 4 BCE near the end of the reign of Herod the Great and was crucified sometime between 31 and 33 CE. There was no trial and certainly no jury. The Romans didn't believe in juries. Even the idea of a trial would have been novel to them. Instead,

Jesus was taken before the Roman governor of Judea, Pontius Pilate, for a cursory hearing.

Pilate found that Jesus was a heretic who claimed to be the King of the Jews. In reality, of course, his teachings were threatening because they could incite rebellion—the last thing the Romans needed. So Pilate sentenced Jesus to die on the cross. What happened next doomed cremation as a burial practice for the next eighteen hundred years.

Since Jesus was a Jew, he was not cremated. Instead, Jesus' body was entombed, a huge stone rolled over the entrance to his final resting place. It was later said that it would take many strong men just to move the rock. The next day, religious leaders met with Pontius Pilate and told him that Jesus had predicted he would once again walk among the living three days after his death.

In response, Pilate ordered legionnaires to stand guard outside his tomb. No one was allowed in or out. The Roman guards purportedly stayed alert—falling asleep on watch meant instant death. On Sunday morning, three days after he died, Jesus' followers entered the tomb for the purpose of anointing his body. They discovered that the huge stone guarding the entrance had been moved. The Romans on guard had fled without explanation. Whatever had happened, one thing was certain—Jesus' body was gone. All that was left was his burial garment, which many Christians believe to be the Shroud of Turin.

Today, the question still lingers as it did with our ancestors of two centuries ago—what really happened? Was Jesus raised from the dead to walk once again among the living? Or, did Jesus' followers move the stone guarding his tomb, spirit the body away, and replace it with the legend of the Resurrection?

Whatever the answer, the Resurrection of Jesus is the cornerstone of Christianity. Had Jesus been cremated, there would have been no body to resurrect. God would have had to do it from ashes. While an all-powerful God should be able to resurrect from anything, followers likely found it more credible and visually appealing for Jesus to be resurrected from an intact body.

The resurrection of Jesus led to the doctrine of the Second

Coming, which the disciple Matthew explains in Matt. 24:36: "No one knows about that *day* or *hour*, not even the angels in heaven, nor the Son, but only the Father." Matthew goes on to state in 24:42–44, "Therefore keep watch, because you do not know on what day your Lord will come. But understand this: If the owner of the house had known at what time of night the thief was coming, he would have kept watch and would not have let his house be broken into. So you also must be ready, because the Son of Man will come at an hour when you do not expect him."

In 90 CE, barely sixty years after Jesus' mortal death, biblical scholars believe the Book of Revelation was written. The last book of the New Testament, it is its only apocalyptic text. Addressing "the scattered Christians of Asia Minor in their hour of affliction"—those who came to Jesus after his martyrdom—the text vividly details the way God will save his people from their suffering at the hands of Satan: "God shall wipe away all tears from their eyes; and there shall be no more death, neither sorrow, nor crying; neither shall there be any more pain; for the former things are passed away."[5]

The words are beautiful, the future dire. The Book of Revelation says that there will be wars, famine, epidemics of disease, and signs from heaven indicating that the world has come to apocalyptic crisis. The Antichrist will come, a political ruler that will establish control over the whole earth. His backup will be a religious ruler, the false prophet. Together, they will establish "a unified social, economic and religious system that dominates the world."[6] Opposing them are God's people, in particular, two prophets, referred to as the two witnesses. Appearing in Jerusalem, they speak against this evil power.

The last half of the Book of Revelation is primarily about the overthrow of the Antichrist and his evil regime. This involves plagues of cosmic proportion, including asteroids hitting the earth. At the end, Jesus Christ returns as a warrior on a white horse and sets up the kingdom of God.[7]

The Book of Revelation solidified the idea of the Resurrection in the emerging Christian imagination. The body was in some elemental way necessary for entry into the next world. The idea of earth burial caught on again. Cremation as a funeral practice became marginalized.

A little over two hundred years later, a man came along whose legacy once and for all obliterated the practice of cremation for the next fifteen centuries. His name was Flavius Valerius Constantinus, more commonly known as Constantine.

Constantine was born at Naissus between 271 and 273 in the province of Moesia Superior, in what is today Serbia and Montenegro.

His father was a military officer named Constantius, his mother Helena, a woman of nonroyal lineage. It is unclear whether Helena was Constantius's concubine or wife. Regardless, Constantius made his way up through the rank of tribune, provincial governor, and probably praetorian prefect.

On March 1, 293, Constantius attained the rank of Caesar in the emperor Diocletian's first tetrarchy. For political reasons, Constantius had to leave Helena to marry Theodora, the daughter of the emperor Maximian. When Diocletian and Maximian retired on May 1, 305, Constantius attained the rank of Augustus.

Constantine had served with distinction with Roman forces in the east. Joining his father in Britain, he assisted him in a campaign against the Picts, a barbarian horde who lived in what today is Scotland. Constantius died on July 25, 306, at Eburacum (York), his son by his side. By unanimous proclamation, the Roman legions heralded Constantine as Augustus, thus carrying his father's mantle.

Returning to the continent after settling matters in Britain, Constantine lived in the city of Augusta Treverorum (modern Trier, Germany) for the next six years. In 307, he married Maximian's other daughter, Fausta, forsaking his mistress Minervina, who had given him Crispus, his first son.

Meanwhile, intrigue was afoot. The Roman senate and the praetorian guard in Rome had allied themselves with Maxentius, son of Maximian. On October 28, 306, they proclaimed Maxentius emperor of Rome, initially with the lower rank of *princeps*, although later he claimed the rank of Augustus.

Maxentius and Constantine didn't trust each other. It didn't help matters that their relationship had been further strained by Maximian's schemes to gain power. The schism became a chasm when Maximian died in 310. Active warfare between the two rivals broke out in 312. The Battle of the Milvian Bridge in 312 would decide who ruled the western half of the Roman Empire. Unknowingly, the stakes for Constantine took on a larger meaning.

He believed that his very soul rested on the outcome.

Prior to the battle, Constantine had appointed a teacher, Lactantius, to tutor his son Crispus. Lactantius would later report that the night before the battle, Constantine had a dream in which he was commanded to place the sign of Christ, the Cross, on the shields of his soldiers. Constantine beat Maxentius, which made Constantine sole ruler of the western half of the empire. He attributed his victory to the power of "the God of the Christians."[8] Right then and there on that battlefield, in 312, Constantine began his lifelong commitment to the Christian faith.

The following year, 313, Constantine's half-sister Constantia married another rival, Licinius. This bond, however, did nothing to quell Licinius's raging drive to power. Constantine and Licinius made war with each other, over and over and over again until their climactic battles in 324. First, Constantine defeated Licinius at Adrianople in Thrace, and then at Chrysopolis on the Bosporus.

Constantia pleaded with her brother to spare her husband's life. Initially, Constantine did. Months later, he changed his mind and had Licinius executed. It was a good move, making Constantine the sole and undisputed ruler of what would become known as the Holy Roman Empire.

The Christian belief system evolved to endorse earth burial over cremation, condemning cremation as a pagan custom. As emperor, Constantine suppressed paganism, including cremation. Emperor for thirty-one years, Constantine died on May 27, 337. The year of his birth is not known for certain; however, he was probably between sixty-four and sixty-six at the time of his death. That gave him plenty of time to enforce Christian edicts throughout his empire, including the one against cremation.

Per Constantine's directive, his body was conveyed to Constantinople to lay in state in the imperial palace. Later, Constantine's sarcophagus was placed in the Church of the Holy Apostles.[9]

By 400 CE, barely sixty-three years after Constantine's death, earth burial had completely replaced cremation. Except for plague or war, when the number of dead was too great to dig graves for, earth burial and entombment remained the accepted mode of bodily disposition throughout Europe. Only in the north countries, where the pagan Vikings ruled, was cremation employed regularly.[10]

The Scandinavians cremated their dead to prevent their spirits from harming the living. They believed that if the body was burned, the spirit could then be released to the afterlife, where it entered into the realm of the gods.[11] Contrary to cinematic depictions of Viking funerals—most notably in the 1958 film *The Vikings*, in which Kirk Douglas's body is borne out to sea on a flaming ship—elaborate funerals were only for those of the higher social class. Vikings not of high station or who were not warriors were burned on funeral pyres—no last voyage. The bone fragments were then buried.[12]

It was not until the seventh century, however, that missionaries from Ireland brought Christianity to parts of northern Europe. Still, the Norwegian and Danish Vikings, who in the eighth to tenth centuries were busy raiding and settling areas of Britain, France, Germany, and the Netherlands, did not adopt Christianity until the eleventh century. For all that time, they had practiced cremation.

By the end of the eleventh century, cremation as a method of bodily disposal ceased. The practice was at its historical low point in popularity. It simmered on history's back burner, waiting for another reformer to bring it out of the shadows to ignite history.

Chapter Three

Sir Henry to the Rescue

"*F*ew people love the writings of Sir Thomas Browne, but those who do are of the salt of the Earth," Virginia Woolf once wrote about the seventeenth-century author, philosopher, and physician.[1]

Some time around 1658, forty to fifty Bronze Age burial urns—historians are not certain exactly how many—were discovered in Walsingham, Norfolk, England. Word of the discovery quickly spread. What Thomas Browne, a physician practicing in Norwich, found especially interesting was that in addition to ashes, the urns contained pieces of charred human bones. Browne was so deeply moved, he wrote a meditation titled "Hydriotaphia," or urn-burial.

The full title of the work, published in 1658, is "Hydriotaphia, Urn-Burial; or, a Discourse of the Sepulchral Urns Lately Found in Norfolk." It is arguably Western history's most famous meditation on burial customs, life's brevity, death's certainty, and the fear of oblivion. This is how it began:

HYDRIOTAPHIA.

URN BURIAL; OR, A DISCOURSE OF THE SEPULCHRAL URNS LATELY FOUND IN NORFOLK.

TO MY WORTHY AND HONOURED FRIEND, THOMAS LE GROS, OF CROSTWICK, ESQUIRE.

WHEN the general pyre was out, and the last valediction over, men took a lasting adieu of their interred friends, little expecting the curiosity of future ages should comment upon their ashes; and, having no old experience of the duration of their relicks, held no opinion of such after-considerations.

But who knows the fate of his bones, or how often he is to be buried? Who hath the oracle of his ashes, or whither they are to be scattered? The relicks of many lie like the ruins of Pompey's,* in all parts of the earth; and when they arrive at your hands these may seem to have wandered far, who, in a direct and meridian travel, † have but few miles of known earth between yourself and the pole.

That the bones of Theseus should be seen again in Athens‡ was not beyond conjecture and hopeful expectation: but that these should arise so opportunely to serve yourself was an hit of fate, and honour beyond prediction.

We cannot but wish these urns might have the effect of theatrical vessels and great Hippodrome urns§ in Rome, to resound the acclamations and honour due unto you. But these are sad and sepulchral pitchers, which have no joyful voices; silently expressing old mortality, the ruins of forgotten times, and can only speak with life, how

---

* " Pompeios juvenes Asia atque Europa, sed ipsum terra tegit Libyos."
† Little directly but sea, between your house and Greenland.
‡ Brought back by Cimon Plutarch.
§ The great urns at the Hippodrome at Rome, conceived to resound the voices of people at their shows.

long in this corruptible frame some parts may be uncorrupted; yet able to outlast bones long unborn, and noblest pile among us.

We present not these as any strange sight or spectacle unknown to your eyes, who have beheld the best of urns and noblest variety of ashes; who are yourself no slender master of antiquities, and can daily command the view of so many imperial faces; which raiseth your thoughts unto old things and consideration of times before you, when even living men were antiquities; when the living might exceed the dead, and to depart this world could not be properly said to go unto the greater number.* And so run up your thoughts upon the ancient of days, the antiquary's truest object, unto whom the eldest parcels are young, and earth itself an infant, and without Egyptian† account makes but small noise in thousands.

We were hinted by the occasion, not catched the opportunity to write of old things, or intrude upon the antiquary. We are coldly drawn unto discourses of antiquities, who have scarce time before us to comprehend new things, or make out learned novelties. But seeing they arose, as they lay almost in silence among us, at least in short account suddenly passed over, we were very unwilling they should die again, and be buried twice among us.

Beside, to preserve the living, and make the dead to live, to keep men out of their urns, and discourse of human fragments in them, is not impertinent unto our profession; whose study is life and death, who daily behold examples of mortality, and of all men least need artificial *mementos,* or coffins by our bedside, to mind us of our graves.

'Tis time to observe occurrences, and let nothing remarkable escape us: the supinity of elder days hath left so much in silence, or time hath so martyred the records, that the most industrious heads do find no easy work to erect a new Britannia.

'Tis opportune to look back upon old times, and contemplate our forefathers. Great examples grow thin, and to be fetched from the passed world. Simplicity flies away, and iniquity comes at long strides upon us. We have enough to do to make up ourselves from present and passed times, and the whole stage of things scarce

---

* " Abiit ad plures."

† Which makes the world so many years old.

serveth for our instruction. A complete piece of virtue must be made from the Centos of all ages, as all the beauties of Greece could make but one handsome Venus.

When the bones of King Arthur were digged up,* the old race might think they beheld therein some originals of themselves; unto these of our urns none here can pretend relation, and can only behold the relicks of those persons who, in their life giving the laws unto their predecessors, after long obscurity, now lie at their mercies. But, remembering the early civility they brought upon these countries, and forgetting long-passed mischiefs, we mercifully preserve their bones, and piss not upon their ashes.

In the offer of these antiquities we drive not at ancient families, so long outlasted by them. We are far from erecting your worth upon the pillars of your forefathers, whose merits you illustrate. We honour your old virtues, conformable unto times before you, which are the noblest armoury. And, having long experience of your friendly conversation, void of empty formality, full of freedom, constant and generous honesty, I look upon you as a gem of the old rock,† and must profess myself even to urn and ashes.—Your ever faithful Friend and Servant,

THOMAS BROWNE. NORWICH, *May 1st.*[2]

Browne's words are infused with an otherworldly understanding of the meaning of death. "Hydriotaphia" is really a philosophical discourse on death, cremation, and the immortal. Browne is in awe of the sight of these urns of human remains from antiquity. In reflecting on them, he salutes them and their past deeds. He is wrestling with the existential realities every person has to face.

Browne was ahead of his time by two full centuries in accepting cremation as a dignified funerary method. While Browne's meditation is celebrated to this day, it did nothing in his time to advance cremation in British society; Browne found little acceptance of his ideas.

A few years later, in 1664, a group of French intellectuals published a book called *Philosophical Discourses of the Virtuosi of France,*

---

* In the time of Henry the Second.

† " Adamas de rupe veteri præstantissimus."

in which they advocated cremation as an alternative to burial. Then, in the 1670s, Anton van Leeuwenhoek, a Dutch cloth merchant and amateur lens grinder, used magnifying lenses to observe microorganisms for the first time. What he was looking at, though he didn't know it, were germs. His discovery would prove to be the key, two centuries later, to seeing cremation finally accepted back into society as a means of body disposal.

During the Victorian era that lasted most of the nineteenth century, England was the dominant world power. The world looked to England to lead.

The British were the first to promote in modern times what to many had been considered heretical: the idea of burning a human body instead of burying or entombing it. Some members of the upper class, doctors, lawyers, physicians, men, and, yes, women of mettle and means advocated cremation as an answer to society's sanitary health problems.

The English, who by then had enjoyed a long history, had cemeteries bursting at the seams. Many of these cemeteries were situated in or near cities. Nineteenth-century construction crews, intent on building new edifices, would find themselves digging up bones and corpses. For some, it had never occurred to them that they weren't the first Britons to occupy the spot. The builders' zeal to bring about modern times through construction had led them to unknowingly defile centuries-old burial grounds.

In the 1860s, French scientist Louis Pasteur developed the germ theory of disease. His idea was that diseases were spread by the microorganisms van Leeuwenhoek had seen under his lenses. Seizing on this discovery as the rationale for a return to cremation, cremation advocates in England argued that burying the dead inside populated areas should be banned for health reasons. Rotting corpses, with their vile gases and putrefying flesh, were a breeding ground for germs and disease; they should be nowhere near their human counterparts.

Since nineteenth-century cemeteries were frequently situated in beautiful areas, it was the practice to cluster homes around them. Contemporary accounts are filled with cemetery-area residents complaining of frequent headaches, ulcerated sore throats, and numerous other maladies that could easily have been spread from the germs of the putrefying bodies. Newborns regularly died from infections and diseases of all types, though it is not known what percentage died as a result of proximity to cemeteries. People often died from what today are treatable diseases, including measles, influenza, and tuberculosis. Prior to the advent of the Salk polio vaccine, society regularly suffered outbreaks. If the victims survived, they would be crippled, forced to the alleys of cities, begging for small change.

And what happened when these people finally died from disease, neglect, and a broken heart? Then as now, it was up to the state to dispose of the bodies of the indigent. Where would they keep getting the land, the cremation advocates asked? Wouldn't cremation be an easier and less expensive alternative? Wouldn't it be healthier and better for society to sanction cremation? But Great Britain could not allow bodies to be burned. It was against the law.

Following on the heels of Pasteur's theory, Professors Coletti and Castiglioni in 1869 presented to the Medical International Congress of Florence papers that advocated cremation "in the name of public health and civilization." Unfortunately, they didn't describe a functional method of cremating the body.[3]

Besides the various religious proscriptions against cremation, a practical matter stood in its way. In order for cremation to be performed effectively in the modern era, the Victorians would have to improve on the centuries-old funeral pyre method. This latter method required that the remains be buried, remains such as charred bones like the ones dug up in Norwich. Quite simply, someone needed to take moral charge of what was a growing reform movement.

That man was Sir Henry Thompson.

♦♦♦

Any person today who has stipulated in his will that he is to be cremated owes a debt to Henry Thompson. Before Thompson turned his considerable charm and intellect to the cause, cremation was still considered a pagan practice in Europe and the United States.

Henry Thompson was born in 1820 in Framingham, England, the only son of Henry Thompson, a grocer and draper on Market Street. As a child he had some health problems and for that reason went to the seaside town of Southwold. Under the care of a Dr. Wake, what might later be considered an ironic name, he made the decision to enter the medical profession.

Thompson apprenticed himself to a Croydon surgeon, and then went to University College where he was awarded his medical doctorate. In 1850, at the age of thirty, he refined an existing surgical device called a lithotrite, a crude machine used to crush bladder stones. What Thompson did was simplify it and at the same time strengthen the shaft to crush larger stones. Using his invention, Thompson successfully operated on the king of Belgium in 1863 and removed his bladder stones. The operation and its success were big news. With his fame thus ensured, Thompson decided to use it to advance society.

Along with Major Rev. C. Voysey and Sir T. Spencer Wells, and other prominent members of British society, Thompson spearheaded the reform movement to promote the healthful and economic practice of cremation. It was the best way, they argued, to dispose of a human body. But how to do it effectively? The technology still did not exist to incinerate a human body completely.

The question, as Thompson saw it, was what would it take "given a dead body, to resolve it into carbonic acid, water and ammonia, rapidly, safely and not unpleasantly?"[4] Scientists resolved to find out the answer. Using coal-gas mixed with atmospheric air, applied to a cylindrical retort of refracting clay, "so as to consume the gaseous products of combustion," Dr. Pietra Polli in Milan, Italy, completely incinerated dead dogs. It took two hours to do it. When the cremation of the dogs was over, all that remained were ashes that weighed 5 percent of the animals' body weight before cremation.[5]

But that was an animal. What would it take to incinerate a

human being? The long-awaited answer finally came at the Machinery Hall of the Vienna Exposition of 1873. One of ten exhibit halls at this world's fair, the Machinery Hall showcased the latest inventions. Included was the modern world's first furnace built especially for cremation by Dr. Bruno Brunetti of Italy.

Brunetti had designed an oblong furnace of refracting brick. The body was cremated by placing it on a metal plate suspended on an iron wire. Underneath was the bed of the furnace where the heat-generating wood was burned. As the fire got going, the heat was raised and concentrated. To regulate the draft, he'd built in side doors above a cast-iron dome with movable shutters. The gases escaped through the shutters, as designed. Four hours later, all that was left was ashes.[6]

But there was no body on display. Brunetti's exhibit was only the prototype for an idea. Since most countries outlawed cremation, no body had been used for a demonstration. The laws needed to be changed to allow it. More important, Brunetti's invention needed to be demonstrated to show its practicality. None of this made a difference to Thompson and his friends.

The cremation advocates knew they were one step closer to a working and successful crematory furnace. They were certain that modern cremation would soon become a reality. And they were right. In 1874, in Dresden, Germany, the first modern cremation occurred in a furnace constructed by Frederick Siemens.[7]

Siemens's furnace used coal-gas and air as fuel. Once ignited, the flames first passed through a regenerator, which consisted of numerous layers of fire bricks, with intervals between them, and then to the cremation chamber, into which the remains had been placed. This chamber had a floor made of fire bricks; the flame passed between these and then into a flue leading to the chimney. The process took about one hour. In the end, all that was left was what the Bible says is left—ashes and dust. The ashes remaining weighed five or six pounds. The total cost for the cremation was about 6 pounds.[8] Siemens's invention was a resounding success. That was enough for Sir Henry Thompson.

Thompson was so impressed that he wrote a paper titled "The

Treatment of the Body after Death," published in the *Contemporary Review*, January 1874. His main reason for supporting cremation, he wrote, was that "it was becoming a necessary sanitary precaution against the propagation of disease among a population daily growing larger in relation to the area it occupied."[9]

Thompson wrote that cremation would reduce the expense of funerals and would spare mourners the necessity of standing exposed to the weather during interment. But his main argument was for sanitary reasons: cremation would prevent the spread of disease from dead bodies. As for the question of where to keep the ashes, Thompson advocated keeping the ashes in urns and putting the urns in a columbarium. A columbarium is brick or stone construction, with niches in which the urn can be placed. Thompson also boldly advanced a further economically based and ecological argument, namely, that the ashes might be used as fertilizer.

The Medical Inspector of Burials for England and Wales wrote in opposition to Thompson's arguments. He said cremation was not a sanitary necessity. Thompson wrote back countering his arguments and focusing on the damage that the dead do to the living by spreading germs. This written war of words provoked a lively discussion and intense controversy in the press. Soon, Thompson received over eight hundred letters from the public making their views known.[10]

What happened next became a part of history. According to the Cremation Society of Great Britain, "encouraged by the reception of his articles, Sir Henry Thompson called a meeting of a number of his friends at his house at 35 Wimpole Street on 13th January, 1874, when a declaration was drawn up and signed by those present," all of whom would become founders of what would become the first modern reform movement in funeral practice. The document titled "The Declaration," said: "We, the undersigned, disapprove the present custom of burying the dead, and we desire to substitute some mode which shall rapidly resolve the body into its component elements, by a process which cannot offend the living, and shall render the remains perfectly innocuous. Until some better method is devised we desire to adopt that usually known as cremation."[11]

This document is particularly interesting because of the list of signatures, including, in addition to that of Sir Henry Thompson, those of Shirley Brooks, editor of *Punch* magazine; painter Frederick Lehmann; painter John Everett Millais; novelist Anthony Trollope; and surgeon Sir T. Spencer Wells. The group aptly represented the realms of art, science, literature, and medicine.

On April 29, 1874, Thompson was elected president and chairman of the Cremation Society of Great Britain. That same year, new members joined the society: Mrs. Rose Mary Crawshay, Mr. Higford Burr, Rev. J. Long, Mr. W. Robinson, and the Reverend Brooke Lambert. Others subsequently followed, including English judge Lord Bramwell, Sir Charles Cameron, Sir Douglas Galton, Lord Playfair, Martin Ridley, Edmund Yates, Mr. J. S. Fletcher, Mr. J. C. Swinburne-Hanham, the duke of Westminster (on Lord Bramwell's death), and Sir Arthur Arnold. Members were responsible for an annual contribution to defray expenses. Of course, this elite group had no problem with money. Society's acceptance of the group was something else.

Many of the meetings were concerned with legal strategies to effect their goal since cremation was still outlawed in England. The group immediately ran into trouble when it was unable to purchase land to construct their crematory. Eventually, in 1878, an acre was obtained at Woking, near the town's cemetery.

With the land settled on, the next step for the society was constructing the furnace. Since Brunetti's introduction of the modern cremation furnace five years before, and Siemens's version in 1874, Professor Paolo Gorini of Lodi, Italy, came forward with his own version, which worked on the small scale that the society was seeking. They bought it, and Gorini was invited to supervise his furnace's construction in England.

The inhabitants of Woking, however, hated having a crematorium in the neighborhood. Led by their vicar, a small but zealous group appealed to the home secretary, Sir Richard Cross, to prohibit the use of the building. Cross was particularly afraid that cremation might be used to prevent determining the cause of death following violence or poison. He requested that Sir Henry Thompson come in for a personal chat.

When the two knights sat down to talk, Cross warned Sir Henry that until Parliament authorized cremation by either a general or a special act, the activity was still outlawed. With the threat of either legal or parliamentary proceedings against them, the Cremation Society of Great Britain was forced to abandon further plans. By March 1879, therefore, the function of the society was restricted to disseminating information and trying to change the public's attitude toward cremation.

In 1880, Sir Spencer Wells brought a petition to adopt cremation before the annual meeting of the British Medical Association. It went to Parliament's Home Secretary's office, where it was ignored. In 1882, Captain Hanham of Dorsetshire applied to the Home Secretary's office for permission to cremate two deceased relatives who, before they died, wrote down specific instructions for their cremation after death. The Home Secretary refused. Having no choice but to bury his relatives or embalm them, Captain Hanham chose the latter. Then, he quickly built a crematorium on his own estate. On October 8 and 9, 1882, Hanham defied the government and cremated his relatives, the first cremations in England in centuries. Hanham himself died about a year later and was also cremated.

Although these events excited much comment in the press, the Home Office of Parliament took no action. Cremation was still against the law, but the government decided to look the other way. As with any repressive law, there had to be a test case before the courts to see if the old law against cremation could hold up under contemporary scrutiny. That test case emerged in 1883.

William Price, an eccentric eighty-three-year-old doctor who claimed to be a Druid high priest, had a baby boy whom he christened Jesus Christ. When the boy died at five months, Price attempted to cremate him, dressed in a white tunic over green trousers—what he claimed was Druid dress for the occasion. The police stopped him before the cremation was completed. Arrested, Price was put on trial at the South Glamorgan Assizes in Cardiff, Wales.

Price claimed at trial that he was performing the cremation in accordance with the Druid religious belief system. In February 1884,

Justice Stephen, who had heard the case, pronounced the verdict: "Not guilty." Stephen delivered his opinion that cremation is legal, provided no nuisance is caused in the process to others.

Price then tried to claim that he be awarded £3,120 in damages against the police for preventing the completion of his son's cremation. The justice awarded the nominal sum of only one farthing. But the legal precedent had been established. Cremation was, finally, legal in Great Britain. Thompson had won.

The Cremation Society of Great Britain publicly offered to perform cremation for the general population, but only after cause of death had been firmly established to the society's satisfaction. The society knew that one of the principal objections to cremation came from police officers, barristers, and magistrates who were still afraid that cremation would obliterate evidence in a homicide. Thompson responded to that criticism.

Being a physician, Thompson did not write what was specified as "cause of death" on a death certificate unless a coroner's inquest had already been held. Instead, Thompson and the society adopted a system of scientific inquiry, at the end of which each case/request for cremation was put on the society president's desk. The president, Thompson, then signed off unless he thought something was questionable.

Finally, on March 26, 1885, Mrs. Jeannette C. Pickersgill became the first person legally cremated in Great Britain, when her body was cremated at the society's Woking Crematorium. From then on, cremation gained in popularity in England. The process would be slower in the United States.

Chapter Four

Baron De Palm Gets Hot

$\mathcal{A}$mericans did not live in a vacuum. They knew from reading their newspapers of Henry Thompson's exploits. They also knew about Brunetti's furnace exhibit at the 1873 Vienna Exposition. More important, 1874 was the year that Thompson published "Cremation: The Treatment of the Body after Death."[1] Those events acting together "created a plausible case for what was coming to be known as modern and scientific cremation."[2] While the exposition display proved the technological feasibility of the practice, Thompson's article trumpeted it as a sanitary necessity.

Seizing on Thompson's public-health-oriented arguments, U.S. cremation advocates sought to promote their cause in the press. The *New York World*, the *Boston Globe*, the *Sacramento Record*, and the *Jewish Times*, among others, all published articles about cremation in 1874, as did the popular magazine *Harper's New Weekly*.

The "modern" idea of cremating a body instead of burying it fit right in with the nation's fascination for the lurid. As far back as pre-Revolutionary America, vivid, sometimes first-person accounts of major crimes began appearing in pamphlets that focused on the bloody deaths of the victims. The pamphlets gave way to the "penny dreadfuls" of the nineteenth century and newspaper accounts of any story involving death.

The idea of burning a person, what Joseph Conrad called the "fascination with the abomination," now *that* sold newspapers. But it was just that, an idea. The newspapers wouldn't continue to run stories about the possibility of cremation unless someone followed through and actually did it in the United States. Cremationists in turn needed someone not only to articulate their ideas but also to make them a reality. Once again, cremation found a champion, this time in the Reverend Octavius Frothingham.

An acknowledged and outspoken abolitionist, Frothingham was a Unitarian minister. He moved beyond that religion's liberal teachings to become a founding member of the Free Religion Association in 1867. The group dedicated itself to an open discussion of religion within a scientific context. It encouraged freedom of thought and questioning established religious practices.[3]

Frothingham's mentors were the Reverend Theodore Parker and Gerrit Smith. Smith and Parker were wealthy abolitionists who, with four others of like mind, formed "The Secret Six," a group that financed John Brown's mad plan to bring about an armed slave rebellion. Brown's 1859 takeover in Virginia of the Harpers Ferry arsenal inspired a now incongruous sight: Colonel Robert E. Lee of the federal army commanding the troops that brought the insurrectionist to ground and led to his execution.[4]

While his friends Smith and Parker narrowly avoided imprisonment for their acknowledged funding of Brown's sedition, Frothingham managed to skirt their more radical abolitionist teachings as well as Brown's deadly fantasy. Instead, his attention was focused on the grave. Frothingham did not believe, as did most in his profession, that laying a body in a grave resulted in eternal rest. Frothingham strongly felt that decomposition produced "a laboratory where are manufactured the poisons that waste the fair places of existence."[5]

In 1874, Frothingham courageously delivered the first procremation sermon by a minister in the United States at Lyric Hall in New York City. Titled "The Disposal of the Dead," the sermon argued that cremation was essentially a purification proceeding, whereas burial resulted in polluting the environment. It was a radical argument by a radical minister.[6] But just as in England, arguments would not suffice to make cremation in the United States a reality.

The newspapers began cutting back on their cremation articles. Until someone actually tried a modern cremation, there really was nothing new to report to an ever-demanding public. For the cremation movement to gain momentum and seize headlines, it needed a true leader, someone willing to make it happen: to actually go ahead and legally cremate a body.

It wasn't that the technology didn't exist to do the job; it obviously did. Brunetti had seen to that. What was needed was a corpse that could be consigned to the flames. Two years later, in 1876, the cremationists and the newspapers finally got what they wanted.

Washington, Pennsylvania, is located on one of the lower spurs of the Laurel Range of the Allegheny Mountains, just thirty miles southwest of Pittsburgh. Today there is absolutely nothing prepossessing about it—a sleepy little town no different from any other. Only this town just happened to be the host of a unique exhibition on December 5, 1876.

Gallows Hill is outside the center of the town. In 1876, when Dr. Julius LeMoyne built his crematory, there was nothing else there. Now LeMoyne's Crematory still stands but is ringed by a nursing home and a hospital. Upon first seeing LeMoyne's crematory on December 5, 1876, an unnamed *New York Times* reporter wrote in the next day's edition: "The splendid hills, the deep vales and woodlands, the happy faces trudging along the rough country road, the sweep of snow sparkling cheerily in the bright sunlight and the keen, invigorating air were a bad preparation for encountering a reception room for the dead, the silent occupant and the curiously sad ceremony of reducing to dust, by means of a fiery furnace, what was so lately a fellow human being."[7]

For months since Baron De Palm had died, America's newspapers had been full of stories about his impending cremation at LeMoyne's Crematory. It had taken months to make the arrangements, to get the proper permits, but things were finally ready to go on the first cremation in the history of the Republic. The body of Baron Charles De Palm had been brought there the night before so it would be ready the next morning for its entry into the fiery pages of history.

On that cold day, December 6, 1876, all eyes in the United States focused on the event about to occur in Pennsylvania. For this was the America edging toward enlightenment and modern invention, the America bursting at the seams during the age of Manifest Destiny, an America angry to get even with the hostiles who only six months before killed Custer and his men at the Battle of the Little Big Horn.

This was also a conservative America, where the very idea of burning a body rather than burying or entombing it was absolutely revolutionary. Dr. Samuel LeMoyne, the man who built the crematory in his own name, was a real-life "Dr. Stockman." Stockman, Henrik Ibsen's physician hero in his 1882 play *An Enemy of the People*, tries to show how water pollution is adversely affecting the health of his town's citizens. For his efforts he is vilified. LeMoyne faced public criticism, too, of the most virulent form, for exposing his town's health crisis.

A practicing physician, devoted husband, and loving father of eight, LeMoyne founded Washington's Citizens Library and was a cofounder of the Washington Female Seminary. But his greatest contribution to his community was as a doctor. When Washington's residents kept getting sick with the same or similar symptoms, some fatally, LeMoyne became convinced that the culprit was the town's burial practices.

He believed contaminated matter containing disease-spreading germs, from buried and decomposing bodies, was running off into the town's streams and wells. He was convinced this was the cause of the diseases that were spreading to victim after victim. LeMoyne reasoned that cremation would eliminate disease-ridden contaminants from leaching into the soil and water supplies and spreading the oftentimes fatal illnesses.

Determined to stop the cycle of disease, LeMoyne decided to build his own crematory. Approaching the trustees of the town's public cemetery, LeMoyne proposed that if they would give him permission, he would donate the money necessary for the construction of a crematory on cemetery property. But the trustees never even considered LeMoyne's offer.

Frustrated that his town had turned its back on what he perceived as a very real public health problem, Dr. LeMoyne built the crematory in 1876 on his own land, on high ground that had been named a century before as Gallows Hill. Construction cost $1500. An elegantly simple, 30-by-20-foot brick building, the crematory had a reception room and a furnace room. Washington resident John Dye planned and constructed the crematory building, using the Siemens's crematorium as his model. LeMoyne himself designed an oven where flames would never touch the body being cremated.[8]

With the crematorium built, the next step was finding someone to put in it. Cremation was not a popular concept in Pennsylvania or any other state for that matter. It was an unpopular idea advanced by a group of intellectuals and freethinkers who believed that cremation was the best way to dispose of a body.

A heated battle between the pro- and anticremation forces ensued. The latter group had ignorance and religious dogma on their side, the former, intelligence and money. Most if not all of the early U.S. advocates were, like their British counterparts, well educated and financially independent. That caused resentment toward both them and their ideas. And then, the Baron De Palm obfuscated matters even further with his dying wish.

The Baron De Palm was an Austrian nobleman who immigrated to New York in the winter of 1875. The kind of nobility that uses his royal lineage for obtaining financial support, he had no money of his own and relied like Blanche DuBois on the kindness of strangers. A contemporary of De Palm described him as a "tramp."[9] But he was an intelligent fellow who became fast friends with Colonel Henry Steel Olcott.

Dr. Julius LeMoyne. (*Courtesy of Washington County Historical Society, PA.*)

Modern-day photos of LeMoyne's Crematory on Gallows Hill. (*Courtesy of Washington County Historical Society, PA.*)

During the War between the States, Olcott had served the Union as a military investigator of fraud and corruption. This was followed by a career in law, which he later combined with journalism, to report on spiritualistic phenomena. He soon became a Spiritualist, consumed with finding a way to reach beyond the grave and contact the dead. As president and cofounder in 1875 of the Theosophical Society, Olcott was a social reformer who championed free thought.[10] When he befriended De Palm, he found a man of kindred spirit.

Unfortunately, De Palm had come to America's shores ill and became worse soon after his arrival. His friend Olcott stayed by his side and became his confidante and executor of his meager estate. Knowing death was imminent, De Palm instructed Olcott to arrange his funeral in accordance with the rites of Eastern religions. Once the service was over, he wished to have his body cremated.

Olcott was faced with a conundrum. On the one hand, he wanted to honor his friend's wishes, but on the other, cremation had not been performed in the United States. It would take time to get the necessary permits to allow the disposition of a human body through flames, not to mention the construction of a real crematorium that could do the job in a modern way.

Nineteenth-century American cremation advocates wanted to show the public that there was a big difference between the old funeral-pyre style of partial cremation, which then required interment of the remains, and modern cremation, which used either the Siemens or the Brunetti furnace models to incinerate the corpse. But as far as Olcott knew, there was no furnace in the United States that had been built to complete the process. Until he found one, Olcott needed to preserve De Palm's body. Otherwise, there would be nothing left to cremate except a decomposing body with the flesh rotting off it.

De Palm was therefore embalmed, and a funeral service was held on May 28, 1876, at the Masonic Temple presided over by its minister, the Reverend Octavius Frothingham. In keeping with Frothingham's style, the service was noteworthy for its lack of orthodoxy. Darwin's theory of evolution, Egyptian mystery cults, Hindu scriptures, and spiritualism were all part of the liturgy at De Palm's last rites. It was attended by two thousand people, including Olcott, the Theosophists' president.[11]

The reporters who attended the service universally condemned it as a "high falutin' farce."[12] Selling Americans on the benefits of cremation was clearly not going to be easy for Olcott. Even the New York Cremation Society, which initially offered support for De Palm's cremation, removed it after all the public furor. Undaunted, Olcott pressed forward to honor his friend's last wishes.

While reading the *New York Herald Tribune* one day, Olcott came across an article about the building of LeMoyne's Crematory in Pennsylvania. He wrote LeMoyne and told him he had the first candidate for his new facility. Olcott's argument, that this would be the first modern scientific cremation—which would certainly be covered by the press—made LeMoyne realize that this was his chance to show the benefit of cremation: by burning a body rather than letting it go into the ground, humanity could avoid polluting its environment.

Olcott applied his legal background and connections to this opportunity, obtaining all the necessary permits to transport the body to Pennsylvania where he made sure in advance it could be legally cremated. Gathering around him like-minded scientists, clergy, teachers, and journalists, he set out for Pennsylvania by railroad with De Palm's corpse. It was a similar odyssey to the one made by Woodrow Call in Larry McMurtry's epic western, *Lonesome Dove*. In the book, Call makes the long and difficult trek from Montana to Texas, carrying, pulling, and sometimes dragging the body of his friend Gus McRae, because he had promised McRae to bury him in Texas. In Olcott's case, he took De Palm's body by train to the smoky steel town of Pittsburgh, Pennsylvania. They arrived there on December 5, 1876.[13]

Upon arrival, August Brunckhorst, the undertaker who had embalmed De Palm with arsenic, was the first to discover that the body was mysteriously missing from its wooden coffin, a disappearance verified by others. Baggage handlers went back into the boxcars to search for it. Inexplicably De Palm turned up a short while later back in the coffin. No explanation was ever given for the Baron's disappearance and later reappearance. Considering the almost surreal nature of the preceding, none was apparently needed.

From Pittsburgh, the strange entourage of Olcott, the Baron—now safely back in his coffin—Olcott's friends, and reporters all rode by horse-drawn carriage and hearse the thirty miles to Washington, Pennsylvania, where De Palm's corpse was delivered to the crematory. There, on the afternoon of December 5, Olcott opened the coffin for all to see how the Baron was doing. It turned out, not well.

Despite embalmer Brunckhorst's best efforts, the Baron looked awful. He was thin and emaciated, and his skin had what pathologists refer to as "slippage": the skin was literally slipping off the body. Olcott closed the coffin. Regardless of the Baron's appearance, Olcott needed to make preparations for the following day's event.

That night, friends of De Palm's removed his corpse from the coffin. It was wrapped in a white linen shroud that was covered with aromatic herbs and spices. The latter, it was thought, would mediate the smell of the burning flesh. After these ministrations, the body was placed on a cradle made out of iron. The cradle would contain the Baron's ashes, ensuring that they did not mix with the coke that fueled the furnace. One final time, the linen covering was pulled back from the Baron's face. Embalmer Brunckhorst had worked a miracle. In some manner of cosmetic wizardry, he had made the Baron seem alive.

Well, almost.

DE PALM'S INCINERATION.
CREMATION OF THE LATE BARON
AT WASHINGTON, PENN.

The "De Palm Incineration," as the *New York Times* called it on December 6, 1876, might be considered one of the first media events. Besides the *Times*, newspapers from coast to coast contained coverage of it on their front pages. But to the *New York Times* reporter who covered it, De Palm's cremation was nothing so much as a macabre celebration of the dead.

As he arrived at LeMoyne's Crematory that morning for the event, the reporter noticed, "Around the building was a noisy, pushing crowd of the young women and men of the place, some of them had been waiting hopelessly (for Dr. LeMoyne only issued thirty invitations) pressing for a place for hours. They were passably orderly, but coarse in their ideas and conduct. Many a brutal joke concerned the dead man went through the crowd to the disgust of the more respectable visitors. The scene was as repulsive, though on a smaller scale, as that to be witnessed before an execution or a prize fight. This was just what Col. Olcott wished of all things to avoid."[14]

Earlier that morning, the furnace had been fired up at seven AM By eight it was ready. The observers were in the twenty-foot-square reception room; it fit only about six or seven. There were a few wooden chairs, "a columbarium very much like [a] modern book-case, for the temporary disposition of urns containing the remains of those who may thereafter be cremated there."[15]

The word *columbarium* is derived from the Latin word *columba* for "dove." The dove, of course, is a symbol of peace. As mentioned earlier, a columbarium is a structure designed with niches—much like a dovecote—to contain the receptacle in which the ashes repose.

The furnace itself was constructed "on the Martin Sieman's prin-ciple, where an escape flue carries off the carbon gases and also the gases generated from the body during cremation, into a chimney. Ten feet long, six feet wide and six feet high, inclosing [sic] a fire-clay retort of semi-cylindrical shape, into which the body to be cremated is thrust after the retort is properly heated by the fire below. The fur-nace heat, generated by coke could be raised by means of a simple hand-worked fan blast."

All the witnesses examined the furnace, and then went back to the reception room where the Baron's corpse, still linen-enshrouded and smelling from incense, was ready for the cremation to begin. "This morning, when the body lay in its winding sheet in the iron cradle, ready for being placed in the crematory, the entire face was exposed to view." When they pulled back the cloth, "the features [of the Baron] gave me the idea of having in life possessed refined lin-eaments . . . a high broad forehead, nose straight and the Grecian type. The body was generally very emaciated, and, as all fluids had long ago been removed from the intestine, it was very light." Aro-matic flowers and branches were placed around the body.

A plate that had been on the coffin had been removed and placed on the windowsill in the small room. It read:

JOSEPH HENRY LOUIS CHARLES BARON DE PALM,

Died May 20, 1876, aged sixty-seven

The cremation was ready to begin. The furnace door was open. According to the *Times* reporter, "The further end of the clay retort was only what is called a 'cherry red heat,' while toward the mouth, there were no signs of even that amount of heat." But LeMoyne knew what he was doing. He had the furnace operator stoke the heat up to 2,000 degrees,

by firing and the use of the fan-blast. When all was ready, the body was quietly and reverentially slid in to the retort. There were no religious services, no addresses, no music, no climax. There was not one iota of ceremony.

At 8:20 o'clock, Dr. LeMoyne, Col. Olcott [and a few others] took their stations on either side of the body and raising the cradle, bore it at once to the retort and slid it in with his unearthly burden, head foremost. As the cradle reached the further and hottest end of the furnace, the evergreens round the head burst into a blaze and were quickly consumed, but the flowers and evergreens on the other part of the body remained untouched.

The flames formed a crown of glory for the dead man. The door of the retort was quickly closed, bolted and screwed up tight, and the furnace man immediately went to work on the fire and fan blast so as to increase the heat. For some minutes nothing could be seen through the little peep-hole. All was dark as night in consequence of the steam created by the saturated winding sheet; but after the steam had all passed away through the flue for the escape of gases, the body wrapped in its winding sheet could be distinctly seen, as also the evergreens at the feet.

Fifteen minutes had gone by since the furnace door had been

slammed shut and the heat increased. The reporter placed his face close to the peephole, where he detected the unmistakable odor of burning flesh. But the odor lasted only a second and was "lost in the more pungent odor of the aromatics." By that time, the retort "presented the appearance of a radiant solar disk of a very warm rather than brilliant color. Though every flower and evergreen was reduced to red-hot ash, they retained their individual forms, the pointed branches of the evergreens arching over the body."

The winding sheet still enfolded the corpse, putting to rest one of "the avowed objections to cremation—the possibility of indecent exposure of the body." This was, of course, Victorian times, when the idea of a body's being naked even for burial was objectionable. But half an hour later, the sheet was clearly charred, the reporter observed. "Around the head the material was blackened and ragged. All were, however, rejoiced to see that the heat was increasing."

This was the crucial point. If the body wasn't completely incinerated, then modern cremation had done nothing to improve on the same practice that took place during the Stone Age.

"Just at this time, a remarkable muscular action of the corpse, almost amounting to a phenomenon, occurred. The left hand, which had been lying by the side of the body, was gradually raised and three of the fingers pointed upward. Although a little startling at the moment, the action was of course the mere result of intense burning heart producing muscular contraction."

The reporter looked at his pocket watch; it was 9:25. After the draft in the retort was tested and found ample, "the left hand began to fall back slowly into its normal position while a luminous rose-colored light surrounded the remains, and a slight aromatic odor found its way through the vent-hole of the furnace."

The Baron continued to burn until an hour later, when "the body presented the appearance of absolute incandescence. It looked red hot. This was the result of extra firing, the heat of the furnace now being far more unpleasant than it was before. As the retort became hotter, the rosy mist assumed a golden tinge and a very curious effect was noticed in the feet." The reporter saw that the soles of the Baron's burning feet "assumed a certain transparency, similar in character, but very much more luminous, to the appearance of the hand when the fingers are held between the eye and a brilliant light."

At 10:40 AM, Dr. LeMoyne and the state's and town's health officers that were present convened to the furnace room, where they discussed, behind closed doors, how long to keep the furnace going, "On reappearing, they announced that the cremation of the body was practically complete. Any one looking into the retort at this moment would think it ought to have been."

While dead sheep had been initially used to test the furnace, John Dye, the furnace's builder, told the *Times*, "The body was more thoroughly cremated at the end of two hours and forty minutes than [the animals] were in five or six hours. About this time, the body was beginning to subside, that though incandescent to a degree, it was nevertheless a mere structure of powdery ashes which the lungs of a child might blow away. The red hot filmy shroud still covered the remains and the twigs of evergreen still remained standing, though they had sunk with the subsidence of the body."

It was all over by 11:15 AM.

"The last vestige of the form of a body had disappeared in the general mass. The pelvis, which had hitherto kept its shape, had fallen in, and nothing now remained but a mass of incandescent ashes, or irregular formation. At the bottom of the retort though up to the last there were some indications of the twigs and of the winding sheet."

To make sure the process was complete, LeMoyne kept the furnace going an hour longer, just in case the heat had missed an errant bone. At noon, "the firemen commenced to draw the fires from the furnace" by closing the vent hole, preventing oxygen from continuing to fuel the fire. The Baron's remains were left "to quietly cool by themselves" until the following day, when "the ashes [would] then be collected and placed in Col. Olcott's ancient Hindu burial urn and taken to New York."

The following day, when the remains were retrieved, all that was left—except for a few small bits of bone—were ashes. The first modern cremation in the United States using science had been a resounding success! As for cost, it had been a bargain. "The direct outlay for the cremation," the *Times* reporter wrote, "was forty bushels of coke at four cents a bushel, and thirty-four hours labor, at sixteen cents an hour: total, $7.04."

Not only did the cremation of Baron De Palm make history as the first of its kind in modern North America, but it had been achieved so cheaply; it was a fraction of the cost even then, when a dollar meant something, of earth burial.

Chapter Five

Dr. LeMoyne Fights for the American Retort

The *Times* reporter was quite thankful that De Palm's incineration had been complete. "Because all the fluids from the Baron's body had been removed, there was not the slightest approach to anything like disruption from the generation of steam in the body itself. Had this necessary part of embalmment not been carried out, there is no doubt that the body would have exploded soon after being placed in the retort."[1]

That, of course, is not true. First, the Baron had had embalming fluid in his veins. Second, cremation literally dehydrates the body; it falls in on itself rather than exploding out. The *Times* reporter had seen this but did not realize what he had seen. Still, the damage had been done. Anyone reading the story on December 6, whether in New York, Pennsylvania, or anywhere else the paper was distributed, would have thought twice about cremation, lest the body "explode." It was the spreading of this type of misinformation that Henry Olcott, Julius LeMoyne, and the cremationists had been trying to avoid. But none of that took away from what a wonderful morning it had been.

Walking down from Gallows Hill to the town hall, Colonel

Olcott and Dr. LeMoyne were exultant. The cremation had worked better than they had ever dreamed it would.

In the afternoon, there was a meeting at the town hall of those interested in cremation. Various addresses were delivered. Colonel Olcott gave a short history of cremation. Dr. LeMoyne talked about reconciling the scriptural and scientific issues raised by the cremation. It was typical of LeMoyne, who was known as a "maverick" personality, to deal with spiritual concerns while at the same time promoting the medical needs of cremation. And yet, despite LeMoyne's best intentions, the media covering the event made it out to be some sort of sensational, barbaric funeral rite.

The *New York World* called cremation "objectionable."[2] The *New York Herald* said it was "part 'folly,' part 'farce.'"[3] The other papers covering the event, including the *Boston Herald*, *New Orleans Times Picayune*, *San Francisco Chronicle*, and *Philadelphia Inquirer*, were no less critical. Still, cremation as an alternative to earth burial might still have made inroads into America's consciousness based simply on the day's publicity.

The cremationists earnestly believed that their arguments, and the physical example of De Palm's cremation, would usher in a new era of enlightenment. It didn't. Even the "scientific professionals" who had been invited by LeMoyne and Olcott had their own axes to grind. For example, Dr. A. Otterson, who attended as a representative of the Brooklyn Board of Health, was not convinced of the public health benefits of cremation or "of the necessity or adaptability of the process to our times and country."[4]

LeMoyne, Olcott, and the rest had made a fundamental mistake— they had underestimated the ignorance of the American public regarding their long-held beliefs. As members of the upper class, they had the benefit of education as well as money. They assumed those less fortunate would cast aside disbeliefs, superstitions, and, most important, religion to embrace the burning light of progress that cremation provided. But precisely for those reasons—and the fact that the majority of the U.S. population had little education—cremation in the United States seemed doomed. The argument that cremation prevented disease did not convince any significant portion of the public.

The germ theory of disease and the cremationists' embracing of that theory and its significance to public health, was lost on a public slow to embrace any kind of scientific reform. This was an America where bleeding was still practiced in some venues as a means to combat disease. People were actually bled using a variety of spring-loaded lancets in order to extract what was thought to be disease-ridden blood. As late as 1889, George Tiemann & Company, the venerable and respected supplier of surgical instruments to the trade, made a complete bloodletting kit composed of eleven medieval-looking instruments.[5]

The cremationists' only hope was that America's love affair with the grave and the cemetery would not last forever. It was only a matter of time before America's immigrant class moved up the economic and social ladder. With that ascendancy came increased knowledge through the reading of newspapers, magazines, and by attending public schools. The cremationists reasoned that a better-educated and more upwardly mobile populace would eventually understand and rally to the cremationist cause. Until then, however, the cremationists weren't about to give up their attempt at reform.

Dr. Charles F. Winslow became the first American put into the furnace in Salt Lake City, Utah, on July 31, 1877.[6] A freethinker who hailed from Boston, Massachusetts, he had elected before he died to have himself cremated in Utah. His friends saw to his last wishes. Afterwards, they found that iron chips from the furnace had mixed in with the doctor's ashes. They were removed one by one, an act that predicted a later technology that would make it possible to remove metal from cremation ashes with the aid of a powerful magnet.

Newspapers, responding to the cremationists' arguments by continuing their coverage of the occasional "burning," shifted their attention to New York City, where Julius Kitcher, a German-American of the Lutheran faith, lived with his Jewish wife. In November 1877, she gave birth to a baby boy who died eight days later.[7]

Kitcher's wife wanted an interment in a Jewish cemetery; Kitcher in one of the Lutheran faith. Shattered by his grief and tired of arguing, Kitcher took his son's corpse and cremated it in a furnace in the paint factory where he worked. "Baby Boy" Kitcher thus became the first child cremated in the United States.[8]

The only cremation "first" remaining was for a woman's corpse to enter the retort. To Mrs. Benjamin Pittman went this honor. A well-educated eccentric from Cincinnati, Ohio, she had told her husband that when she died she wanted to be cremated. After her death, her body was "displayed at her Cincinnati home in a beautiful cherry and mahogany casket—an elegant resample, custom carved with the monogram 'P' at the foot and a large cross at the head."[9]

Her family then transported her coffin and its inhabitant to Washington, Pennsylvania, for a rendezvous on Gallows Hill with Dr. LeMoyne, who was only too happy to fire up his crematory once again. This time, there was a viewing in the small reception area. A eulogy was delivered, a poem read. The body, wrapped with a white, alum-laced shroud, was removed from the coffin and laid on the catafalque, a decorated platform on which the coffin rested in state during the funeral. LeMoyne's attendants shoved the coffin into the furnace's flames head first, as had been done to De Palm. Once again, the *New York Times* covered the cremation at LeMoyne's Crematory; once again, cremation got a bad review with the headline "An Unceremonious Right" on February 16, 1878.[10]

The reporter wrote that the ceremony lacked heart and prayer, a bleak, joyless exercise in flaming futility. The *Philadelphia Inquirer*, *Chicago Tribune*, and the *Boston Globe* chimed in with similar sentiments. But that didn't stop enlightened individuals who, in several states, formed local cremation societies, like this one in Indianapolis, Indiana: "Three hundred men and women met in a hall in Indianapolis, Indiana Tuesday night, and organized the Indiana Cremation Society," said the small item on page 5 of the *New York Times*, December 6, 1878.[11]

Besides Indiana, New York had its own cremation society. And then, Dr. LeMoyne gave the practice a boost when he decided to avail himself of his own hospitality.

Dr. Julius LeMoyne was born on September 4, 1798, when John Adams was president. His life spanned those of the Founding

Fathers and in many ways paralleled their revolutionary fervor as well. His attempt to introduce cremation into American society was no less revolutionary than introducing democracy to a people raised under a monarchy. But Thomas Jefferson realized something that LeMoyne did not.

In 1817, when LeMoyne was nineteen and studying to be a doctor, Thomas Jefferson had retired at his Monticello estate, where he wrote his old friend the Marquis de Lafayette, "What government can bear depends not on the state of science, however exalted, in a select band of enlightened men, but on the condition of the general mind."[12]

Even with the cremationists' best efforts, "the general mind" was against them. And still LeMoyne forged on. A strong and robust man during his lifetime, LeMoyne developed diabetes, for which there was no known treatment. Being the enlightened scientist he was, LeMoyne tracked the symptoms of the disease and the progressive deterioration of his organs. He succumbed to the disease at eighty-one, an impressive age in 1879 when the average life span was about fifty.

Prior to his death, LeMoyne had requested an autopsy. After the autopsy proved that the diabetes had decimated his organs as he had suspected, LeMoyne's heirs carried out his second instruction, to cremate his body. Once again, reporters traipsed to Gallows Hill, once again the firemen stoked up the furnace. Ironically, the newspapers once again hailed cremation as a godless rite, though LeMoyne himself was a Christian. In a "cremation treatise" he drafted before his death, LeMoyne stated that he wrote it "from a Christian standpoint." References to "the great creator," Jesus Christ as the "Savior" and the Bible as "revealing the will of God" were peppered throughout.[13] For a man perceived by the press as decidedly unreligious, he was anything but in the manner of disposing of his body.

LeMoyne saw nothing wrong with combining the science of cremation and his belief in God and the hereafter. To him, the body was nothing more than a vessel for the soul, a vessel that if committed to the ground could play havoc with the living when it released its deadly germs into the earth. He was not about to contribute to this hazardous problem.

The furnace door was opened. Wrapped in an aromatic winding

sheet like De Palm, LeMoyne's body was committed head first to the flames. The furnace was stoked up to over 2,000 degrees. This time, it didn't take four hours. Within three, it was over. LeMoyne's last instruction to his heirs was to find a rose bed into which his ashes were to be scattered, "so that the queen of flowers might seek sustenance in his cinerary remains and scent the air with her message of beauty and fragrance."[14]

The ashes were gathered from the bottom of the retort and placed in an urn. There is no record of any of LeMoyne's ashes actually being scattered, or an explanation for why his family did not carry out this last wish if, indeed, they did not. In its records, the Washington County Historical Society states that "the ashes were placed in an urn under a simple stone monument in front of the crematory."[15] The inscription reads:

F. JULIUS LEMOYNE, M.D.
BORN SEPT. 4, 1798 DIED OCT. 14, 1879
A FEARLESS ADVOCATE OF THE RIGHT

The newspapers, of course, had a field day. The *Philadelphia Inquirer* reported that "the great difficulty [with] this reform . . . has been the impracticable character of the persons who have been foremost in urging its adoption."[16]

The paper pointed out that the people who championed the cause, like LeMoyne and Olcott, tended to be "a body of mystics who rejoiced in the learned title of Theosophists and in whom every vestige of common sense was obliterated. . . . They were the very last class of men and women who should have been picked out to introduce a reform of any kind among a sober and intelligent people, and more especially, a reform which, to most minds, seems barbarous and inhuman."[17]

While the paper was essentially correct, it failed to point out that any reform is usually effected by reformers who appear to be impractical if not crazy to the society they are trying to reform. It was the kind of criticism lodged at LeMoyne that he had to tolerate for much of his adult life, and yet, it never deterred him.

In 1884 the second crematory opened in Lancaster, Pennsylvania. As was true of many of the early crematories, it was owned and operated by a cremation society. Crematories were soon built in major U.S. cities, including New York City, Buffalo, and Cincinnati, but they didn't get much business. In the eight years from 1876 to 1884, only forty-one cremations were performed in the United States.[18]

ChrisTina Leimer, author of *The Tombstone Traveller's Guide*, paints an even bleaker picture of the practice's popularity, claiming only twenty-eight "formally recorded cremations in the U.S." during that same period.[19] Still, the figures supplied by the Cremation Association of America, "an association of persons, principally cemetery operators, who are in the cremation business," show a slow rise in the following fifteen years until 1899, when 1,996 cremations were performed.[20]

Despite these low figures, the cremationists strove onward. Following LeMoyne's lead, a group among the Protestant clergy throughout New England and the Great Lakes area promoted cremation as a means of burial reform. More crematoriums were built in cities as far-flung as Detroit and Los Angeles. LeMoyne's legacy, the task of advancing cremation as a health reform, eventually fell to the members of his own profession.

Doctors by and large were educated and rational. Committing a diseased body to fire would seem to immediately neutralize its ability to spread disease through its putrefying flesh. The American Medical Association (AMA) weighed in with its official opinion.

The AMA had created a committee to look into the cremation controversy. On May 6, 1886, the AMA's Cremation Committee delivered its report at the organization's annual meeting in St. Louis, Missouri. In the report, committee members argued that earth burial "propagated the germs of disease and death, and spread desolation and pestilence over the human race."[21] The AMA reformers argued that "God's half acre [the grave] must become a thing of the past. The graveyard must be abandoned . . . [since] the earth was made for the living and not for the dead. . . . Pure air; pure water and pure soil are absolutely necessary for perfect health."[22]

Despite these findings, the AMA's full membership refused to adopt an official position. As to the argument that corpses spread disease, even doctors began to debunk it. Science would later confirm that dead bodies were indeed a breeding ground for germs, but it was another matter for late-nineteenth-century scientists to accept this idea. Cremation's critics claimed that as long as a body was buried in a rural cemetery, away from people, no one's health was in danger. If no people were around to be immediately affected by corpses' germs, no matter how they putrefied, there was no need to worry.

The missing issue in all of the arguments, which clearly flowed across religious and pubic health lines, was the cost—cremation was clearly cheaper than earth burial. Cremating a body was inexpensive. The body didn't even have to be in a coffin; if the family didn't want one, any box would do. In those early days of cremation in the United States, the body was usually taken out of its coffin and committed to the flames without it, which therefore made the investment in a fancy coffin even more extravagant and unnecessary.

The only real cost involved were the wages for the firemen and the cost of the coke or other fuel. De Palm's incineration had proven how cheap the whole process was. Yet Americans, raised on and used to rituals, saw nothing ritualistic about cremation. Again, the cremationists had not taken fully into account that the funeral takes place at an emotional time. Scientific arguments be damned—most relatives can't imagine their loved ones being consumed by fire, even if they were dead. They felt more comfortable with an elaborate funeral full of fancy oratory, fancy flowers, fancy coffin, fancy hearse, fancy interment, and fancy gravestone, all of which cost the kind of fancy money most people don't have.

If people were going to change their minds, they needed to be convinced that funeral rituals could stand an overhauling. They needed to be persuaded that there was nothing wrong with burning a dead body and that they weren't going to hell for burning it. Unfortunately, the pope and others had different thoughts on the matter.

In 1886, in the Vatican, Pope Leo XIII officially banned cremation among Catholics. Calling cremation a "detestable abuse" of the human body, the pope vilified the practice.[23] He proclaimed, "The body which lies in death naturally recalls the personal story of faith, the loving family bonds, the friendships, and the words and acts of kindness of the deceased person. It is the body whose hands clothed the poor and embraced the sorrowing."[24]

While cremationists were freethinkers—many of whom preferred Eastern religions to Western ones—the fact that the leader of one of the world's most influential religions had officially banned cremation among his flock was a tremendous blow to the cremation movement in the United States. Catholics might make up a minority of the population, but that minority still represented millions of Americans. And now, the pope was saying to them that if their bodies burned, so would their souls. A trip into the flames of the retort was a trip into the everlasting fires of hell. That left only the freethinkers, medical people, and non-Catholics to advance the cremation argument.

From 1890 to 1899, cremations in the United States increased slowly. In 1899 1,996 Americans who died were cremated.[25] That same year, the *Journal of the American Medical Association* (JAMA) published a letter to the editor from Dr. J. O. Malsbury that reflected the growing impatience with the medical community to see the practice sanctioned by its organization.

CREMATION VS. BURIAL

PERU, IND., May 13, 1899.

To the Editor:—Regardless of what may have been the ancient customs or are the modern methods of disposing of the dead, regardless of whims and fancies pro and con, there is but one sanitary method, but one method which is safe for the living, but one method which is acceptable to the dead, and but one method which is justice to nature—that of cremation.

From a sanitary standpoint, what is more elegant, more beautiful, more esthetic and cleanly than resolving the organized body into its original elements by a rapid, safe and thorough method—cremation—as against the disgusting, horrifying, slow, unsafe and inelegant method—putrefaction? Death is robbed of many of its horrors when we remember that our dear old body, even though it may have been an aching and ugly one, is to be rapidly transformed or changed, as it were, into oxygen, hydrogen, nitrogen and carbon, the four elements of which all living organisms are in the main constructed. It is pleasing to know that our bodies may thus be restored to nature, ready to again be claimed by organized life.

When we regard the lives, health and safety of the living, there is no choice—cremation, and that alone, offers security from infection and transmission of disease from this source, that of the dead. A body after interment must sooner or later undergo putrefaction, the elements of which, together with such disease germs as may be present, are carried to the surface in various and many ways, and thence to the air and water-channels, and he who escapes is more lucky than wise. It is thus that disease is being rejuvenated without a cause apparent. The cemetery is a menace to the living, an enemy to nature, and an usurper of the dead.

The cemetery, with all its paraphernalia, should be abolished, and in its stead parks established, which should be beautiful and rendered comfortable and inviting with the money which has heretofore been spent for tombstones, vaults, etc.; that the living may have a beautiful place of assemblage where they may muse, with safety and surroundings of cheerfulness, of the happy disposal of the bodies of their dead relatives and friends; as against the mournful and hazardous visit of the cemetery, where everything is suggestive of sadness, and we are forced to remember the imprisonment of our dead friend's body in a putrid tomb.

The modern faddist is not content to imprison or inter the body in the ordinary way in light casket and thin outward box, which requires from two to five years for the elements to be liberated, but he insists on having a stone or brick vault enforced by a metallic casket, which combination drags out and prolongs the term of imprisonment to an indefinite period. Nature, having dealt with us so generously and kindly in yielding up her elements to form us a physical being or body during our journey from the hilltop on the left to that of the right, should, now that the journey is ended, be allowed, yea, assisted, to claim her own without hindrance or delay. While it may seem a little shocking to think of or see the incineration of a body, it is horrifying to think of or see a body in state of putrefaction. Incineration need not interfere with the religious belief which calls for resurrection of the body; if the elements can and are to be collected after the process of putrefaction, the same may be equally true of cremation.[26]

In his letter, Dr. Malsbury went all out in making a compelling case. Not only did he advocate cremation on scientific grounds, but he hoped to appeal to the aesthetes reading his words in proposing "cremation parks" where relatives could scatter their loved ones' ashes while enjoying a day out. It was an idea ahead of its time, but in 1899, cremationists had a much bigger problem than what to do with the ashes.

As the new century dawned, cremation was no longer unique to modern times. By 1900, there were twenty crematories in operation in the United States. Still, in actual figures, the number of individuals being cremated compared to the death rate was miniscule. If cremation was going to make inroads into the twentieth century, the practice had to find itself, once again, on the front pages of America's newspapers. But a lone cremation, like De Palm's, would no longer suffice. Twenty-four years had passed. It had to be something bigger for the papers to cover it.

Which was how the water begat the flames.

Part Two

Chapter Six

The Fire after the Hurricane

The United States did not treat Jean Lafitte well.

Lafitte helped save the United States during the War of 1812. During the decisive engagement, the battle of New Orleans in 1815, Lafitte and his pirates changed the course of the battle in America's favor. The United States won the battle and the war; the British were defeated. Hailed an American hero and offered a full pardon for his legendary career as a pirate and smuggler, Lafitte went back to his island stronghold of Barataria, outside New Orleans. From there, his ships went out again to prey upon foreign shipping in the Gulf of Mexico.

However, the federal government didn't like that arrangement. Lafitte had served his purpose. He had saved America. Now that he had returned to being a pirate, they sent warships into the Gulf of Mexico, then up to the western shore. In 1817, they bombed Lafitte's island stronghold at Barataria, forcing him to flee after slaughtering many of his men. Lafitte later wound up on Galveston Island, off the coast of Texas in the Gulf of Mexico. Here he established his new headquarters. While owned by Spain, Galveston was part of Texas, which was a province of Mexico. Lafitte made a mutually beneficial deal with the Mexicans, who were eager to gain their independence from Spain.

In return for allowing him to continue his pirating activities, Lafitte agreed to the Mexicans' request that he concentrate his efforts on Spanish ships. Lafitte readily agreed and was back in business as *bos* (leader). Lafitte built a big, fine house for his family. This time, he placed cannon in the upper windows of the house, training their sights on the water through which his enemies might choose to attack him. America, aware of his move, allowed him to live there briefly.

Lafitte's new venture did not last long. His ranks deprived of professional pirates, he was forced to rely on the depraved Gulf jetsam and flotsam that found its way to his little village on the island. Most of these men were cutthroats without a vestige of honor or a sense of responsibility in serving the *bos* for the good of the greater whole. Even the *bos* could not control some of them when they went out drinking and whoring, and soon, not only the Americans but the Mexicans turned on Lafitte as the depredations of his pirates added up.

In the latter part of 1820, the USS *Enterprise* docked in Campeche Bay adjacent to Galveston Island. Aboard was a naval diplomat, Lt. Larry Kearney, who had been dispatched by President Madison himself. Kearney ordered Lafitte off Galveston Island. Lafitte stalled but eventually was forced to give in. He didn't want the slaughter of Barataria to be repeated.

In May 1821, the U.S. fleet landed on Galveston Island, finding Lafitte's village in ruins, burned to the ground. Lafitte and the remnants of his pirate fleet had left, burning their homes in their wake so no one could benefit. As for Lafitte himself, he was never found; he vanished into the pages of history.[1] Lafitte's exploits would become part of Galveston's local folklore.

But that was not the worst disaster to afflict Galveston. After the fall of the Alamo in 1836, Texas gained its independence from Mexico. In 1837, the Congress of the Republic of Texas made Galveston a port of entry. By the end of the nineteenth century, Galveston thrived as a shipping port. That all changed on September 10, 1900.

That night, the deadliest hurricane in United States history struck Galveston Island. After the storm passed, John D. Blagden, serving a temporary assignment at the Galveston Weather Bureau office, wrote to his family in Duluth, Minnesota:

Weather Bureau
Galveston Tex
Sept 10, 1900
To All at home

Very probably you little expect to get a letter from me from here but here I am alive and without a scratch. That is what few can say in this storm swept City. I have been here two weeks, to take the place of a man who is on a three months leave, after which I go back to Memphis.

Of course you have heard of the storm that passed over this place last Friday night, but you cannot realize what it really was. I have seen many severe storms but never one like this. I remained in the office all night. It was in a building that stood the storm better than any other in the town, though it was badly damaged and rocked frightfully in some of the blasts. In the quarter of the city where I lodged (south part) everything was swept and nearly all drowned. The family with whom I roomed were all lost. I lost everything I brought with me from Memphis and a little money, but I think eighty Dollars will cover my entire loss: I am among the fortunate ones.

The Local Forecast Official, Dr. Cline, lives in the same part of the City and his brother (one of the observers here) boarded with him. They did not fare so well. Their house went with the rest and were out in the wreckage nearly all night. Dr. Cline lost his wife but after being nearly drowned themselves they saved the three children. As soon as possible the next morning after the waters went down I went out to the south end to see how they fared out there. I had to go through the wreckage of buildings nearly the entire distance (one mile) and when I got there I found everything swept clean. Part of it was still under water.

I could not even find the place where I had been staying. One that did not know would hardly believe that that had been a part of the city twenty-four hours before. I could not help seeing many bodies though I was not desirous of seeing them. I at once gave up the family with whom I stayed as lost which has proved true as their bodies have all been found, but the Clines I had more confidence in regard to their ability to come out of it. I soon got sick of the sights out there and returned to the office to put things in order as best I could. When I got to the office I found a note from the younger Cline telling me of the safety of all except the Drs. wife. They were all badly bruised from falling and drifting timber and one of the children was very badly hurt and they have some fears as to her recovery.

Mr. Broncasiel, our printer, lives in another part of the town that suffered as badly is still missing and we have given him up as lost. There is not a building in town that is uninjured. Hundreds are busy day and night clearing away the debris and recovering the dead. It is awful. Every few minutes a wagon load of corpses passes by on the street. . . . [2]

According to a writer of the time,

After the hurricane, bodies floated everywhere. Bodies hung in trees and bodies littered the little high ground left in town. An orphans' home demolished by the storm had 90 of its young charges and 10 nuns perish in the roiling waters. If there had been a viable undertaking business left on the island, it would have grown fat with grief and money. Up to 10,000 people died.

City leaders turned to fire after they tried sea burials, loading 700 corpses onto a barge taken 18 miles out into the Gulf of Mexico. They tried weighing down the bodies, but scores of bloated corpses washed back onto the beach, carried on "waves like hearses."[3]

The ruined city had no furnaces with which to cremate the dead. Instead, Stone Age–style funeral pyres were set up around Galveston to deal with the problem. Bodies were burned by Galveston's "dead gangs," members of which were plied with whiskey and threatened at gunpoint to keep at their horrifying task.

The Cremation Association of North America (CANA) lists the 2,414 cremations that took place in 1900, but these were "official" cremations, that is, taking place in one of the twenty crematories then in existence.[4] CANA does not include in its statistics the Galve-

Body on stretcher being carried to the funeral pyre after the Galveston hurricane of 1900. (*Reproduced from the Collections of the Library of Congress.*)

ston cremations because the numbers are hard to estimate since record-keeping at the time was incomplete. Considering that approximately ten thousand died, and few of that number were actually interred—much of the city was under water, making burial impossible—the cremation total is probably in the thousands. Americans who needed to be convinced that cremation was a viable alternative to burial didn't have farther to look than the front pages of their daily newspapers.

For the next few years, cremation as an alternative to burial made steadier gains than it ever had before. It is hard to say whether the coverage of the Galveston hurricane was what served to energize the cremationist movement, but it was clear that the mass cremations had stayed the tide of inevitable disease that would have resulted had the bodies rotted while awaiting burial.

By 1906, the number of cremations in the United States had almost doubled from 1900, up to an official total of 4,518.[5] The official cremation rate once again comes into question because of a strange rumbling San Francisco residents felt on the morning of April 18, 1906. The next day's paper reported the cataclysmic event this way:

> Death and destruction have been the fate of San Francisco. Shaken by a temblor at 5:13 o'clock yesterday morning, the shock lasting 48 seconds, and scourged by flames that raged diametrically in all directions, the city is a mass of smoldering ruins. At six o'clock last evening the flames seemingly playing with increased vigor, threatened to destroy such sections as their fury had spared during the earlier portion of the day. Building their path in a triangular circuit from the start in the early morning, they jockeyed as the day waned, left the business section, which they had entirely devastated, and skipped in a dozen directions to the residence portions. As night fell they had made their way over into the North Beach section and springing anew to the south they reached out along the shipping section down the bay shore, over the hills and across toward Third and Townsend streets.
>
> Warehouses, wholesale houses and manufacturing concerns fell in their path. This completed the destruction of the entire district known as the "South of Market Street." How far they are reaching to the south across the channel cannot be told as this part of the city is shut off from San Francisco papers.
>
> After darkness, thousands of the homeless were making their way with their blankets and scant provisions to Golden Gate Park and the beach to find shelter. Those in the homes on the hills just north of the Hayes Valley wrecked section piled their belongings in

the streets and express wagons and automobiles were hauling the things away to the sparsely settled sections. Everybody in San Francisco is prepared to leave the city, for the belief is firm that San Francisco will be totally destroyed.

Downtown everything is ruined. Not a business house stands. Theaters are crumbled into heaps. Factories and commission houses lie smoldering on their former sites. All of the newspaper plants have been rendered useless, the "Call" and the "Examiner" buildings, excluding the "Call's" editorial rooms on Stevenson Street, being entirely destroyed. It is estimated that the loss in San Francisco will reach from $150,000,000 to $200,000,000. These figures are in the rough and nothing can be told until partial accounting is taken.

On every side there was death and suffering yesterday. Hundreds were injured, either burned, crushed or struck by falling pieces from the buildings, and one died while on the operating table at Mechanics' Pavilion, improvised as a hospital for the comfort and care of 300 of the injured. The number of dead is not known but it is estimated that at least 500 met their death in the horror. . . .[6]

Unlike contemporary accounts that likely sought to allay panic and underestimated casualties to around five hundred, Gladys Hansen, San Francisco's archivist emeritus and curator of the Museum of the City of San Francisco, has estimated there were over three thousand deaths.[7] Of that number, there are no official figures of what percentage of the bodies was actually buried versus cremated. Considering the literal lack of space within the city for interment and the difficulty in simply transporting the dead through the burned-out hulk of the city into outlying areas that were also devastated by the quake, it does not seem unlikely that at least half of those who died were committed to the flames.

Four years earlier, in 1902, the city had passed an ordinance prohibiting burials within the city. The city's graveyards were filled up. Only cremation and the burial of cremation remains were still legally allowed within the city. Despite that ordinance, some of the bodies after the quake were buried within the city limits. However, the bodies that were burned in mass cremations at funeral pyres set up around the city were done so according to statute.[8] For a change, the cremationists actually had the legal and moral high ground. Cremation was legal there, plus it was a health necessity. If the bodies sat around they would putrefy and easily breed germs harmful to the living. Because the earthquake, the deaths and the subsequent cremations were big news, the story stayed on the nation's front pages throughout April 1906 and surely made inroads into the popular consciousness.

While Henry Thompson's paper "The Treatment of the Body after Death," published in the *Contemporary Review* of January 1874, did more to popularize cremation in the United Kingdom than any other piece of similar writing, the United States could not make the same claim.[9] There was no one single piece of writing among the nineteenth-century cremationist's papers, articles, letters to the editor, and today what would be known as "Op Ed" pieces that influenced people as much as Thompson's writing did. None of the U.S. cremationists' writings permeated society enough to resonate and throw into doubt the popularity of burial and the efficacy of cremation.

That all changed in 1907 with the publication of Robert Service's epic poem, *The Cremation of Sam McGee.*

During the late nineteenth and early twentieth centuries, the American frontier west of the Mississippi had been settled. When the 1898 Gold Rush in Canada's far northern province of the Yukon beckoned, the scoundrels and scalawags who had literally been ridden out of existence in the Old West fled to the northern climes to see if the pickings there would be any better than at home. But the Gold Rush attracted people of all types as well, from all over the world, including one young man from Canada via Britain—Robert W. Service.

Service was born in Preston, England, on January 16, 1874. In 1894, at the age of twenty, he went to Canada, living for a short while on Vancouver Island. Employed by the Canadian Bank of Commerce in Victoria, British Columbia, he was transferred to Whitehorse and then, finally, to Dawson in the Yukon.[10] Dawson

Makeshift funeral pyres set up around San Francisco after the 1906 earthquake. *(Reproduced from the Collections of the Library of Congress.)*

was a town right in the middle of the Gold Rush that attracted miners, trappers, hunters, Old West outlaws, anyone who thought they could make a buck in the frigid environs.

It was in the Yukon that Service's natural instincts as a writer took over. Inspired and impressed by the frigid cold weather, he wrote an epic poem about those feelings:

THE CREMATION OF SAM MCGEE

Robert W. Service

There are strange things done in the midnight sun
By the men who moil for gold;
The Arctic trails have their secret tales
That would make your blood run cold;
The Northern Lights have seen queer sights,
But the queerest they ever did see
Was that night on the marge of Lake Lebarge
I cremated Sam McGee.

Now Sam McGee was from Tennessee,
where the cotton blooms and blows
Why he left his home in the South to roam
'round the Pole, God only knows.
He was always cold but the land of gold
seemed to hold him like a spell;
Though he'd often say in his homely way
that he'd sooner live in Hell.

On a Christmas Day we were mushing our way
over the Dawson trail.
Talk of your cold! through the parka's fold
it stabbed like a driven nail.
If our eyes we'd close, then the lashes froze
till sometimes we couldn't see,
It wasn't much fun, but the only one
to whimper was Sam McGee.

And that very night, as we lay packed tight
in our robes beneath the snow,
And the dogs were fed, and the stars o'erhead
were dancing heel and toe,
He turned to me, and "Cap," says he,

"I'll cash in this trip, I guess;
And if I do, I'm asking that you
won't refuse my last request."

Well, he seemed so low that I couldn't say no;
then he says with a sort of moan,
"It's the cursed cold, and it's got right hold
till I'm chilled clean through to the bone
Yet 'taint being dead—it's my awful dread
of the icy grave that pains;
So I want you to swear that, foul or fair,
you'll cremate my last remains.

A pal's last need is a thing to heed,
so I swore I would not fail;
And we started on at the streak of dawn
but God! he looked ghastly pale.
He crouched on the sleigh, and he raved all day
of his home in Tennessee;
And before nightfall a corpse was all
that was left of Sam McGee.

There wasn't a breath in that land of death,
and I hurried, horror-driven
With a corpse half hid that I couldn't get rid,
because of a promise given;
It was lashed to the sleigh, and it seemed to say,
"You may tax your brawn and brains,
But you promised true, and it's up to you
to cremate these last remains."

Now a promise made is a debt unpaid,
and the trail has its own stern code,
In the days to come, though my lips were dumb
in my heart how I cursed that load!
In the long, long night, by the lone firelight,

while the huskies, round in a ring,
Howled out their woes to the homeless snows—
Oh God, how I loathed the thing!

And every day that quiet clay
seemed to heavy and heavier grow;
And on I went, though the dogs were spent
and the grub was getting low.
The trail was bad, and I felt half mad,
but I swore I would not give in;
And I'd often sing to the hateful thing,
and it hearkened with a grin.

Till I came to the marge of Lake Lebarge,
and a derelict there lay;
It was jammed in the ice, but I saw in a trice
it was called the Alice May,
And I looked at it, and I thought a bit,
and I looked at my frozen chum;
Then "Here," said I, with a sudden cry, "is my
cre-ma-tor-eum!"

Some planks I tore from the cabin floor
and I lit the boiler fire;
Some coal I found that was lying around,
and I heaped the fuel higher;
The flames just soared, and the furnace roared
such a blaze you seldom see,
And I burrowed a hole in the glowing coal,
and I stuffed in Sam McGee.

Then I made a hike, for I didn't like
to hear him sizzle so;
And the heavens scowled, and the huskies howled,
and the wind began to blow,
It was icy cold, but the hot sweat rolled

down my cheeks, and I don't know why;
And the greasy smoke in an inky cloak
went streaking down the sky.

I do not know how long in the snow
I wrestled with grisly fear;
But the stars came out and they danced about
ere again I ventured near;
I was sick with dread, but I bravely said,
"I'll just take a peep inside.
I guess he's cooked, and it's time I looked."
Then the door I opened wide

And there sat Sam, looking cool and calm,
in the heart of the furnace roar;
And he wore a smile you could see a mile,
and he said, "Please close that door.
It's fine in here, but I greatly fear
you'll let in the cold and storm—
Since I left Plumtree, down in Tennessee,
it's the first time I've been warm."

There are strange things done in the midnight sun
By the men who moil for gold;
The Arctic trails have their secret tales
That would make your blood run cold;
The Northern Lights have seen queer sights,
But the queerest they ever did see
Was that night on the marge of Lake Lebarge
I cremated Sam McGee.[11]

It was the heartfelt expression of Service's experiences in the Yukon coupled with the poem's surreal ending that drove cremation straight into the consciousness of the American public. When Sam McGee sits upright to say how happy he is to be in the flames, it serves to humanize cremation. The poem would go on to become intensely popular in America; it is still taught today in poetry classes. It is equally ironic that, once again, it was an Englishman who had such a profound impact on cremation in the United States.

Service would go on to become a war correspondent for the *Toronto Star* during the Balkan War of 1912–13 as well as World War I. Like Ernest Hemingway, Service was also an ambulance driver during the war for the Canadian Army Medical Corps.[12]

After World War I, he returned to Vancouver province for a time and settled in Victoria, the province's capital city. Service eventually retired to the French Riviera, where he died in Monte Carlo on September 14, 1958.[13] Lost to history is the fact that Service's famous protagonist, Sam McGee, was a real person. McGee was one of Service's customers at the Bank of Commerce. As for the *Alice May*, whose boiler served as the story's retort, it was named after the *Olive May*, a real derelict ship on Lake Lebarge.

By 1913, the number of cremations in the United States had climbed above the 10,000 mark for the first time in history. That year, 10,119 cremations occurred, up over 300 percent since the beginning of the century. While still lagging far behind burial and entombment, the numbers showed that cremation was gradually becoming an accepted part of the American death ritual. As such, it had achieved the epitome of American distinction—it had become a business. Dr. Hugo Erichsen saw cremation as a legitimate business providing an alternative for the bereaved.

Erichsen was born in Detroit in 1860. The son of immigrant parents, Erichsen was educated at Detroit's German-American Seminary, the Realschule in Kiel, Germany, later receiving his medical doctor degree from the University of Vermont. A lifelong Unitarian, like so many cremationists, he was sixteen at the time of De Palm's incineration. After reading about it in the newspaper, he became a convert to cremation. Erichsen was a hybrid: he had the reformist's zeal in a pragmatist's body.[14]

Erichsen condemned Pope Leo XIII's 1886 ban on cremation,

characterizing the pope as the "ancient personage with the threefold crown and the alderman's stick." Of course Unitarians had never been advocates of the pope. In 1887, Erichsen published "The Cremation of the Dead Considered from an Aesthetic, Sanitary Religious, Historical, Medico-Legal and Economical Standpoint." It "was the first great pro-cremation work written by an American."

By 1896, the debate between cremationists and burial advocates began to come to an end. The question was not whether cremationists could convince their fellow Americans that cremation was an alternative; they were doing that. The real question was how to make cremation more efficient and functional.

In 1913, Erichsen helped organize the Cremation Association of America (renamed the Cremation Association of North America in 1975). Some early members operated crematories inside cemeteries. Others were funeral directors with on-site crematories. Still others were independents. Most, though, were not worried about public attitudes toward cremation. What concerned them was the cremation industry's bottom line. This was what historian Stephen Prothero calls "the bricks and mortar stage" of the history of American cremation, when cremationists began pondering the practical.

Erichsen became the organization's first president and helped set the new organization's agenda. Like his fellow bottom-line cremationists, he wondered which was the best method for powering the furnace—electricity, gas, oil, coke, or something else. He wondered what a crematory should look like. Should it be the functional brick of LeMoyne's or something more elaborate?

Cremationists had finally arrived. They were no longer on the outside looking in. After decades of struggle, they were becoming part of the funeral establishment. Now, they had to try and find their place within it.

Chapter Seven

Villa, Shorter, and the Vatican

By the early twentieth century, all the early cremationists had passed into the retort. Sir Henry Thompson, Dr. Julius LeMoyne, the Reverend Octavius Frothingham, Colonel Henry Olcott, all dead. With the idealists dead, the businessmen like Hugo Erichsen took over.

Since Erichsen's Cremation Association of America included many members who were also in the cemetery business, by criticizing burial in favor of cremation, they were hurting their own business. Rather than do that and spoil profits, these early-twentieth-century cremationists eliminated the antiburial rhetoric from their arguments. Instead, a new argument was developed.

It was lucky that Thompson and LeMoyne had been cremated by the time the cremationists/businessmen developed the concept of "memorialization." Had it developed in their time, they might have been so outraged that they'd have opted for earth burial.

Looking at the bottom line, the cremationist/businessman figured that since the cost of the actual cremation was so low, they had to make their money some other way. That way took the form of memorializing the dead. The dead who were buried had a headstone to memorialize them. What about those who were cremated? The answer was to sell urns, buildings in which to place the urns, and, strangely enough, a plot of ground in which to bury the ashes.

The late-twentieth- and early-twenty-first-century practice of scattering ashes on land or a body of water that had meant something to the deceased didn't exist at the end of the Victorian period. It was rebellious enough to plan to have your corpse cremated, let alone having the ashes scattered. There had to be some propriety.

Many of the early cremationists eschewed scattering and had their ashes buried in cemeteries. They felt it was more dignified. They may not have wanted their bodies in the ground, but ashes were okay because they were environmentally safe and took up a lot less space. As the nineteenth century wore into the twentieth, burial of ashes in cemeteries became a commonplace event.

Yet no matter how hard they tried to commercialize the process, between overhead and other costs, businessmen had a difficult time making a profit. They needed more volume. Once again, it would be world events that brought cremation back to the front pages.

In 1913, in Mexico, President Francisco Madero was assassinated. After Victoriano Huerta's brief term as head of government, Francisco "Pancho" Villa and his chief rival, Venestia Carranza, lobbied the United States for official recognition as Mexico's leader. Villa sent his representative to Washington to argue his case. While Villa partook of Washington's hospitality, President Wilson embarrassed Villa by choosing Carranza for diplomatic recognition.

An angered Villa already had his men engaged in fighting Carranza's forces at Agua Prieta, right below the border at Douglas, Arizona. Seeing that the battle would be lost without reinforcements, Carranza got the president to back up his decision with action. President Wilson allowed Mexican federales to cross into the United States at El Paso, Texas. From there, they boarded a special train that took them to Douglas, where they went back across the border and reinforced their compadres to fight Villa's men.

Merely angry before, Villa was now furious. The United States needed to be taught a lesson. He began hatching a plan. The original idea Villa had was to attack from the south into Texas, but some of his men who heard rumors of the scheme did not want to be a part of it and deserted. Afraid of discovery, Villa abandoned this first plan. Villa then chose Columbus, New Mexico, as the point of attack, but this time told only a few trusted lieutenants.

Columbus was a town where Villa felt the merchants had cheated him on past munitions deals. German agents, whose job it was to keep the United States occupied elsewhere so they couldn't enter the war in Europe, told Villa that the bank he did business with in Columbus claimed there was no more money left in Villa's account.

Villa wanted revenge and the money.

On March 9, 1916, at approximately 2 AM, Pancho Villa and his men attacked the United States Army garrison stationed at Columbus. The sleeping soldiers awoke to the sounds of killing and screaming. According to eyewitnesses who survived the attack, the five hundred men under Villa's command shouted, "Viva Villa! Viva Mexico! Muerte a los Americanos [Death to Americans]!"

The U.S. soldiers, confused at first, regrouped. Over the course of the next three hours, the two sides shot away at each other. When their sense of revenge was finally satiated, Villa and his army set the town afire. Riding back across the border, they left twenty-four Americans dead in their wake, ten civilians and fourteen soldiers.[1]

In the end, Villa suffered the most. At least one hundred of his men, fully 20 percent of the raiding force, had been killed.[2] While surprised by the enemy, the Americans had fought back hard. The Columbus raid became nationwide news. The *New York Times* bannered it with a front-page headline on March 10, 1916, that read:

9 SOLDIERS, 8 CIVILIANS KILLED

Night Attack on Border

Snipers Shoot Down Inhabitants as they rush from the buildings

Beaten Back by Regulars

Cavalry Force of 250 Pursues Raiders Miles Into Mexico

100 Bandits Slain[3]

Each subhead was more lurid than the previous one. Villa was good for selling papers and so, it turned out, were his men. In describing the fate of Villa's raiders, the unnamed reporter wrote, "The raid on American territory proved costly to the Mexicans. The bodies of 27 bandits including Pablo Lopez, second in command, had been gathered and burned before noon and troopers reported an undetermined number of dead still lying in the brush."[4] These bodies would wind up being cremated.

Photography was not commonly used to cover news events until well into the twentieth century. However, a photographer happened to be present to document the burning of those bandits' bodies, and his picture was seen all across the country. Although it proved expedient for the U.S. Army to burn the bodies—U.S. Army uniformed soldiers are clearly visible in the photograph—the picture of bodies piled up and in flames was the type of publicity that the cremationist/businessman sought to avoid.

They were trying to sell cremation as a *dignified* ceremony, albeit profitable, one using the *modern* technology of the furnace—the funeral pyre was a step backward. While it's hard to analyze the exact effect the Villa cremations had on the psyche of the average American contemplating cremation, CANA's own figures for this time period reflect stagnation.

In 1913, 10,199 Americans were cremated. During the period between 1914 and 1918, an average of 13,114 bodies per year went into

Villa's men being burned after the raid on Columbus, New Mexico. Note the leggings of the soldiers in the photograph. (Reproduced from the Collections of the Library of Congress.)

the retort. By 1922, only 15,563 entered the retort, a mere increase of 50 percent over nine years. Compared to the 150 percent increase during the previous nine years from 1904 to 1912, cremation was clearly on the downswing.[5] Pancho Villa had been bad for business.

Clearly, the industry needed to make things profitable to continue. The cremationist/businessman developed a "pitch" meant to sell the customer on services other than simply cremating the body. The pitch was brilliant in its simplicity.

Cremation was essentially a way of preparing the body's ashes for inurnment. Once the ashes were in the urn, the urn had to be put someplace. The answer, usually, was a columbarium on cemetery grounds, or burial of the inurned ashes in a plot. No cremation was complete, customers were told, without an urn, a final resting place, and a rite of committal.[6]

Crematory and cemetery operators in 1927 and 1928 argued forcefully in public speeches for "memorializing" the cremated dead. What we now call "packages" began to be sold—cremation, memorial service, urn, and columbarium niche. And then, once again, nature intervened.

September is a particularly dangerous time in Florida, when tropical storms roiling the seas threaten to come ashore and attack the sunshine state. While the Galveston hurricane in 1900 was inarguably the worst natural disaster in terms of loss of life the country has ever encountered, the hurricane that hit Florida on September 16, 1928, ranks second.

On that windy, overcast Sunday, the weather grew progressively gloomier as the day wore on. That was not unusual because the month had been particularly wet—twenty-one inches of rain had fallen into Lake Okeechobee. Water had already reached the top of the earthen levee that the Army Corps of engineers had constructed around the southern and eastern parts of the lake, meant to stop adjacent farmlands from being flooded.

As the day progressed, so did the strength of the wind, reaching hurricane force. The wind and the rain pounded at the towns in the glades near the levee. Eventually, the levee gave way and the flood began. By the time it was over, more than two thousand people had died. The inevitable question, of course, was what to do with the bodies. The land was soaked, flooded. Burial was impossible. There would be a public health crisis unless something was done and fast. With the many rotting corpses strewn about, disease would spread rapidly among the survivors, disease that could easily spread beyond the state's borders.

The solution, of course, was cremation.

America's papers blared the news. Sixteen hundred victims of the hurricane were cremated on funeral pyres and their bones interred in a mass grave. To the new breed of cremationist, this was an outrage! Bodies unceremoniously dumped on funeral pyres, burned, and not memorialized? It was undignified. Worse, it was bad for business. There might be people in the country who actually believed cremation occurred over open fire, bodies tossed on like so much meat to be cooked. What then? Would they seriously consider cremation upon their deaths?[7]

Perhaps it is just coincidence, but CANA figures are not available for only the year 1928, as was the case for 1916, the year of Villa's Columbus raid. Instead, the periods 1914–18 and 1924–28 are statistically grouped together with figures that show cremation to be slumping. For example, from 1924 to 1928 about twenty thousand Americans were cremated each year. That is only a slight 25 percent rise from the 1923 figure of 16,516.[8]

There was no question—cremation needed to be marketed to the public in an effective manner. In the 1930s, cremationists created their first marketing campaign. "Cremation as memorialization" was the idea they sold to the American public. Figures for this period show that the campaign had moderate success.

During the period from 1934 to 1938, of 7,100,000 Americans who died, 182,054 were cremated. That meant that by 1938, 2.56 percent of Americans had chosen cremation. With further aggressive marketing, that figure had climbed to 4.05 percent in 1953. Within this time period, the funeral industry fought the battle over pulverization.

It had come to the attention of crematory and cemetery operators that some individuals were trying to "beat the system" by scattering the ashes themselves without paying for urns and the other
accoutrements of the trade. To combat this trend, some cremationists refused to pulverize the remains from the cremation. This way,
the unfortunate next of kin got ashes mixed in with unpulverized
bone fragments. If the sound of their loved one's bones rattling
around in the container wasn't enough to get the bereaved to change
their minds and opt for the full package, nothing was.

Not all cremationists had forgotten about the ideals of the earlier movement, however. The problem was, how could ideals and
business be reconciled? As it has throughout history, cremation
found a champion. This time, he emerged from the depths of the
Great Depression in the Pacific Northwest. His name was Fred
Shorter.

Like the rest of the country, the Pacific Northwest suffered through
the Great Depression in the 1930s. Unemployment was staggering.
Families were uprooted constantly in the search for work. People
began to lose hope. It was during this period that "radical" political
ideologies worldwide began to take hold. In the United States, communism and other left-leaning political beliefs found their way into
the American fabric.

Karl Yoneda, a Japanese American and a communist, had lived
for years with his lover, Elaine Black, in California. Also a communist, Black wanted to marry Yoneda but couldn't, because she was
white. California's antimiscegenation law made such marriages
illegal. The couple finally left the Golden State and went to Seattle
in 1935 to be married in the Reverend Fred Shorter's Church of the
People.[9]

Shorter was a radical minister, cut from the same cloth as the
Reverend Octavius Frothingham. He served as president of the local
branch of the National Association for the Advancement of Colored
People, and as pastor of the Pilgrim Congregational Church. He

directed numerous charity efforts, including the establishment of a "skid row" mission to feed the hungry. As in the case of many reformers, his own people eventually gave him the boot. Because of his radical views, he was ousted from his church.

Undaunted, Shorter went on to do something different. In 1935, he established the Church of the People, sharing space with a radical theater company. His church would become a place for those like him, who felt dispossessed and needed a place to seek succor. Politically savvy, Shorter maintained high-level political contacts throughout the city.

In August 1936, Seattle's populist congressman Marion Zioncheck committed suicide by throwing himself out the sixth-floor window of the Arctic Building in downtown Seattle. A manic depressive who self-medicated with alcohol, Zioncheck championed civil liberties and labor rights. His friend, Fred Shorter, eulogized him.

Marion Zioncheck and Fred Shorter shared liberal political philosophies. Shorter said that Zioncheck was "a shell-shocked comrade who died at the barricades fighting to the very last for the poor and dispossessed."[10] After Zioncheck's death, Shorter's attention turned to the disposition of the dispossessed.

Throughout the 1930s, political and religious radicals started questioning and attempting to redefine the rituals and practices associated with death. Articles were published in many publications, including the *Nation*, criticizing the funeral practices of Americans. In a 1934 article in the *Forum and the Century* magazine, for example, writer Marion J. Castle said that a decent Christian burial is seldom decent or Christian.[11] Castle criticized everything about the modern funeral, from the high cost of embalming to earth burials in overcrowded cemeteries.

Fred Shorter felt the same way. He began to endorse publicly cremation and memorial services over elaborate funerals and earth burial. Unlike traditional funerals, memorial services took place without the body being present. Shorter's congregation endorsed putting his ideas into action.

The Church of the People parishioners established a committee to look into opening their own crematory. It was a radical idea, since the rate of cremation was still low. Precisely because cremation was practiced by a single-digit percentage of the public, the idea of Shorter's church establishing its own crematory was doomed. It just wasn't practical. Instead, in 1939, Shorter established the People's Memorial Association (PMA), the first memorial society in the country.

The PMA was a cooperative "that promoted memorial services and functioned as a collective bargaining group for mortuary consumers. The difference between a cooperatively owned crematory and access to a commercial one at discounted rates was significant, since it was the model that the memorial society movement would adopt."[12] Shorter's view, like the early cremationists, was that cremation should be done as quickly and expeditiously as possible and at the least expense. The Shorter-led PMA entered into a working agreement with James C. Bleitz, a Seattle mortician who was willing to work with the group.

Despite being labeled as communists and radicals, the PMA would survive and prosper. Throughout the 1940s, the memorial society movement sought to provide inexpensive cremations and funerals to consumers. Though they offered discounted services, more consumers still chose the traditional funeral home route. Despite this, cremation continued to make inroads. As for Shorter, Don Shay of Leavenworth, Washington, remembers him vividly.

"He was a very nice man," says Shay, who last saw Shorter fifty years ago. "He was the pastor at the Great Falls Montana Church that my parents went to. He baptized me. He was a good friend of my parents. Growing up, he and his family were always very kind to me. I saw him two or three times a year."[13]

When Shay's mother grew ill, he lived with Shorter and his family for a short while. To the young Shay, Shorter did not seem different. He certainly never came across as a radical cremationist. "To my mind, he was a good friend of the family and a typical minister concerned about people and his church.

"After my mother died, I didn't see him for years and years and years. He married my father and my stepmother and next time I saw him was when he did a memorial service for my stepmother when she died in 1955. I know he had two kids and haven't heard from Clayburn or Mary Alice. I understand he died during a boat cruise."[14]

In many ways, the Reverend Fred Shorter of the twentieth century and the Reverend Octavius Frothingham of the nineteenth were one and the same, men of the cloth devoted not only to the individuals in their flock but to advancing humanity, especially in death.

William Kephart, a sociologist studying class differentials in death customs in Philadelphians, discovered that members of the upper crust, especially the well-educated ones, had been looking for years to reduce funeral expenses; more and more they were opting for cremation. Still, by 1962, cremation had not become popular with the general public.[15]

CANA figures show that in 1962 out of 1,814,000 deaths in the United States, only 63,435 cremations took place—just 3.71 percent of total deaths.[16] For the industry, this was not promising, a point noted at the Congress of the International Cremation Federation in Berlin in June 1963.[17] When Cremation Association of America past-president Paul O'Bryan addressed the group from the podium, he said that the acceptance of cremation was dying among the American populace.[18]

LeMoyne and Olcott's dream was going up in smoke, but not from crematoriums. The dream was failing because of public apathy. Amid the turbulent 1960s, when a president and a presidential candidate were assassinated, an unpopular war was raging in Vietnam, and the civil rights struggle was being fought in the blood of the innocent, a hand reached out from, of all places, the Vatican.

The pope emerged to save and eventually help to promulgate the practice of cremation. How ironic then, that the occupier of this same position had, in a very real sense only three-quarters of a century before, been cremation's greatest foe.

Twenty-one times since Christ's crucifixion, the Vatican has held ecumenical councils. These councils are assemblies of ecclesiastical dignitaries and theological experts for the purpose of discussing and regulating matters of church doctrine and discipline. In 1963, Pope John Paul XXIII convened the last of these councils. The Catholic Church called it the Second Vatican Council.

Though John Paul XXIII would die that summer, Pope Paul VI would embrace the council's work. Both popes wanted the church to respond to the modern world with less of a reactionary tone, to try to see if some of its more rigid positions could be moderated.

On May 8, 1963, while the Second Vatican Council was taking place, the Vatican suddenly reversed Pope Leo XIII's 1886 ban on cremation. The church accepted the practice, but with two stipulations: the funeral rites could not be performed at the place of cremation, and the actual decision to cremate did not run counter to Christian belief.[19] While the church still preferred whole body burial, cremationists and their beliefs were accepted by the Holy See.[20]

The Vatican was saying, in essence, that Catholics had as much right as anyone else to choose the way they disposed of their bodies. The church then overturned a centuries-old prohibition.

By putting its imprimatur on the practice, the church provided invaluable support to the cremationist industry that could now market to the Catholic community. That plus the fact that most other religions look closely at and are in some way influenced by papal decrees could only mean that good times were ahead for the cremationist/businessman.

Helping out the cremation cause further was the 1983 Revision of the Code of Canon Law. Modifying its stance even further, the Catholic Church said that cremation was allowed when simply chosen in good conscience.[21] The church backpedaled a bit in 1989 when the Order of Christian Funerals, which priests used to perform funerals, failed to include a provision allowing for remains to be present in the church for the funeral liturgy.

In the 1990s, U.S. bishops of the Roman Catholic Church took a look at the statistics and recognized cremation's growing popularity. By 1996, cremation was performed on 21.27 percent of Americans. Among 2,314,690 Americans who died that year, 492,434 had found their way into the retort.[22] It was an absolutely astonishing gain. In the thirty-three years since the Second Vatican Council allowed cremation, the practice had become an accepted part of American funeral practice. Now, it was actually common. Certainly the church's imprimatur didn't hurt.

On March 27, 1997, the bishops of the United States sought and obtained an indult (an exemption from a general rule) that allowed for cremation remains to be present, in the church, for the funeral liturgy.[23] Nineteen hundred and ninety-seven years after Jesus' crucifixion and resurrection, cremation was finally accepted fully by the Roman Catholic Church. In the rest of the world, Buddhists have been practicing cremation since Buddha was cremated circa 480 BCE. Hindus, whose founding goes back even further, circa 1500 BCE, also practice cremation. But the practice is forbidden in Islam. Protestants had long since accepted the practice. As for Jews, cremation was still frowned upon as a method of body disposal.

Chapter Eight

"I'll Give It a Shot"
Arranging My Own Cremation

here's a line in a Bellamy Brothers song, "Kids of the Baby Boom," that goes "And we watched John Kennedy die one afternoon, kids of the baby boom." Kennedy's assassination at the hands of Lee Harvey Oswald changed a whole generation's concept of death.

How could it happen? we wondered. Who would want to kill a U.S. president? And Kennedy? The man was mythic and loved. At a young age, we were forced to confront death and what happens afterward to the body and the soul.

Preteen kids like me remember vividly where we were and what we were doing when the news came that our handsome, revered president had been shot to death. I was home sick from school that day, watching a quiz show on NBC called *PDQ*, hosted by Dennis James, who used to do the Cerebral Palsy Telethon. The "Special Report" graphic suddenly flashed on the screen. There was dead air; you knew it was something bad. It was always something bad when the "Special Report" graphic came on and the television stopped talking and showing pictures.

Newscaster Frank McGee came on and reported that the president had been shot in Dallas. I didn't know McGee that well, so I turned to CBS and Walter Cronkite. He was wearing on earplug. He sat at a desk with someone else; I don't recall who it was. About an hour later, Cronkite heard on his earphone that the president was dead. He delivered the news with a choked voice and tearful eyes.

I couldn't believe it. JFK was like part of the family. He was all over the place on television. It seemed like he came into my living room every night.

The weekend after he died, I was very worried. I was ten years old and worried because the president, whom I had been taught in school runs the country, had fallen. What was going to happen? I cried by myself, wondering if anyone else felt the same way. To a kid who doesn't understand the Constitution, all I knew was that there was a handsome man in the office one day who you innately trusted and the next day there was this horse-faced Texan named Lyndon who looked like he wasn't smart enough to run a school let alone a country.

But if JFK's assassination wasn't traumatic enough, how about the murder of his assassin, Lee Harvey Oswald, on national television? After Oswald was caught, he was being transported for booking when Jack Ruby broke through a small crowd and delivered the fatal shot to Oswald's abdomen. I can still see the expression of pain on Oswald's face as he fell.

After that, nothing was safe anymore.

The Vietnam War escalated. When they reached draft age, U.S. males eighteen years of age had to make a very real confrontation with death. They could easily be drafted and sent to Vietnam to die in some rice paddy. That's exactly what happened to over 58,000 Americans.

I confess in print right now to my everlasting regret that I voted for Nixon in 1972 when I was a know-nothing eighteen-year-old. Had I known something, I wouldn't have voted at all. Watergate dogged Nixon in his second term. When he resigned, that was pretty much it for a generation.

Baby boomers were now about as cynical as you could get. We knew that we were vulnerable and could die young; we knew it from a young age since Kennedy got shot. Our collective subconscious said that if a young, handsome, vital guy like JFK could die, we could too. We just didn't want to believe we would die. I never believed that I would die until the day I was seventeen and I walked into the Oceana Theater in Brooklyn and saw James Bond about to be cremated.

What had really scared me about Bond's trip through the retort was the look of fear on actor Sean Connery's face. Though the character was of course indestructible, Connery played Bond as a man who felt fear. *He* didn't know he couldn't die because *he* wasn't in on the joke. What I had been putting off for so long was facing up to my own mortality.

I approached my fiftieth birthday. I knew damn well that I was probably a lot closer to my death than my birth. Of course, if I live to be 101, I'm wrong. One can always hope.

I already had a burial plot for myself, if I wanted, out on Long Island where my father is buried. My mother was supposed to take that space, but, being the ever-practical person that she is, she figured out that it would be less expensive to be buried in Florida than having her body shipped north. She and her surviving brothers, sisters, and brother-in-law, who had always lived within miles of each other, had gotten a good deal on adjacent plots. They had decided to be buried together under the sunshine in the Sunshine State. That left the plot on the island next to my father open.

"You can have it if you want it," my mother said.

I loved my father, but the idea of spending eternity next to him, listening to him pontificate in the afterlife on a variety of subjects as he did in life, just didn't appeal to me. I called the cemetery to see if I could sell it. My father always liked talking to strangers.

"It's part of a joint plot from your father's lodge," I was told. "You'd only get a few hundred dollars for selling it."

"But my parents paid for that plot for years, far more than a few hundred dollars, and now you're telling me it's not worth anything?"

"Sorry," said the lodge official sincerely.

That "sorry" wasn't good enough. I decided to compare the cost of burial versus cremation. First things first though. Whether opting for earth or flame, you have to die.

Growing up in Brooklyn, I had heard a lot about Green-Wood Cemetery. It was the last resting place of generals and publishers, actors and politicians (the same), as well as gangsters. Located in the borough's Dyker Heights neighborhood about two and a half miles from the Brooklyn Bridge, it is arguably one of the world's most beautiful cemeteries.

It was founded in 1838 as the third rural cemetery in the United States, and by the 1850s its beautiful grounds and statuary had made it a leading tourist attraction, bringing in five hundred thousand visitors per year. In the 1860s, the *New York Times* reported, "It is the ambition of the New Yorker to live upon the Fifth Avenue, to take his airings in the [Central] Park, and to sleep with his fathers in Greenwood."[1] From 1850 to 1900, Green-Wood claimed that "no American cemetery interred more political leaders than Green-Wood. They came by the thousands and the hundreds of thousands, first as tourists, then as permanent residents: Civil War generals, murder victims, and victims of mass tragedies, inventors, artists, the famous, and the infamous. And they have continued to come to Greenwood Cemetery, bringing their lively stories and dark secrets with them. In all, almost 600,000 people have chosen Greenwood as their final resting place."[2]

New York World publisher Horace Greeley; abolitionist Henry Ward Beecher; composer Leonard Bernstein; F. A. O. Schwartz of toy store fame; Samuel Reid, the man who designed the American flag; Alice Roosevelt, T. R. Roosevelt's first wife; Henry Brockholst Livingston, President Thomas Jefferson's second Supreme Court appointee; Governor DeWitt Clinton, who ran against James Madison in 1812 and lost; Thomas Hastings, who wrote the music for the classic hymn "Rock of Ages"; Samuel Morse, inventor of the telegraph; and Frank Morgan, who played the wizard in the film *The Wizard of Oz*—all are interred in Green-Wood.

The cemetery's carefully landscaped grounds, which make it look like a park complete with statuary, was a model used by Frederick Law Olmsted in the design of Central Park. Here's a listing of its current interment charges:

So, let's say you are buried on a Saturday ($260 extra), in an underground vault covered by earth. You can expect to pay approximately $3,489 for the interment of your body. That doesn't include the cost of the clergyman officiating or the coffin.

Interment Charges

Charges for Opening Graves, Vaults, etc.:

Maximum depth including use of lowering device	
Adult *#	$1,284.00
Children(10 years or less) *#	659.00
Saturday burials - extra charge	260.00
(additional charge for each half hour or portion thereof for arrival after 11:30 AM)	56.00
Wooden outer case or non-metal casket only - extra charge	62.00
Additional charge for grave openings by hand when made necessary by the lot being enclosed Maximum depth	445.00
Interment of cremated remains in customary container *#	334.00
Interment of cremated remains extra depth *#	379.00
Inurnment of cremated remains in niches, private mausoleums and recessed foundations *#	157.00
Vaults, underground when covered by exposed slab *#	606.00
Vaults, underground when covered by earth *#	768.00
Tombs in side hills and above ground *#	581.00
Sealing end catacombs	179.00
Sealing side catacombs	225.00
Opening and closing crypt (Community Mausoleums) *#	829.00
Use of Chapel	171.00
Use of Shelter Tent	81.00
Use of Grass Lining	81.00
Funerals arriving after 4 PM or waiting time over 30 minutes, for each half hour or portion thereof	56.00
When necessary to raise remains an additional charge will be made:	
when remains are to be lowered into the same grave	349.00
when remains are disinterred to another location	755.00
Receiving Tomb - for each body	324.00
Additional charge after 6 months for each 6 months thereafter	114.00

Caskets are available in all kinds of woods and metals. Prices vary according to the type of container and its composition. Typically caskets start at around $650 and go up to $4,000 and beyond for "better" models, that is, sturdier and more beautiful wood or metal. If you select a $4,000 coffin, that, plus the cost of interment at Green-Wood, totals $7,489.

Compare that to the cost of being cremated. Green-Wood charges $330 for a cremation, and that includes the use of the chapel. Throw in $35 for the temporary storage of the cremation remains ("cremains") until the ashes are either disposed of or inurned and the cost is up to $365.

Now let's take a look at the types of urns. Urns come in a variety of materials including wood, metal, and granite, in a variety of styles from the classic one on the cover of this book to keepsakes like a pendant that contains your loved one's ashes. Cost ranges from $79

Cremation Charges

Adults (including use of Chapel for service) *	$330.00
Direct Cremation (no service - no family in attendance)*	280.00
Direct Cremation using Alternative Container (no service, no family in attendance)*	250.00
Children (10 years or less) (includes use of chapel)*	225.00
Direct Cremation (no service - no family in attendance)*	189.00
Direct Cremation using Alternative Container (no service, no family in attendance) (metallic cases or metal lined cases are prohibited)*	170.00
Temporary storage of cremated remains for one month or less	35.00
Disposal of cremated remains	84.00
Shipping of Cremated Remains via registered mail	33.00

* Includes $5.00 New York State Cemetery Vandalism and Abandoned Cemetery Property Fund

for a pendant to bronze urns at $749. Even if you choose the most costly bronze urn and add that to the actual cost of cremation, the total is only $1,079.

Compared with burial, that's a difference of $6,410. Looked at financially, without religious, emotional, or health issues factored in, cremation is a bargain. I then wondered what the cost would be for similar services from my local undertaker. I drove into town to find out.

The doorbell at Brit Ponsit's Funeral Home was the figure of a male lion etched in brass. I depressed his tongue, which rang the bell inside. After a moment, a rather attractive woman in white high-heeled pumps answered the door. I wondered if white high-heeled pumps were de rigueur in the funeral business during the day.

"I'm here to find out about arranging a funeral," I said.

"Oh, is someone ill?" she asked sympathetically.

"No," I answered as brightly as I could. "It's for me."

That didn't seem to faze her. She led me up a dark corridor, off which was a maze of rooms with folding chairs. Some of the ante-rooms had Queen Anne chairs upholstered in rich fabric and settees that looked like something from a turn-of-the-century parlor.

"Brit will be right up to talk to you," she said. She left me in a small conference room with a teakwood table, desk, and chair. It's a good thing I like teakwood, otherwise I might have looked for the undertaker who favored mahogany.

"Hi," said Brit, bustling in with a rustle of papers and extending a firm hand. Brit was a wearing a short-sleeved dress shirt with a carefully knotted tie and slacks of indeterminate lineage. His manner was straight and direct.

"I'm making out my will," I explained, which was true, "and I'd like to find out about arranging my own funeral," which was sort of true. After telling him that I was Jewish, Brit, who was not, spoke eloquently on the Jewish tradition of *Taharah*, the ceremonial washing of the body, prayers said over the body, and dressing it in a plain linen burial shroud before the memorial service and the interment.

As an alternative, my body could be disinfected with a topical disinfectant prior to burial. Great. In death I get to wear *eau de l'hôpital*.

"Most families choose one or the other," Brit explained.

The cost was actually the least of Brit's concerns. "Life insurance will cover it," he said. "Some people also open up an account with us in their name to pay for things when they die. The account is portable; you have complete access to it. We never touch a penny until you die."

"Do you watch *Six Feet Under*?" I asked, referring to the HBO show about the quirky Fisher family who run a Southern California funeral home.

"It's my life," said Brit, his cherubic cheeks glowing.

I really had confidence in Brit.

"I'm having trouble choosing between cremation and earth burial," I explained.

"You know, people tell an undertaker all kinds of things they'd never tell anybody else. You have to take into consideration that the whole funeral is for the family, the survivors, not the person who died."

Brit slid a blue brochure across the table. It was a "General Price List." The way Brit explained it, if I chose an earth burial, the cost would be as follows:

Transfer of remains to funeral home—$220
Dressing/Casketing—$75
Taharah—$75
Supervision by staff—$650
Funeral Service—$375
Supervision by religious body—$125
Facilities for Funeral Service—$400
For Religious Committee—$225
Hearse $210
Burial Clothing—$100
Steel Anodized Temporary Grave Marker—$60
Acknowledgment Cards—$25
Traditional Plain Pine Casket—$700
Vault Opening—$425

The total cost Brit would charge for my burial came to $3,665. The cost of the plot and the marker, of course, was extra. That was between me and the cemetery and the stone carver. Each cemetery has physical requirements for the headstones. Cemeteries generally have some sort of relationship with the local headstones makers, which can be seen scattered around most urban cemeteries. But there are also national or regional headstone makers whose services could be employed.

If I chose cremation, I had options too. Brit could just collect me at my house—Brit does many of the collections himself—and drive me by minivan to the crematory, which is actually in one of my town's cemeteries. After the cremation, my family could pick up my ashes from Brit. The total cost for this type of cremation service is $1,020.

As much as I like to think of myself as a no-frills kind of guy, I'd like somebody to say some nice things about me, just in case I'm listening. For that pleasure and really for the sake of my family, the price has to go up if my memorial service takes place at Brit's funeral home. Here's the cost breakdown for a cremation that includes a memorial service:

Transfer of remains to funeral establishment—$210
Dressing/Casketing—$75
Rental Casket—$575 (I could opt to be housed in the cardboard container that I'd later be cremated in, which only costs $75, but I just can't bring myself to be that cheap for my own funeral)
Supervision by the staff—$650
Funeral Service $375
Supervision by religious body—$125
Facilities for Funeral Service—$400
For Religious Committee—$225
Hearse $210
Guest Registry Book—$25
Acknowledgment Cards—$25
Steel Anodized Temporary Grave Marker—$60
Burial Clothing $100
Cremation Fee—$225
Cremation Urn—$55 (the cheapest)

The total cost Brit would charge for my cremation would be $3,280. Why the mere difference of $385 between cremation and earth burial? Because of the cost of the coffin rental. Should I choose to be laid out in a cremation cardboard box, the price obviously decreases. Even in death, it appears to be better to buy than rent.

I noticed that there were other costs that wouldn't apply to me. Jews don't get embalmed, so I would save $375 for that service. "The embalming is actually for a viewing," Brit explained. So is the additional cosmetology charge of $75.[3] Even in death you are charged for looking your best.

Thanking Brit for his time, I decided to take a ride up to Reynolds Cemetery where my congregation had bought burial land. As I drove through the streets of the city, past the hospital and the high school, I wondered if my family would actually take this route following my hearse when I died. I turned on some Creedence Clearwater Revival to blot out the thought. As John Fogerty wailed on "Who'll Stop the Rain," I drove through the gates of Reynolds Cemetery. It happened to be raining. I swear.

Reynolds is a throwback cemetery like Green-Wood, with beautiful, manicured paths for strolling, and its origins date back to the middle 1800s too. The place is full of rolling green hills and ornate statuary. Brit had drawn me a map of the cemetery so I wouldn't get lost. I followed it, turning left at the fork in the road and drove down a rutted, pockmarked road that had turned to mud from the constant rain.

The gravestones were of myriad design and age, everything from the plain granite markers of the nineteenth century to the clean and elegant lines of late-twentieth-century etchings. One family had put up a granite totem pole as a marker, with a picture of the deceased implanted in the middle. I stopped to admire it. The air smelled fresh and clean from the rain and the spring.

The Jewish section of the cemetery was in the rear, over a narrow, rutted road. *I hope my hearse has good springs,* I thought. Then it was through some sheltering oaks that overhung the road. If I chose earth burial, the space my congregation had already chosen was up ahead on the right, a small pasture ringed by blooming poplars in a serene and lovely vista. Beyond were the rolling green hills of a golf course. Mine is a new congregation, so there were just a few head-stones. The space would no doubt fill up in the future.

I remembered where my father was buried on Long Island, a cookie-cutter cemetery with indistinct cookie-cutter plots. I hated the place. There was nothing serene about it. Would my family feel the same way if I was buried in Reynolds? Brit had said that a funeral was for the living and so was the interment. But who is a cremation for? The dead or the living?

On the way out, I got lost and passed by a granite statue of three women. The one in the middle was standing, her breasts exposed by a tunic wrapped around her waist. What looked like handmaidens were on either side, fawning over her. I continued to drive until finally a blessed "This Way Out" sign came up on the right. I followed it out to the road and began the drive home.

Brit had said that some rabbis refuse to perform funeral services for a person being cremated. And while the Catholic Church allows cremation, earth burial is still preferred. In both religions, you have to be a little bit of the maverick to enter the retort.

I wonder if I am.

When somebody dies, be it in a hospital or at home, at some point family and friends have to physically let go of the body. However, death has occurred, and from the moment of death on, the body begins to decompose. It has to be transported as quickly as possible for disposal and/or embalming.

If earth burial and embalming have been chosen, there's an additional stop at the mortician's table, where the blood is drained and embalming (preservation) fluid is pumped through the veins. Cosmetic additions and corrections might be done to the features, if necessary, for an open-casket viewing. For someone who is going to be cremated, their next of kin needs to sign a cremation authorization certificate. The cremation of Suzy Berg, a woman who died in Tampa, Florida, provides an example of such a procedure.

Though no statistics exist, anecdotal evidence from families of the Jewish deceased in Florida show that while it is still not acceptable to the Orthodox and Conservative groups, many Jews today are opting for cremation. Senior citizens in particular seem to like the idea that they can save money—and leave more for their relatives—by opting for the retort over earth burial.

The Bogardus Brothers Funeral Home had picked up Suzy Berg's body at her house where she died. As is typical when someone dies at home, the funeral home picks up the body and transports it back for eventual disposition.

Once Suzy got to the crematory, her body had to be prepared to go into the retort. While the process is more or less the same as it was in LeMoyne's time, it is more closely monitored today. So, the body was placed "on ice," in a refrigerated chamber. When the crematorium was ready, the body was removed and placed on a gurney.

Berg's body was examined for a pacemaker or any implanted medical device that could blow up or melt under the intense heat. Any jewelry she might have been wearing was also removed. Her body was taken from the gurney and placed on an insertion machine. Suzy was slowly lifted and propelled forward on hydraulically and electrically powered rails. The insertion door was opened by an electric motor and the insertion machine continued moving toward the furnace. The body was carefully lowered into the cradle inside the furnace. The insertion machine slowly retracted, and the door was closed and made airtight. All of these maneuvers were operated by the assistant who actually handles the insertion of the body into the retort.

Since Julius LeMoyne's time, crematoriums have become regulated by state law. The Florida Department of Environmental Protection (DEP) requires crematoriums to meet their requirements in the building and testing of the facility. The DEP even employs an air toxins program manager responsible for, among other things, making sure that the cremation process doesn't pollute the air.[4]

The biggest change in the process of cremation since LeMoyne's time is the way it has been automated. No longer required is a furnace man with a skilled hand at raising and lowering temperature through the manual use of the flue and bellows. A contemporary crematory operator uses an operating board. On the board there is a schematic picture that shows time, temperatures, process air, and amount of oxygen in the flue gas. The operator can see if ventilators, ash-room air, and burners are running and make adjustments accordingly.

Different programs can be chosen from the operating board on the furnace front. For example, in the Tabo Incinerator, a popular brand from Sweden, the uptempering program heats the furnace to operating temperature. A built-in clock enables the uptempering program to start automatically. The downtempering program finishes the furnace operation and puts it in resting position.[5]

During the actual burning of the body, a microprocessor keeps track of time, temperatures, process airs, furnace pressure, and amount of oxygen in the flue gas. Depending on what happens in the furnace, the processor sends signals to the various units. It is also possible to connect a terminal in another room at the crematorium and read the values from the operating board there.

It took two to three hours to cremate Suzy Berg. When the job was finished the ash was emptied through a movable grate down into an ash pan. After cooling off, the ash pan was taken to an ash processor and put in. Powered by an electric motor, the processor took about twenty minutes to grind up the bone fragments and ash until they reached the grayish, sandy consistency of cremains. When the milling was finished, the ash pan containing the cremains was emptied into a container that was delivered to the funeral home.

On the cremation authorization form Suzy's husband Sol had signed, a heading at the bottom of the page said, "Disposition of Cremated Ashes." The funeral chapel did as instructed. Sol took possession of Suzy's cremains for scattering.

Chapter Nine

John F. Kennedy Jr.
Icon of Cremation

*F*or all their foresight, the early cremationists forgot one thing—even though the body is reduced to ashes, something still has to be done with the ashes. So, what do you do with the ashes? Do you take them home, scatter them, inter them, what?

Whether or not you think the body is an unimportant vessel for the soul, the end product needs to be disposed of. Ashes can literally last a millennium if packaged the correct way. Thomas Browne's seventeenth-century work "Hydriotaphia" was predicated on the discovery of Stone Age urns containing cremated human remains. But today's family or friend who collects the ashes of the dearly departed has a variety of options.

Some wordsmith in the funeral industry, perhaps to make the idea of the end product more palatable, combined the words *remains* and *cremated* and came up with cremains, the ashes remaining after the body has been pulverized by the machine. When the retort door is opened, a magnet goes through the remains and picks out any unmelted metal, leaving only bone fragments and a coarse powder. The fragments and powder are then carefully transferred to a machine that pulverizes them. What eventually comes out through a spout at the bottom is a finely ground powder, light gray to white in color: cremains.

For an extra fee, the crematory can split the ashes if several loved ones would like cremains for memorial purposes. If the deceased lived in California, for example, but came from New York, half the ashes could be buried in California, the other half back home in New York. There are, however, other options if the loved one chooses to keep the ashes.

The ashes can be stored in their original plastic container, though it is a good idea to label them as such so no one confuses them with another substance such as flour. The last thing you'd want to do is make a cake out of grandma's ashes. Family members have shown thoughtfulness in placing the ashes in items of meaning to them. One Florida insurance salesman, for example, placed the ashes of his beloved wife in a ceramic jar, one of many she had made and of which she was justly proud.

"We heard of one person who had the ashes put into her mother's favorite cookie jar. A family member who does wood-working could make an attractive box for the ashes. If the cremains will be visible, perhaps combining the ashes with seashells would be a nice touch. What you should consider is potential leakage or break-ability of the container, however," advises the Funeral Consumers Alliance of San Mateo and Santa Clara Counties in California.[1]

The most common method of storage, of course, is placing the ashes in an urn. Urns are made from metal, wood, china, and other materials. Some are of extremely elaborate design, others quite simple and stark. If you choose, the cremains can be stored at a cemetery of your choice that provides this service. Urns can also be placed in a wall or indoor niches in a columbarium. Cemeteries impose different charges depending on location, height, glass or solid door for the niches, and size. The usual niches are about ten inches wide, twelve inches high, and fifteen inches deep.

As with Thomas Brown's Stone Age urns, some individuals prefer having their ashes interred in the ground. In this kind of sce-nario, the ashes, in the urn or other container, are placed in the earth. Up to four sets of cremains can generally be placed in one reg-ular-sized burial plot, with markers erected accordingly.

Even in death, just like any piece of real estate, location is everything. If the ashes are placed near a nice view, a lake or garden, for example, you pay more, as opposed to ashes interred in a columbarium with a view of the opposite wall. The fact that the individual has passed into another realm and no longer has the usual senses makes no difference to some people.

The living have trouble thinking of their loved ones without their five senses even in death, and readily pay for proximity to fragrant rose gardens, verdant fields, and silvery lakes. Expect to pay extra for a bronze or brass plaque inscribed with the name, birth and death dates, and epitaph of the deceased, which is placed next to the niche in the columbarium or next to the plot of ground where the ashes, in the urn, are interred. Of course, the ashes can be scattered. Some cemeteries maintain gardens where this can be accomplished for an extra fee.

If scattering is done privately, the ashes can be scattered just about anywhere. The laws governing the scattering of ashes differ from state to state, so consult your state laws before embarking on this practice. In California, for example, the passage of a law in 1998 allowed cremains to be scattered or buried on private land with the permission of the landowner.[2] The state's new governor, Arnold Schwarzenegger, is a liberal Republican and Kennedy in-law. It wouldn't be surprising if he loosened even further the law regarding scattering. Cremains can be scattered near a beloved rose bush, under an apple tree, on your own property or that of a relative's, on a golf course (Harpo Marx, who was Jewish, had his ashes scattered on the seventh hole of a California golf course), or along a favorite hiking trail in a county, state, or national park.

For obvious reasons, you should avoid scattering ashes on a windy day. Ashes blowing back into your face would not be pleasant. If you can't wait for the perfect weather conditions, throw the ashes downwind. The color of the cremains is different from that of dirt, so they will be noticeable. You may want to cover the area with dirt or leaves to prevent the ashes from blowing away or being too evident.

One of the recent trends in scattering is the development of memorial gardens adjacent to churches. The memorial gardens are places to scatter the ashes in a religious setting that the surviving family and friends may revisit. Expect to pay a one-time fee or donation for this privilege and the perpetual maintenance of the garden itself. Perpetual maintenance usually involves mowing the lawn under which the ashes are interred.

Regardless of the method and location, the laws governing disposal of cremains are state-based, in most cases without special permits. However, laws come into play when a decision is made, either by the deceased or by family members, to do the scattering on an open body of water. Then, the federal government gets involved. It is fitting, then, that it was the son of a president of the United States who, in death, did more to promote the scattering of ashes at sea than anyone else.

The last thing in the world John F. Kennedy Jr. likely desired was to be seen as an icon of cremation. He had absolutely no wish to be another Baron De Palm. Right before he died, his mind was on making his magazine *George* a major player in the New York publishing sweepstakes. The magazine was struggling to find its niche.

With barely a year's worth of piloting experience—but possessed of a reckless, devil-may-care attitude—Kennedy, his wife, Carolyn, and her sister, Lauren, took off in John's single-engine Piper Saratoga on July 16, 1999. They were supposed to leave earlier than their 8:38 PM departure, but Carolyn's sister got stuck in New York traffic. As they traveled from New Jersey to Martha's Vineyard, darkness soon set in. It became a hazy, overcast night.

The next day when news blared that the plane had crashed in the ocean off the coast of New England and all aboard had perished, many experienced pilots around the country reacted in the same way—the kid never should have taken off. It turned out that one of his flying instructors offered to accompany him. Kennedy purportedly said he wanted to do it alone.

The National Transportation Safety Board (NTSB) investigates every accident involving a plane in U.S. air space. Their accident report begins as follows:

14 CFR Part 91: General Aviation
Accident occurred Friday, July 16, 1999 in VINEYARD HAVEN, MA
Aircraft: Piper PA-32R-301, registration: N9253N
Injuries: 3 Fatal.

The noninstrument-rated pilot obtained weather forecasts for a cross-country flight, which indicated visual flight rules (VFR) conditions with clear skies and visibilities that varied between 4 to 10 miles along his intended route. The pilot then departed on a dark night.[3]

Because Kennedy was not instrument-rated to fly under conditions of haze and darkness, he was disoriented. More experienced pilots flying similar routes on the night of the accident reported no visual horizon while flying over the water because of haze.

According to a performance study of radar data, the airplane proceeded over land at 5,500 feet. About 34 miles west of Martha's Vineyard Airport, while crossing a 30-mile stretch of water to its destination, the airplane began a descent that varied between 400 to 800 feet per minute (fpm). About 7 miles from the approaching shore, the airplane began a right turn. The airplane stopped its descent at 2,200 feet, then climbed back to 2,600 feet and entered a left turn. While in the left turn, the airplane began another descent that reached about 900 fpm. While still in the descent, the airplane entered a right turn. During this turn, the airplane's rate of descent and airspeed increased. The airplane's rate of descent eventually exceeded 4,700 fpm, and the airplane struck the water in a nose-down attitude.[4]

Kennedy flew erratically and then hit the water like a freight train colliding with a wall. But what exactly caused the crash? The National Transportation Safety Board "determines the probable cause(s) of this accident as follows: The pilot's failure to maintain control of the airplane during a descent over water at night, which was a result of spatial disorientation. Factors in the accident were haze, and the dark night."[5]

A pilot suffering from spatial disorientation cannot accurately determine the altitude or motion of the aircraft in relation to the earth's surface. Pilots literally have illusions about what's up and what's down. Federal Aviation Administration Advisory Circular 61-27C states that "spatial disorientation, as a result of continued VFR flight into adverse weather conditions, is regularly near the top of the cause/factor list in annual statistics on fatal aircraft accidents."[6] Thus Kennedy, his wife, and his sister-in-law, all in their prime of life, died suddenly when Kennedy crashed into the ocean, thinking he was still in the air.

Cremationists nationwide felt pride when they heard that John Kennedy Jr. had chosen cremation. Because he was a Kennedy, the nation's media covered his cremation and the scattering of his ashes. Pictures appeared in newspapers as well as full footage on television of the USS *Briscoe*, a navy destroyer, steaming out to the open ocean, away from the prying eyes of the nation. But a description appeared in every major paper of what happened next.

Kennedy was a devout Catholic, aware that U.S. bishops forbade the scattering of ashes at sea. That is because the church allows cremation providing the process does not demonstrate a denial of faith in the resurrection of the body, which it might if the ashes—the body—are scattered.[7] An urn containing the full set of remains must be placed into the water.

Two years earlier, in 1997, the Catholic Church allowed for an indult to allow the presence of the cremated remains of a body at the funeral mass. The mass was said over Kennedy's body, and his urn was dropped into the ocean. Someplace out in the Atlantic Ocean, the ashes of John F. Kennedy Jr. were committed to the water that he loved so much as a child and an adult. Yet the inaccurate story of the *scattering* of Kennedy's ashes was spread through the media like wildfire.

In the wake of Kennedy's death, scatterings at sea became popular. The Code of Federal Regulations Sec. 229.1 (see Appendix C) sets out the procedures for burial at sea. You cannot just dump the ashes in the water. A general permit is required to transport the cremains to the sea. The vessel doing the dispersal must be three miles out from land. Most funeral homes can arrange to have the ashes scattered at sea or over some wilderness area by a licensed pilot or boat captain. Some, however, will not provide this service for fear of lawsuits if something goes wrong.

Another way of scattering ashes in water is the "do-it-yourself" option. Family or friends may scatter the ashes if they have a sailboat or motorboat, as long as the scattering is done five hundred yards or more from the shore of the ocean or navigable inland waterways (for example, San Francisco Bay, a big lake, or wide river). It must not be done from a wharf or pier. The ashes must be removed from the container, in other words, scattered overboard.

Some families choose to personalize the scattering with a religious or spiritual ceremony. One or several relatives, a clergy member, or even a whole boatload of friends may get together for a send-off that is as simple or elaborate as desired. The federal law also licenses professional scatterers, who advertise on the Internet and in the Yellow Pages. On the East Coast, for example, there's Gus Hald, while on the West Coast, there's Ken and Anya Shortridge.

The captain of the forty-three-foot-long motor yacht *Determination*, Gus Hald arranges maritime funerals. The ashes, which are sometimes sent to him by mail, are scattered on the waters off the coast of Long Island. Hald recently charged $150 for such a service; charters generally start at about $675 for six passengers. Hald supplies a certificate specifying the longitude and latitude of the site where the ashes were scattered.[8]

On the West Coast, Ken and Anya Shortridge operate a scattering service out of San Diego called Ashes on the Sea. They actually go one step further by providing a virtual attendance service. Right before the scattering they'll call you on a cell phone and describe what's happening. This service, including the filing of burial permits, was recently $300. The basic unattended service was $125, while attended services began at $425.[9]

Mindful of the Georgia crematory scandal, every unattended scattering is videotaped and Global Positioning Satellites (GPS) are used to verify the exact longitude and latitude where the ashes are scattered. The person or people arranging the scattering are provided with a memorial certificate with the exact location of the scattering, as well as time and date.

If the deceased is a war veteran, the navy or coast guard will conduct a sea burial at no cost to the family. A flag is required, which the family can obtain from the Veterans Administration. The flag will be returned to the family upon conclusion of the service, which the deceased's family or friends have the option of witnessing. If the funeral home is inland and the ashes have to be shipped to either coast for dispersal, the funeral home will charge postage to send the cremains to the nearest navy/coast guard base.

For those living in a landlocked state who want their ashes scattered on the water, they may contact Gus Hald, Ashes on the Sea, or another reputable scattering service listed on the Internet or in the Yellow Pages. These services will scatter the ashes at sea and no family member need be present. Just tell them what you want and they'll do it (see Appendix C) as long as you pay the price, of course.

Before engaging a scattering service, check with the local state funerary board to make sure the service you are engaging is properly licensed. Also, pay attention to any complaints that might have been filed against the service and then use your best judgment in deciding what to do.

A century and a quarter after Henry Thompson's revolutionary championing of cremation for its low cost, he would be happy to know how affordable even the shipping of the remains has become. I used to have a standing joke with my mother that when she died (she lives in Florida), we'd wait till rigor mortis set in and then buy an economy one-way seat from Fort Lauderdale to New York. That would be a helluvalot cheaper than shipping her in a casket. What I didn't know was how much cheaper it would be to ship cremated remains.

The only thing the United States Postal Service (USPS) requires to ship cremains is that the ashes be in "sift proof containers or other containers that are sealed in durable sift proof outer containers. The original plastic bag provided by the crematory is sufficient for a sift proof container."[10] The identity of the contents must be noted on the address label, and the container must be sent via registered mail with return receipt. Current shipping rates can be found online at http://www.usps.com.[11] Neither Federal Express nor United Parcel Service will ship cremains.

If scattering on sea or land is too pedestrian, there are still other alternatives. One of the most creative is the one offered by the Association Française d'Information Funéraire (AFIF). The association will scatter the ashes over three different sites in the French Alps: Mont Blanc's summit, Vallée Blanche, and Mer de Glace. For the contents of one urn scattered across all three peaks, the cost is approximately 1,410 Eurodollars, or $1,627. The ashes are carried out by helicopter, and, subject to weather conditions, the AFIF confirms the scattering as soon as it is completed.[12]

In 1999 in California, a new law was instituted that made it legal for the first time to scatter ashes on the ground and close to shore. The law came about because of a 1997 scandal in which the cremated remains of five thousand people were found in a Contra Costa County, California, shed.[13] Before the law passed, California had some of the strictest cremation laws in the country, requiring that ashes could be scattered only three miles offshore or in a cemetery and then only by a registered disposer of cremation remains.[14]

The new law made it possible to innovate, which is something Californians do very well. San Diego–based Celebrate Life, a company specializing in scattering ashes, came up with an alternative to the traditional approaches and was able in the summer of 1999 to perform a cremation first: ashes scattered by fireworks. The ashes were those of rocket scientist John Kotowski, an engineer who worked on the lunar drill that was used to take samples during the first moon landings.[15]

When the eighty-five-year-old Kotowski died, his relatives wanted a ceremony appropriate to Kotowski's profession and personality. Because of the new law, Kotowski's family was able to place his ashes in fireworks, which were then launched over San Francisco Bay on July 17, 1999. The deceased's family and friends observed the celebration on a sixty-foot yacht in the harbor while the *William Tell Overture* blared over the ship's loudspeakers. Apparently, the engineer had been a fan of *The Lone Ranger*.

Then there's the matter of the receptacle. If urns, plastic containers, or coffins aren't to your liking, Creative Remains, a San Francisco–based operation, specializes in making unique receptacles for ashes. They use a network of local artists working in a variety of media: ceramics, clay, sculpture, stained glass, memorial plaques, and bronze portrait busts. They can also modify existing objects to hold the ashes—collectibles, sports equipment, jewelry, books, statues, musical instruments, walking sticks, fishing rods, and picture frames.[16]

It's not surprising that California has led the way in innovative and creative scatterings. According to CANA figures for 1998 alone, 42 percent of those who died in the Golden State entered the retort. Hawaii's 58.5 percent and Nevada's 56.5 percent lead the nation. However, Mississippi with 5.1 percent and West Virginia with 5.5 percent are at the bottom of the pack.[17] Interestingly, many of these states opt for relatively simple cremations while California definitely leads the Union in extravagant and creative approaches to cremation

A final variation for happily married couples is for the surviving spouse to keep the ashes of the deceased. When both are dead, a loved one can mix the cremains in one container for burial or scattering, bury separate urns at the same time, or put the urn into the same casket.

Part Three

Chapter Ten

Diamonds Are a Girl's/Man's Best Friend

*A*s the new millennium was about to begin, Sir Henry Thompson, Dr. Julius LeMoyne, Reverend Fred Shorter, and all the early cremationists were, like Sam McGee, smiling from the retort.

According to the Cremation Association of North America, in the year 2000, 26.19 percent of deaths resulted in cremations. This means that out of a total of 2,403,351 Americans who died that year, 629,362 were cremated in one of 1,601 crematories scattered throughout the fifty states.[1]

With the popularity of cremation, the method of disposal of the ashes also changed. The database kept at findagrave.com (see Appendixes A and B) clearly indicates the popularity of interring the ashes in urns. But baby boomers have begun to indulge in many different ways of containing the ashes and celebrating the lives of loved ones who have entered the retort.

Baby boomers have come up with a variety of ways to celebrate the lives of their loved ones by putting their ashes into something other than the usual. One of the more unique ideas is to make a diamond out of the ashes. Called a LifeGem, it is not quite the phoenix of legend, but it sure is beautiful. What makes the product interesting is that its origin stems from two young boys' confrontation with death.

"Our mother is a German citizen," explains Dean VandenBiesen, LifeGem's vice president of operations. His brother Rusty is the company's chief operating officer. "Every summer we'd go to Germany to spend time with our family. Our father was a pilot so it made getting there that much easier." While they were there, the boys stayed with their grandmother. Rusty was four at the time.

> Rusty was sleeping in grandmother's spare bedroom. She was a very religious woman, a Roman Catholic. On all four walls were religious icons, including a picture of Jesus after he was crucified. After three nights of being in a strange room in a strange country, staring at those pictures, it dawned on Rusty that he was going to die one day.
>
> Rusty was very upset. He was crying. We had to console him. We told him, "You're only four, you're going to live for another hundred years!"[2]

It didn't work. Over the years, thoughts of death preyed on Rusty's mind. He felt intensely lonely at the thought of being put underground and left there or his ashes being put somewhere.

"Rusty just dreaded the thought of dying," says his brother.

Like Thompson, LeMoyne, and Shorter, Rusty VandenBiesen felt there must be a better way. Time had progressed to the point that cremation was more common, but the question of what to do with the ashes was still in dispute. Some preferred interring them, others scattering them, still others putting them in an urn.

Then one day in 1999 when Rusty was in his late twenties, he was watching a documentary on cable TV about high-quality manmade diamonds created in a laboratory. That's when the moment of gestalt occurred. If carbon is both the basis of human life and the basis of diamonds, Rusty wondered if both could be combined. Could carbon from a human body be taken, in death, and made into a manmade diamond as a memorial to the departed?

He found the idea rather comforting. He commissioned some studies that indicated it might be possible. Rusty worked for four years to develop the product, discovering along the way that the technology already existed to make it possible.

"We solved the technical problems," said Dean, "and figured out how to collect the carbon from the ashes and make diamonds out of it. And then we realized we could make a lot of people happy by doing this. People just weren't satisfied placing ashes in urns or other keepsakes. They wanted something valuable, portable and especially something that wasn't weird. People have a lot of funny feelings about ashes," said Dean.

Rusty VandenBiesen's issues with mortality were finally laid to rest as the diamond/cremains process was perfected. In 2001, Rusty, along with his brother Dean and two other principals, formed LifeGem, a company that would provide the service of turning cremains into diamonds.

"Rusty made the connection between human carbon and diamonds as a memorial. The idea born out of pain. That's why it's been successful," his brother continued.

The actual diamond created by LifeGem can measure anywhere between .25 carats and 1.3 carats. It possesses the same quality as diamonds found at high-end jewelers. Rusty had succeeded in extending the work of the cremationists into the twenty-first century, where disposal of the cremains was more of a problem than anything else.

"Most of the carbon is in tissues. It doesn't really matter if it comes from organs or muscle but for our purposes, most of it comes from organ tissue," explained Dean.

After the client has signed the order form/authorization, which authorizes LifeGem to collect the carbon of the deceased, midway through the cremation process a special carbon collection kit is employed. The door to the retort is opened. Four ounces of organ tissue are separated from the body and moved to a special sealed container. Once the tissue is in the container, a cover is put on the container and it is placed back in the retort. The door is closed and the cremation continues.

At the end of the process, the door is opened and the container is removed. The tissue inside has been reduced to dry, crispy flakes of carbon. The carbon flakes are then put into a grinder and turned into a fine powder. That carbon powder is placed in a special graphite crucible that is engraved with a unique sixteen-digit tracking number. Next comes the diamond creation process.

A crucible is placed in a vacuum induction furnace. All oxygen is pumped out and the furnace is then heated to a temperature of 3,000 degrees Fahrenheit. This high temperature removes impurities such as calcium, ash, iron, aluminum, and oxygen. Because there is no oxygen in the furnace, the carbon is preserved through the purification. The carbon is also transformed into graphite from the high temperature.

It is the graphite that goes into the diamond press and will later form the diamond. Interestingly enough, the element boron, which is present in the carbon that is collected, survives the purification process. Boron is an extremely tough element that has a boiling point of about 3,200 degrees Fahrenheit. Boron is also extremely common, found in products such as detergents, clothing, glass, paper, wood, and dishware. In this case, boron is what gives the LifeGem diamonds their blue tint.

Baby boomers might remember the episode of the original TV show *Superman* with George Reeves in which the Man of Steel takes a piece of coal in his hand and crushes it so hard he makes a sparkling diamond out of it. LifeGem employs basically the same process—without Superman, of course.

The graphite powder is then placed into a diamond press, where it is subjected to pressure in the range of 800,000 to 900,000 pounds per square inch, and temperatures ranging from 2,000 to 3,000 degrees Fahrenheit. These conditions replicate the forces beneath the earth that form natural diamonds. What takes nature millions of years to complete can be achieved in the lab in a matter of weeks. The size of the diamond is controlled by how much time the graphite stays in the press. The longer the press time, the larger the diamond. The diamond that comes out of the press is a raw crystal that needs to be polished and faceted per customer specifications by a skilled diamond cutter.

Then the diamond is certified. The certification lists all of the phys-

Examples of LifeGems, formed from human cremains. (*Photos courtesy of LifeGem.*)

ical and optical characteristics of the LifeGem diamond. The sixteen-digit tracking number will be laser-etched on the girdle of the diamond, which will be placed in a jewelry setting and delivered to the client.

"The whole process takes about twelve weeks from start to finish," says Dean. "Not including the backlog which can sometimes run months."

While LifeGem trains crematories all over the United States on how to use their carbon collecting kits, the brothers VandenBiesen in the earlier days went on carbon collection duty themselves.

> My brother and I went to Detroit once to oversee a cremation and carbon collection. The body first had to be disinterred. We watched it come out of the ground. The body was encased in this concrete vault. We took it back to the crematory and busted open [the] vault. Inside, the metal casket was sweating. We opened it and everybody in the crematory, they stopped, like they were in a train wreck. The person was lying there in pretty good shape all right, but it was the worst smell in my life. That was it for Rusty.[3]

LifeGems are now all over the United States, Canada, and Europe, with several plants working to produce diamonds. The key to the whole process, of course, is that the carbon has to be collected before it is burned up. The ash itself has a lot of calcium but the percentage of carbon is lower, which is why the carbon needs to be collected before the cremation is complete.

"Some people think it's strange but some really love it. Gives people something to look forward to. I'm still amazed to be able to create something this beautiful from the building block of life," Dean VandenBiesen concluded.

LifeGems are expensive. The cheapest LifeGem, at .20–.29 carat, costs $2,299, while the top-of-the-line .70–.79 size gem costs $9,999. In between are other carat/pricing options. Though expensive, the diamonds provide a great comfort to the deceased's loved ones, who can wear the gem and keep it with them at all times. Like the early cremationists, Rusty VandenBiesen turned out to be a visionary. He can be contacted through the Web site LifeGem.com.[4]

But suppose diamonds aren't your best friend. Suppose, for

example, that you want your ashes to be part of the environment when you go. You're not looking for a traditional scattering on the ocean but actually want to be an ongoing part of it. Eternal Reefs, Inc., has the answer.

Eternal Reefs, Inc., has Reef Ball Development Group Ltd. (RBDG) as its "primary strategic partner." RBDG was created by a group of college friends who enjoyed diving but were troubled by the worsening condition of the natural reef formations. A decision was made to do something about the reefs' declining condition. Patented mold systems were developed to create reef modules that closely mimic natural reef formations, and an environmentally friendly concrete formula was developed to make the new reefs, called Reef Balls.[5]

Authorized Reef Ball contractors produce these reefs for state agencies and many private organizations worldwide. By the year 2000, RBDG had over one hundred thousand scientifically designed artificial reefs in the water. Then, Carleton Glen Palmer, a parent of one of the group members, requested that his cremated remains be put in a reef by RBDG.

"I can think of nothing better than having all that action going on around me all the time after I am gone—just make sure that the location has lots of red snapper and grouper," said Carleton.[6]

Carleton got his wish. When he died, his cremated remains were mixed into the concrete as a reef unit was being cast. After being cured for about a month, it was deployed as a memorial reef in a permitted location. Carleton's reef is now teeming with sea life.

Out of this personal experience, Eternal Reefs was created. The company works only in permitted locations that are approved by the federal, state, and local governments. With every memorial reef, the executor of the estate receives two memorial certificates that identify the longitude and latitude of the memorial. The coordinates themselves are recorded when the reef is placed on the ocean floor.

To date, memorial reefs have been placed on Virginia's eastern shore, in the waters off Fort Lauderdale, Marco Island, and Sarasota, Florida, as well as Charleston, North Carolina. In 2004, the company's first placement for the new year will be back in Sarasota.

An Eternal Reef as it appears after set up. (*Courtesy of www.eternalreefs.com. Copyright Eternal Reefs, Inc.*)

The company offers four different sizes of reefs to choose from. At the top end of the line is the Atlantis, 4 inches high by 6 inches wide, weighing between 3,800 and 4,000 pounds. The largest of the company's reef products, the Atlantis "stands out as a pinnacle of the reef and attracts the larger species of sea life."[7] It is a rather exclusive product that can only accommodate up to four sets of remains.

At the other end of the line is the Community Reef, what Eternal Reefs describes as their "most cost effective product."[8] That's because it is a complete reef system the size of two full-sized basketball courts. Individuals who choose this option have their cremated remains mixed *together* and are cast as a complete reef system of multiple modules.

So what does it cost to be part of a natural reef? The company claims that prices are going down and recommends that consumers check with their Web site, http://www.eternalreefs.com. Just as with earth burial, they are developing a program to pay for the cost in advance. George Frankel, an executive with the company, says "[It] now appears that it [the Advance Planning program] will be an insurance based product used for 'final expenses.' These funds will be payable to the estate to be used for the purchasing of the Memorial Reef. It will cover all the expenses from the time we receive the remains until the Memorial Reef is cast and deployed. It will not cover any expenses the family incurs in attending the casting and placement events."[9] That is, the program won't cover the physical manufacturer of the unit or its deployment in the water. The family will have to pay those expenses themselves.

As the century advances, there will be more products like LifeGem and Eternal Reefs. Technology has already solved the problem of how to effectively cremate a body, but no amount of technology can tell a human being how best to remember a loved one.

Chapter Eleven

The Dead Wives Club
How Murderers Use Cremation
to Cover Up Their Crimes

*J*ack Reeves was a handsome soldier deeply in love with his wife, Sharon Johnson. When Jack was posted to Verona, Italy, his devoted wife followed.

One night in Verona, Sharon awoke to the sound of a gunshot. Jack barged into their bedroom with a smoking revolver. An Italian man was peeking in the couple's bedroom, Jack said. Fearful he was a burglar or worse, Jack shot the peeping tom dead.

An Italian court didn't believe his defense and convicted Jack of murder, sentencing him to fifteen years in prison. Jack was astonished; he claimed he was protecting his family like any Texan would. A few months later, Sharon visited him in jail with good news. Jack's hometown of Wichita Falls, Texas, had begun a petition drive to free him.

In Wichita Falls, thousands of signatures were collected on "Free Jack Reeves" petitions. Eventually, even fellow Texan President Lyndon B. Johnson heard about Jack's plight and agreed to help. Months later, Jack was visited in jail by a representative of the U.S. embassy.

Acting at the behest of the president, Italian authorities pardoned Jack Reeves. A jubilant Jack walked out of jail and into the sunlight and loving arms of Sharon. They returned to Texas, hoping to leave all the unpleasantness behind them. Jack and Sharon moved to Copperas Cove in Coryell County, Texas. Over the next few years, Sharon gave birth to two healthy sons. To outsiders, she seemed to have matured into a happy homemaker. But inside the Reeves household, all was not well. Jack had been cheating on Sharon, and she was on the verge of a nervous breakdown.

When Jack was assigned to duty in Korea, Sharon thought the separation might help their marriage. Not really. Jack cheated on Sharon with a Korean woman named Myong Wei. Sharon found out about it, and when Jack returned to the United States, Sharon requested a divorce.

On March 5, 1978, Coryell County police were called to the Reeves home by Jack. When they arrived, Sharon was dead, apparently of a self-inflicted shotgun wound to the chest. The coroner ruled it a suicide, and the police investigated no further. Jack had Sharon embalmed, placed in a steel coffin, and entombed in an airtight vault.

Jack went on to marry his Korean girlfriend, Myong. Myong really loved Jack, and marriage to a U.S. citizen meant instant entry to the United States. She moved to Texas to live with Jack. At first, Myong was very happy there. But after a few years, marriage to Jack Reeves became hard.

Myong complained to her sister Susan that Jack beat her and forced her to engage in humiliating sexual acts. She demanded a divorce. Jack countered with a reconciliation trip to their country cabin. According to Jack's later account to police, Myong took a rubber raft out into the lake and drowned. Jack later called Myong's sister to tell her of the tragedy.

Immediately, Susan grew suspicious. Myong couldn't swim and was afraid of water. So what was she doing sunning herself on an air mattress in the middle of the lake? State park rangers had their doubts too. Their investigation showed that Myong had drowned in only four feet of water. Why hadn't she just stood up—unless she couldn't? Despite the rangers' suspicions, the justice of the peace ruled the drowning accidental. A removal service transported the body to a funeral home for burial.

Arriving at the funeral home, Susan found further fuel for her suspicions when she looked down at her sister in her coffin and discovered bruises on her sister's neck. She questioned Jack about the bruises, and he claimed his wife had gotten them after hitting a rock in the lake. Susan demanded that an autopsy be performed. Instead, Jack abruptly cancelled the next day's funeral and had Myong's body cremated.[1]

That action made Richard Cross turn over in his grave.

History's most principled opponent of cremation was Sir Richard Cross. Cross was the British home secretary during the late 1870s and early 1880s, the period during which Sir Henry Thompson and the seminal British cremationists were trying to get permission to build a crematory and cremate a body if Parliament would make it legal.

Part of the function of the British Home Office was and continues to be reducing crime and "ensuring the effective delivery of justice."[2] As the head of the Home Office, Cross objected to cremation on the grounds that the practice might be used to cover up a homicide. As home secretary, he would not allow it until Justice Stephen weighed in on the matter in 1884.

That was the year that eccentric eighty-three-year-old Druid priest William Price claimed he was within the law when he cremated the body of his five-month-old son (see chapter 3). Never mind the fact that Price had fathered a son at eighty-three—no mean feat. When Justice Stephen ruled that Price's cremation of his son was legal, the octogenarian's place in history as the man who brought back legalized cremation to Great Britain was assured.

Cremation was legalized in Britain. But Cross's opposition to the practice should be respected and taken seriously. Richard Cross was not some ignorant member of the aristocracy but a principled man who helped establish a historical precedent in British criminal law.

Before 1884 it was the frequent practice of the Home Office to offer rewards for the capture of suspected felons. That same year, there was a change of policy when the Home Office decided to stop offering rewards. They did not feel on the basis of past experience it produced results, that is, captures and convictions. The new policy was in effect only one year when Richard Cross came into the mix.

In 1885, the year after the Druid priest Price won his cremation case against the Home Office and Cross, there was "a remarkable case of infanticide at Plymouth."[3] Cross was pressured to offer a reward for the capture of the murderer. Holding to the principles of the Home Office, he refused. Two years later, Cross's precedent was cited by his successor Home Secretary Mathews who refused to offer a reward for the capture and conviction of the murderer soon to be known as Jack the Ripper.

All five of the Ripper's victims were prostitutes, all murdered and mutilated by knife. At twenty-five, Mary Jane Kelly was the youngest of the Ripper's victims. A contemporary publication, the *Illustrated Police News*, reported, "The throat had been cut right across with a knife, nearly severing the head from the body. The abdomen had been partially ripped open, and both of her breasts had been cut from the body, the left arm, like the head hung to body by the skin only. The nose had been cut off, the forehead skinned, and the thighs down to the feet, stripped of flesh."[4]

With such extensive injuries, cremation might have seemed like the best method of body disposal, but that option was closed to Kelly: she was a Roman Catholic, and the pope had banned cremation the previous year. Instead, Mary Jane Kelly was buried at Walthamstow Roman Catholic Cemetery.

As for cremation's legality, Cross never wavered in his suspicion that the practice could be used to cover up a crime. Sir Henry Thompson himself acknowledged the validity of that position. Even after getting state permission for the practice, the Cremation Society of Great Britain adopted a provision into its bylaws that it would not accept for cremation a body that might have met death illegally.[5]

U.S. law enforcement officials have copied their British counterparts. Most states now have some sort of provision in their criminal laws that says a cremation can be stopped if foul play is suspected. How, then, could Jack Reeves kill his wife and cover up the crime by having her cremated?

Susan Wei suspected that Jack Reeves had killed her sister Myong. She needed to get closer to Jack in order to prove he did it. Susan convinced Jack to let her come and live with him. Jack liked the idea and considered marrying her, too—first one sister, and then the other.

Going through Jack's papers after moving in with him, Susan discovered old newspaper clippings describing Sharon's death. In turn, Jack discussed Sharon's death openly. He called it a tragedy but there was nothing of the grieving husband in his voice, much in the same way that he showed little emotion right after Myong died.

Susan now suspected that Jack had killed his two wives after they each requested a divorce. His concern, she assumed, was not wanting to split assets. And if the shooting in Italy were murder, too, Jack had already murdered three people. For his part, Jack had begun to realize that Susan's repeated questions meant she was onto him. One night he raped her, warning her that she would get worse if she went to the police.

Scared out of her mind, Susan stole Jack's car and drove all the way to Michigan. Back home, Jack was alone again. Jack *hated* being alone. He began leafing through a mail-order catalog of Filipino women looking for American husbands. He came across the picture of Emilita Flaminiano, a beautiful eighteen-year-old who lived in a Manila slum.

Amid grinding poverty and open sewers, Emilita shared a one-room hut with her parents and siblings. At night, she dreamed of the America she saw on TV shows like *Dallas* and hoped one day she could lasso a handsome American like Patrick Duffy's character, Bobby. Soon, her ad began paying off.

She got a letter from an American. After several more letters were exchanged, her suitor proposed marriage. Emilita accepted. Her prince said he would come to Manila immediately. He would meet her family and then take her back with him to the United States. Excited, Emilita went to the airport to meet his plane. She expected him to look like handsome and noble Bobby. Instead, what she got was a paunchy man who reminded her more of Larry Hagman's character J. R. He was forty-six, with thinning gray hair. His name, of course, was Jack Reeves.

Emilita could have pulled out of the marriage, but too much was riding on it. Besides her trip to the United States, Jack had agreed to pay her family a monthly stipend that included medical care for her ailing mother. So Emilita accepted his proposal and went to Texas, where she and Jack married. In her new home, she experienced for the first time the luxuries of indoor plumbing and charge cards.

Jack bought her a Nissan Pathfinder Jeep, a cell phone, a pager, and more. Emilita came to love Jack's possessions—the brick house in Arlington, Texas, where they lived; the fishing boat; his Harley-Davidson motorcycle; and the camper he kept parked in the driveway. Worldly comforts, though, exacted a great price.

Emilita didn't find Jack attractive, and they rarely made love. When she became pregnant, Jack hit the roof. He was convinced the baby wasn't his, and, what's more, he didn't want another child. He demanded she get an abortion. A devout Catholic, Emilita refused. She believed, as the church proscribed, that the soul was already present in the fetus and that to abort was the action of killing a human being.

Jack sent her back to the Philippines, where, nine months later, she gave birth to a healthy baby boy. When the child was one year old, Emilita sent Jack a photo. After examining the picture, Jack realized the baby was his. The resemblance was unmistakable. He succumbed to her pleadings and let Emilita come back home.

Leaving the baby behind, Emilita returned, only to discover that while she was away, Jack had been cheating on her. She now knew she had to get a divorce. She confronted Jack and asked him to sign the papers granting her freedom. Jack was stunned. Hadn't he given her a good life? What kind of good Catholic girl would demand a divorce? Wasn't divorce, too, discouraged by the church?

Emilita had learned a thing or two about being a Texan. She stuck to her guns. She wanted a divorce. Jack was defeated. He offered her thirty grand and an apartment if she would stay for just a few more months. Then, he proposed a trip to their cabin at Lake Whitney to seal the bargain. Despite a nagging feeling of dread,

Emilita agreed. She told her friend Sandy Weiss to page her if she didn't hear from her after two days. When no word came, Weiss paged Emilita but received no answer.

On October 12, 1994, Detective Tom LeNoir of the Arlington, Texas, police department was dispatched to Jack's house. A transplanted Louisianan with a taste for all things Creole, he was there to investigate the disappearance of Emilita. The missing person's report had been called in by Sandy Weiss. That immediately made LeNoir suspicious.

Why hadn't her husband called it in himself?

Jack said that his wife had gone camping, had come home, took the Pathfinder out to meet her boyfriend and disappeared. The story smelled fishy to LeNoir, and when he got back to the office he put Jack Reeves's name through the computer. Up came the record from years before of his conviction for the Italian shooting.

Weeks passed with no sign of Emilita. LeNoir got posters made up with her picture and posted them around the area where he assumed she had disappeared, near the couple's cabin at Lake Whitney. During the next few months, in between his more active cases, LeNoir began to investigate Reeves's background further.

He uncovered Sharon's suicide and Myong's drowning and cremation. LeNoir suspected that every time a wife wanted to leave, Jack made sure she turned up dead and then did what he had to do to destroy the evidence of the crime, including cremating Myong's body to prevent an autopsy that almost certainly would have turned up evidence of murder.

The break in the case came in October 1995, one year after Emilita disappeared. A hunter near Lake Whitney discovered a body. Partially unearthed from a shallow grave and ravaged by scavengers, the remains were eventually identified as Emilita Reeves. There was enough circumstantial evidence to charge Jack with Emilita's murder. LeNoir took Reeves into custody. He was indicted and held without bail. LeNoir decided to look further into the circumstances of Sharon's death. That's when he called Sandy Gately.

Appointed by Lyndon Johnson's former protégé Gov. Ann Richards to the post of Coryell County District Attorney, Gately was fascinated by the case. If LeNoir's suspicions were correct, he had a man in custody who had gotten away with murder for almost twenty years. Gately realized that the cops, the justice of the peace, and the district attorney had bungled the case of Sharon's death. They had never investigated. It was a wrong that needed to be righted to clear the name of the county she represented.

An experienced prosecutor, Gately knew that the best witness against Jack Reeves would be his deceased wife Sharon. Modern forensic science might be able to help them if, and only if, the body was in good enough shape to be examined and tested. A short while later, Gately watched as Sharon's remains were disinterred from her grave.

Sharon had been entombed in an airtight vault in a steel coffin and thoroughly embalmed. When the coffin was opened, it was discovered that Sharon's body had been mummified! It was in perfect condition. Using forensic techniques not available in 1978, plus computer simulations, criminalists concluded that the gunshot wound to Sharon's chest was not self-inflicted. She had been murdered.

There is a famous speech given by Edward G. Robinson in Billy Wilder's film *Double Indemnity*. Robinson playes ace insurance investigator Barton Keyes, whose company is being forced to pay off on an accident in which the insured fell off the back of a train. Keyes suspects foul play. His boss, Mr. Norton, thinks it might be a suicide, that the decedent killed himself by throwing himself off the back of a train. Keyes tells his boss,

> You know, you ought to take a look on the statistics on suicide sometime. You might learn a little something about the insurance business. . . . Come now, you've never read an actuarial table in your life have you? Why, they've got 10 volumes on suicide alone. Suicide by race, by color, by occupation, by sex, by seasons of the year, by time of day. Suicide, how committed: by poisons, by firearms, by drowning, by leaps. Suicide by poison, subdivided by types of poison, such as corrosive, irritant, systemic, gaseous, narcotic, alkaloid, protein and so forth. Suicide by leaps, subdivided leaps from high places, under the wheels of train, under the wheels

of trucks, under the feet of horses, from steamboats, but Mr. Norton, of all the cases on record, there's not a single case of suicide by leap from the rear end of a moving train.[6]

LeNoir felt just as suspicious as Keyes about the method Sharon allegedly used for her suicide. While there are many cases of suicide by gunshot to the chest, the more common method is to the brain. Plus, forensic and ballistics tests showed that the angle of the wound could have occurred only if someone shot her; it wasn't self-inflicted.

LeNoir found out that Sharon had wanted a divorce that would have cost Jack a large amount of money. Investigators established that the gun that killed Sharon belonged to Jack and that he was at the scene of the crime. His alibi was that he was sleeping in the other room. This time, nobody bought it. Sandy Gately charged Jack Reeves with the 1978 first-degree murder of his wife Sharon Reeves.

Gately then tracked down Myong Reeve's sister Susan. Susan had since married, had two kids, and was now living in Alabama. Susan told Gately about her suspicions that Jack had killed her sister and that he had her body cremated to cover up the evidence. Had that not happened, had police been smart enough at the time to wonder where those bruises on Myong's neck came from, they would have held up her cremation.

An autopsy would probably have shown that Jack Reeves had strangled his wife. He then faked her drowning in four feet of water. But because Myong's body had been committed to the retort, it would be difficult to charge Reeves with her murder. They had only Susan's word that the bruises were on her neck and no forensic evidence to back it up.

On January 30, after a two-week trial, Jack Reeves was convicted of the first-degree murder of his wife Sharon. The judge sentenced Jack to life in prison without parole. Then, on September 5, 1996, Jack Reeves was found guilty of murdering his third wife, Emilita. For the second time he was sentenced to life in prison. He is not eligible for parole until 2045.

As for Myong, hers is the only murder Jack got away with because her body was cremated.[7]

There is no telling how many cases like that of Myong Reeves exist in the annals of the U.S. criminal justice system in which a murderer had a body cremated to cover up the crime. In the nineteenth century, though, when murderers wanted to get rid of the body, they usually did it by burial or drowning. Cremation was such a new practice at that time, it is doubtful criminals would even have thought of it, unless it was a do-it-yourself funeral pyre, which would still leave lots of evidence.

In the twentieth and twenty-first centuries, however, with cremation more common, it would make perfect sense for a murderer to try to destroy a body by cremating it. It would be especially practical if one family member murdered another, as in the Reeves case. It has never been unusual for criminals to apply modern technology in pursuit of their nefarious goals.

Sir Richard Cross had been right to be suspicious of cremation in certain situations. Separated by a century and a quarter, Tom LeNoir had followed through on Cross's suspicions. He had investigated and put a serial wife killer behind bars.

Chapter Twelve

Tri-State Revisited

*A*ll of the gains that cremationists had made in the United States threatened to be wiped out in one fell swoop by the Tri-State Crematory scandal. Fox News, MSNBC, CNBC, CNN, and CNN Headline News gave the story extensive coverage and why not? Among the lurid details was the existence of an awful stench, though no one bothered to explain that after two weeks of decomposition a body stops smelling, even though it continues to decompose.

As usual, the cable networks offered no perspective on where the scandal fit within the history of American cremation. All they were interested in was sensationalism and ratings. Viewers were left to seriously wonder: If they opted for cremation, would they even get to the retort, or would some greedy and unscrupulous crematory operator take their loved one's money and leave them in the sunshine with their unseeing eyes?

And then, just a few months after the scandal broke, it was old news. The families of the defiled were left to soothe their psychic wounds in private. But even as the story died down, the case itself wound its way through the criminal justice system as the living sought some justice for the dead.

In March 2003, the Georgia Emergency Management Agency had recovered 334 bodies from the property and conclusively identified 222. The state charged Ray Brent Marsh, the crematory operator, with allegedly making money illegally from bereaved families. The state says that he pocketed the money he was given by funeral homes to cremate his clients.[1] In essence, he was accused of running a confidence game—getting people to pay for a product they never received and then hiding the truth.

Marsh's indictment is on literally hundreds of charges. Most, though, are low-level state felonies and misdemeanors. Only federal charges can elevate his crimes to a level commensurate with the government's ability to mete out decades of hard time behind bars. Otherwise, even if found guilty, he'll be out in a few years.

In the wake of the scandal, the Georgia state legislature moved at a lightning-quick pace to pass a bill strengthening crematory regulation rules, at the same time making it a felony for a funerary business to abandon a corpse. The bill's sponsor was Mike Snow, the state representative who had previously championed lack of inspection of Tri-State Crematory (see chapter 1). In the wake of the scandal, Snow wrote a new law for the state of Georgia, which he campaigned to pass.

Snow's bill, HB 1481: Desecration of a Dead Body, "prohibits mutilation, desecration of a dead human body wherever it awaits final disposition, lies in state or is prepared for burial, showing or cremation, whether it's in a funeral home, place of worship, private home or other facility, a grave site or any other place."[2]

Snow's bill also states that a person "commits the abuse of a dead body when he throws away, abandons, or finally disposes of any dead human body or any portion of it, other than by burial, entombment, and inurnment, burial at sea or scattering of cremated remains." This latter section specifically covered crematories, including the ones like Tri-State that did business only with funeral homes and not the consumer directly.

The bill became law in May 2002. Shortly afterward, the first

Senator Chris Dodd (D-CT) chairing a subcommittee hearing in April 2002 that looked critically at the funerary business. (*Courtesy of www.senate.gov/~dodd/.*)

civil suits were field by the families of the decedents who should have been cremated but weren't. Many of these suits would eventually merge into one class-action suit. To prove their case, the plaintiffs in the class-action suit employed Charles Crawford as an expert witness. Crawford is a licensed funeral director in Nashville, Tennessee, and has worked in the funeral industry since 1978. He has operated his own crematory since 1995.

Crawford visited Tri-State Crematory on June 20, 2002. Based upon his observations, he claimed in court documents

> that a reasonably prudent funeral director would notice, upon a visit to Tri-State that the buildings in which cremations were performed were not climate controlled or secure from pests. These deficiencies indicated to Mr. Crawford that Tri-State Crematory did not meet the standard of care for what a funeral director should observe in a third-party crematory and would not have met the standard of care at any prior date when it appeared the same. It would have been a violation of that standard of care for a funeral

director to choose Tri-State to perform cremations on its behalf if Tri-State appeared at any time as it did on June 20, 2002.[3]

Tri-State also got its own expert witness, Alan Kroboth, who stated in a class-action brief that

> under the industry standard of care for operation of a crematory, it has never been acceptable not to keep track of the identity of a body entrusted to a crematory for cremation. Nor, over the past 25 years, has it ever been appropriate for a crematory operator to commingle human remains, or to cremate two sets of remains jointly, without express permission to do so. Over the past 25 years, it has continually been the industry standard of care to ensure that all human remains are contained during the pulverizing process.[4]

The brief goes on to state,

> It has also been the standard of care over the past 25 years to ensure that all visible bone fragments are recovered from the cremation chamber after a cremation, and to ensure that no visible bone fragments are allowed to accumulate in the cremation chamber over time. Finally, over the past 25 years, it has uniformly been the industry standard of care that the cremation facility, its surrounding areas, and its holding facility should be kept in a neat and tidy condition. Again, the evidence reviewed at the class certification hearing showed directly or circumstantially that these standards were not adhered to at Tri-State.[5]

/ Through the second quarter of 2002, police and forensic experts combed every inch of the Marsh property and removed all the remains they could find. On June 20, Ken Poston, Ray Brent Marsh's attorney, voluntarily opened the crematory and its grounds to the many attorneys who were involved in the case.

"Today is a voluntary opening of the crematory to the many attorneys that are involved in the civil side of this matter," Poston said in a local paper. "It [the tour] was slated to last the whole day, but we just had somewhat of a surprise in the middle of it with the discovery of more human remains, mostly in the form of bone."[6]

One of the attorneys had discovered the remains of a vertebra and a digit. The two fragments weighed about six ounces. Attorney Poston speedily informed police and prosecutors of the discovery. If anything, Poston's kind gesture in voluntarily opening the crematory grounds had backfired. He was getting bad publicity for the discovery of the bone, instead of being lauded for an open and conciliatory gesture in a hostile environment.

"When you're in that sort of situation, as an attorney you have an ethical obligation to contact law enforcement, which we did," Poston explained.[7]

Until his trial in 2004, Ray Brent Marsh remains under house arrest at his family's sixteen-acre property at the crematory site in Noble. Marsh has since tried to declare himself indigent so the state would have to pay for his attorneys. The court wouldn't buy it, so Marsh has to pay out of his own pocket.[8] As for Tri-State itself, the crematory has closed. Back on the highway, the signs have been removed. Tri-State is not getting any more business, at least for now.

But for the families of the dead who lay moldering in the sun until their discovery, it has been an uphill battle to come to grips with their victimization. The last thing anyone expects is that the person handling the disposal of a loved one's remains would take the money and not even run, leaving the dead ignored, unattended, and dishonored. The survivors were left to mourn the dead and fight for justice for their loved ones. Meanwhile, the task of identifying all the bodies is ongoing.

In an effort to bring the matter to a conclusion, the Georgia Bureau of Criminal Investigation tried matching bodies through DNA analysis, fingerprint analysis, dental analysis, and the simple means of physical identification when possible. Then they listed the remains that are still unidentified on their Web site.

Please be aware that these descriptions are the best non-medical descriptions of the remains that we can provide. In some cases, limited information is available regarding the remains. This is largely due to the degree of post mortem change. In some cases, certain findings are limited by the extent of remains recovered; as such, some descriptions are purposefully incomplete because no further information is available.

Not all remains lent themselves to a description and as a result, not all unidentified sets of remains are included in these descriptions. Such remains lacked any unique descriptive features to allow for identification. In these cases, no DNA match was made, therefore, unless additional DNA samples are submitted from their kin, these remains are not deemed identifiable. Dates of death are estimates only, based on physical state of remains and recovery parameters. These should be considered as a guide only; if other identifying features are consistent with your loved one, then please make a note of this.

In all cases, for convenience in identifying sets of remains, remains have been separated out on believed race and sex. In all cases, please remember that certain features, especially race and sex, are scientific estimates. If the general description is consistent with a specific individual, except for race and/or sex, please note this information on the possible match form. DNA testing was attempted on all these sets of remains. Due to the low utility of sibling DNA in isolation from direct lineage DNA [parents and children], such samples were not analyzed. These lists have been further separated based on the results of the DNA testing.[9]

The Georgia Bureau of Criminal Investigation's simple explanation of what they were doing was all the more chilling for the lack of drama of the identification process. Here is a typical description of some of the unidentified bodies:

WHITE FEMALES NO DNA MATCH POSSIBLE
Descriptions of Remains—Walker County
#39 older adult, over 50 years, probably white, probably female,
    5 ft 3 in to 5 ft 9 in
missing all teeth (no upper or lower teeth)
possible healed fracture middle left forearm
old fracture left thigh with metal plate (5 screws)
green patterned nylon pullover shirt, size 40/20W, "Anytime" brand
severe arthritis with fused vertebra in neck and middle-lower
    back ("stiff")
died May1998—Mar 1999
NO DNA MATCH POSSIBLE

#47 30–55 years, 5 ft to 5 ft 2 in, small build
missing all wisdom teeth except right lower
missing left upper second molar and right upper first molar
missing right upper outside front tooth
silver fillings left upper first molar, left lower second molar, &
    right lower first molar
mild arthritis right knee
stiff neck (2 fused vertebrae in middle)
died May 1998–June 1999
NO DNA MATCH POSSIBLE

#48 45–65 years, female, 5 ft 1 in to 5 ft 6 in, small build
died May 1998–June 1999
NO DNA MATCH POSSIBLE

#56A older adult
missing all right lower molars and first right lower premolar,
    missing all left lower teeth
missing central lower teeth—only right lower eyetooth and first
    premolar remain
DNA STATUS PENDING

#61A adult female
missing left lower molar and left lower second premolar
porcelain crown left lower first molar
silver filling left lower canine (eye tooth)
died Nov 1999–Dec 2000
NO DNA MATCH POSSIBLE

#61B adult
impacted, unerupted right lower eyetooth
missing right lower second molar and wisdom tooth
missing right lower first premolar
died Nov 1999–Dec 2000
NO DNA MATCH POSSIBLE

#82A female with extreme arthritis in right ankle
died May 1998–Jun 1999

DNA STATUS PENDING
#88 elderly, over 60 years, female, about 5 ft 3 in
missing all teeth
osteoporosis[10]

In California, Michael Brown's alleged body parts/cremation scam was discovered shortly after the Tri-State story broke (see chapter 1). Brown has since been indicted on numerous counts of mutilating human remains and embezzlement, two counts of falsifying death certificates, and two counts of solicitation to commit a felony.[11] "If the state is to be believed, Brown was an opportunist and con man who preyed on the living and the dead. If convicted on all those counts, he'd get two hundred years in prison."

But Brown actually got lucky. Instead of being tried in the press, fate took a hand when an even bigger story emerged in Lake Elsinore, the town where Brown had his business. A Lake Elsinore man was arrested and accused of kidnapping and killing five-year-old Samantha Runnion and leaving her body on a twisting road high above the town. The Runnion case shifted attention away from Brown. By the time it was adjudicated, the national press was nowhere to be seen.

On March 15, 2003, Richard Layton, Brown's attorney, argued before Riverside County Judge Rodney Walker, the presiding judge in the case, that the grand jury "was not given all the necessary information before they indicted his client on charges of illegally selling body parts from dozens of corpses."[12] It didn't work.

A few months later, on July 18, Brown made a deal. He pleaded guilty to sixty-six felony charges for illegally transferring bodies from his cremation business to the anatomical supply house he operated next door. In return for the plea, prosecutors dropped the rest of the charges. Brown wouldn't have to serve two hundred years, but he didn't get off either.

"I'm deeply remorseful for what has happened," Brown said at his October 4, 2003, sentencing hearing. "Something did terribly go wrong."

The judge was not terribly sympathetic. Brown was sentenced to twenty years in prison, a distinct message to those who would make money illegally off the dead. The cremation business was rocked to its core by these scandals, especially the one in Georgia.

"The Cremation Association of North America (CANA) founded in 1913, whose 1,200 plus members represent funeral homes, cemeteries, and crematories from around the world, is appalled at the recent discoveries in Noble, Georgia at the Tri-State Crematory who is not a CANA member," said Jack Springer, CANA's executive director.[13]

There have also been calls for reform.

"I strongly believe that we have an obligation to ensure that no widow or widower, family or community is taken advantage of during times of sorrow and stress," wrote Senator Christopher Dodd, D-CO, in a letter to the General Accounting Office (GAO), the investigative arm of Congress.[14]

Dodd had asked the office to look at funeral homes, mortuaries, and crematories to determine whether the bereaved are being victimized by price gouging, abusive or deceptive trade practices, and health violations. Whether or not the GAO, usually a responsive group, initiates an investigation is under review. Dodd went further, allying himself with his House colleague, Rep. Mark Foley (R-FL), and on April 26, 2002, held a hearing before the Senate Subcommittee on Children and Families, which Dodd chaired.

Senator Dodd in his opening statement said,

> The award-winning television program *Six Feet Under* has popularized the funeral industry and has exposed the public to some of the more interesting contemporary aspects of the business of caring for the dead. Americans are talking about the death care industry around the kitchen table and around the water cooler at work. Unfortunately, all the stories they talk about are not fictional accounts from the TV show. There has been a rash of deeply troubling stories in newspapers across the county. News reports from Noble, Georgia [and] Riverside, California and numerous other places around the country have raised serious concerns about the industry.

Americans are now intimately familiar with stories about cremations that never took place and burials that should have happened, but never did. We've read about inspectors who didn't inspect and families who have been told that the ancient tenets of their religious faiths would be respected in caring for a deceased loved one, only to discover that those tenets were ignored. We've learned that some families, in their moment of greatest grief and vulnerability, have been ripped off by unscrupulous dealers for thousands of dollars. As one of our witnesses will testify, there is a great deal of confusion about funeral products and services and in some cases that confusion has led to terrible consequences for families.

There are those who say that the newspaper articles and consumer complaints are only anecdotes and do not reflect the high level of fairness, care, and propriety that exists in this industry. I am not here to take gratuitous pot shots at an industry and I understand that it is not the habit of the news media to report on the planes that don't fly. However, the sheer volume of these reports and the wide geographic distribution of these incidents make it appropriate for Congress to examine whether consumers are receiving the protection that they deserve when they are making one of the largest purchases of their lives under great emotional distress.[15]

Dodd recognized that Congress has never directly legislated in this area, but "in light of recent events and changes taking place in the industry, [he believes] that it is appropriate for Congress to consider whether the federal government can and should take additional steps to protect American consumers and help maintain the high level of consumer confidence that has historically been enjoyed by the funeral industry."[16]

Dodd feels that the laws regulating the death care industry are "inadequate," essentially "a patchwork of state rules that are neither protecting consumers nor serving the industry well. Currently, the federal role is limited to a single disclosure rule—known as the funeral rule—promulgated decades ago. [Dodd believes] we must modernize these laws."[17]

Even before his hearing opened, Dodd admitted that based on

his preliminary assessments, Congress should consider taking six specific actions:

1. Codify the Funeral Rule because the rule should have the full force of law.

The Funeral Rule, or "the Rule," as it is known in the funerary trade, was adopted by the Federal Trade Commission (FTC) on September 24, 1982. It became fully effective on April 30, 1984, and was later amended on July 19, 1994. The FTC defines it this way:

The Rule, as it stands today, specifies that it is an unfair or deceptive act or practice for a funeral provider to: (1) fail to furnish consumers with accurate price information disclosing the costs of each funeral good or service used in connection with the disposition of dead bodies; (2) require consumers to purchase a casket for direct cremations; (3) condition the provision of any funeral good or service upon the purchase of any other funeral good or service; or (4) embalm the deceased for a fee without authorization.

The Rule also specifies that it is a deceptive act or practice for funeral providers to misrepresent the legal or local cemetery requirements for: (1) embalming; (2) caskets in direct cremations; (3) outer burial containers; or (4) any other funeral good or service, and to misrepresent that cash advance purchases are the same as the cost to the funeral provider when such is not the case. The Rule sets forth preventive requirements in the form of price and information disclosures to ensure funeral providers avoid engaging in the unfair or deceptive acts or practices described above.[18]

The key part of the Rule, the loophole that enables places like Tri-State to function, is that the Rule applies only to funeral providers. The Rule defines a funeral provider as "any person, partnership or corporation that sells or offers to sell funeral goods *and* funeral services to the public."[19] So, people who sell or offer to sell *only* funeral goods or *only* funeral services, like cremations, are not considered funeral provider, thus, they are not

subject to the Rule's provisions. Because Tri-State sold its cremation services directly to funeral homes and not to the public, it
was technically not a funeral provider and therefore outside the
Rule's province.

2. Expand the Funeral Rule. Currently the Rule applies only to
   funeral homes. But the funeral industry has changed in the
   two decades since the Rule was first promulgated. The
   Funeral Rule should be expanded to cover every business that
   sells funeral goods or services directly to consumers.

3. The federal government should become an effective partner
   with the states to promote more frequent and thorough
   inspections of funeral facilities. Senator Dodd believes Congress should consider establishing a grant program to assist
   states to hire and train more inspectors. As a condition of
   receiving federal funds under this program, states would be
   required to adopt clear standards and license requirements
   for funeral service providers.

4. The FTC should be required to maintain a clearinghouse of
   pricing information to help consumers make informed deci-
   sions.

5. Congress needs to consider whether consumer protections
   from other areas of federal law should be adapted to this
   industry. For example, in the area of mortgages, there is a
   prohibition against excessively high interest rates, and consumers have the right of recision, that is, to terminate a contract even after it is signed. An analogous provision could be
   put into a contract with a funeral home/crematory.

6. The FTC should be given enhanced enforcement authority so
   they can more effectively crack down on bad businesses.
   These enhanced enforcement authorities would include the
   power to levy special penalties, issue immediate cease and

desist orders, and in extreme cases to temporarily or permanently close facilities that pose a danger to the public's health or well being.[20]

In the wake of the hearing, Senator Dodd decided to ally himself with his House colleague Mark Foley even further. On November 14, 2002, they introduced S3168 and HR 5743, similar bills, into the U.S. Senate and House of Representatives respectively. The Senate bill was referred to the Commerce, Science and Transportation Committee, and the House version to the Energy and Commerce Committee. Each bill sought "to codify the FTC Funeral Rule into law and extend its regulatory coverage, currently restricted to funeral homes, to cemeteries, crematories and monument retailers. Under the law, funeral service clients would be able to sue such businesses for up to *$5,000 per Funeral Rule violation.*"[21]

Also proposed was the creation of the U.S. Office of Funeral, Burial and Disposition within the Department of Health and Human Resources. The idea behind this office was to ensure that all states regulate and inspect funeral service businesses within their jurisdiction through some type of board, bureau, or governmental department. Dodd and Foley stated publicly that their purpose was "to improve funeral home, cemetery, and crematory inspections, to establish consumer protections relating to funeral service contracts, and for other purposes."[22] However, because all pending legislation expired when Congress adjourned in November 2002, those bills died an untimely death and have not been reintroduced.[23]

But one purpose for introducing these bills was to generate public support for government regulation of funeral services. The funeral industry feels exactly the opposite, and it has the money to lobby Congress to keep things the same.

"The past abuses within this industry can be controlled, but only if the public is willing to speak out and advocate for necessary changes," says Carolyn Hayek, former executive director of Fred Shorter's People's Memorial Association.[24]

And let us hear an "amen" to that.

Chapter Thirteen

Ted Williams, the Future of Cremation, and SARS

Ted Williams's nineteen-year career with the Boston Red Sox began in 1939 and ended in 1960, cut short by six years of military service during World War II and the Korean War. His lifetime batting average of .344 placed him sixth on the all-time list of the game's greatest hitters. He hit 521 homers, landing him in the top ten home-run hitters of all time. In 1941, he hit an average of .406, the last player to do so.[1] For those of us who grew up in Brooklyn, Ted Williams was the only athlete playing for a non–New York team that was spoken of with awe.

The reason for the respect was Williams's astounding success as a hitter. He was brilliant. And it wasn't just the talent. He worked at it. His work ethic was as much admired as his eyesight, purported to be an unerring 20/10. Williams could see the ball curving as it came in, the rotation on the ball, the seams, everything, which was why he hit the ball almost 3.5 out of 10 times. Baseball is the only sport that pays you for failure.

Williams could smell the burn from a foul tip when the ball glanced off the bat. In later years, when talking with contemporary sluggers, he would ask them, "Do you smell the smoke?"

Never a voluble individual, Williams mellowed, even with the press that he never trusted. As he grew older, he thought about what he wanted to be done with his body when he died. On December 22, 1996, Williams's will was filed with the state of Florida.

"I direct that my remains be cremated and my ashes sprinkled at sea off the coast of Florida where the water is very deep," Williams wrote in Article 1—Cremation/Funeral of his Last Will and Testament. Williams lived in Florida and was an avid deep-sea fisherman.

But when Williams died on July 5, 2002, the Splendid Splinter, as he was known in life—a man who shunned publicity—suddenly became in death an unwitting advocate for cremation. Despite his wishes to be cremated, he was frozen . . . headless. Williams's head was frozen in one cryogenic tank, his body in another.

According to Larry Johnson, the former chief operating officer of Alcor Life Extension Foundation in Phoenix, Arizona, Williams's torso is kept in one of the facility's stainless steel tanks. His head has a separate home in a "lobster pot" placed inside a freezer chest.[2] Williams wound up in the "soup" because of a note produced after his death.

The note is dated November 2, 2000. Written on a greasy napkin, it is signed by Williams, his son John Henry, and daughter Claudia Williams. The note says that the three want to be put in "Bio-Stasis after we die" for the opportunity to "be together in the future."[3]

The note's veracity would later be challenged by Williams's daughter Bobby-Jo Williams Ferrell. The Florida State Attorney's Office mounted an investigation to determine the note's veracity. A laboratory analysis later determined that Williams's signature appeared genuine. According to Assistant State Attorney Mark Simpson, forgery could not be proven beyond a reasonable doubt. Charges were not filed.

If at some future date the Williams children agree to honor his original will, he will be cremated. Until then, Ted remains in cold storage.

♦♦♦

2002CP519

Last Will and Testament
of
Theodore S. Williams

I, THEODORE S. WILLIAMS, a resident of Citrus County, Florida, do hereby make, publish and declare this instrument to be my Last Will and Testament, hereby revoking any and all Wills and Codicils I formerly may have made.

ARTICLE 1 - CREMATION/FUNERAL

1.1 Cremation. I direct that my remains be cremated and my ashes sprinkled at sea off the coast of Florida where the water is very deep.

1.2 No Funeral. It is my wish and direction that no funeral or memorial service of any kind be held for me and that neither my family nor my friends sponsor any such service for me.

ARTICLE 2 - PAYMENT OF DEBTS,
TAXES AND EXPENSES OF ADMINISTRATION

I direct that all estate, inheritance, succession and other death taxes of any nature, other than generation skipping transfer taxes, which may be levied or assessed by reason of my death by the laws of any State or of the United States with respect to property passing under this Will or any other property (exclusive of any tax imposed as a result of Section 2041 or Section 2044 of the Code, or a corresponding provision of State law) shall be considered a cost of administration of my estate, and that such taxes, together with all debts and expenses of administration of my estate, shall be paid out of my residuary estate. Provided, however, any excess retirement accumulations in qualified employer plans and individual retirement plans shall bear the increase in estate tax imposed by Section 4980A of the Internal Revenue Code.

In the event my residuary estate lacks sufficient liquidity to pay such debts, expenses, taxes and other charges properly chargeable to my residuary estate, I authorize my Personal Representative to request such amounts from the Trustee of the TED WILLIAMS TRUST OF JULY 1985 as amended and restated on _December 2 2_, 1996, as the same may be amended from time to time before my death, as my Personal Representative deems advisable for the payment in whole or in part of such debts, expenses, taxes and charges (whether due with respect to the trust property or otherwise). Such debts and expenses, however, are not to be a charge against any portion of my property or my trust property constitutionally or otherwise exempt from debt by the laws of the State of Florida. There shall be no right of reimbursement

1

_J.S.W._

Article I of Williams s will states that he wants to be cremated. (*Courtesy of TheSmokingGun.com.*)

It is ironic that as the first decade of the millennium is picking up steam, the future of cremation still hinges on past concern.

Despite the advances in technology, affordable prices, and memorial products, cremation is making headlines only because of health concerns. Advocates are using the same arguments that the fathers of modern cremation—Henry Thompson, Julius LeMoyne, Octavius Frothingham, and Henry Olcott—made over a century ago.

An item appeared on March 13 on the UPI wire with the headline:

MILITARY WON'T CREMATE INFECTED CORPSES

The article went on to state that "the military will not cremate any soldiers who may die from smallpox or other biological weapons if there is a war with Iraq. However, the Defense Department is still working with myriad government agencies to make sure the corpses can be transported and handled safely without spreading the disease in the United States, a top Pentagon health official said."[4]

Despite the fact that certain biological agents could cause corpses to be infectious, the government had ruled out battlefield cremations. Of course, the United States did go to war with Iraq. As of this writing, no weapons of mass destruction, including biological, have been found.[5] But the remains of American soldiers, who continue to die in Iraq, are regularly being sent home for cremation and burial.

On April 3, I picked up my local paper. On the front page was a story that said my town had two suspected cases of the Severe Acute Respiratory Syndrome (SARS) virus. A friend of mine, Isaac Parker, is the local infectious diseases specialist. Quoted in the article, Isaac said that there was little or no chance that the victims came in contact with anyone in town because they were freshly off a plane from the Far East. He, of course, used Centers for Disease Control (CDC) protocol, including protective covering when examining them.[6]

The CDC defines SARS as a respiratory illness recently reported in Asia, North America, and Europe. If not treated quickly, SARS sufferers experience high fever, severe body aches, dry cough, and trouble breathing.[7] It can be fatal, and it is not a pleasant way to die.

The night the story appeared, Isaac was supposed to play in a bridge game. The host of the game called and asked him not to play because his wife was afraid Isaac might have SARS. Isaac was furious, but agreed not to come. Who wants to go where they are not wanted? And yet, he wondered, how do you fight such ignorance?

Half a world away, Thailand was having its own problems with SARS. The Associated Press reported, "Panicky Thai residents and some medical personnel blocked the cremation of a Hong Kong man who had died of SARS in Thailand, fearing the deadly virus would spread through smoke."[8]

Now that didn't make any sense considering that no virus could withstand the blast from the retort's flames. And yet, enough people in Thailand believed the opposite and had stopped a man's cremation because of that belief. The SARS virus can be spread through the air "or by other ways that are currently not known," says the CDC.[9] Potential ways in which SARS can be spread include touching the skin of other people or objects that are contaminated with infectious droplets and then touching your eye(s), nose, or mouth.[10]

Spreading SARS through cremation? The exact opposite is true. Burning is a way to kill the virus. A SARS-infected body would be a breeding ground, allowing the virus to multiply and making handling the corpse that much more dangerous. If Henry Thompson and LeMoyne were still around, they would be arguing for cremation.

Will SARS become the black plague of the millennium? Will American society once again turn to cremation, as it did after the Galveston hurricane and the San Francisco earthquake, as a means of curtailing the spread of disease?

Whatever the answer, cremation is back on the North American continent for good.

It looks like Ray Brent Marsh is going to have company at the docket.

The Associated Press reported on June 20, 2003, that eight

decomposing bodies were found in an Ohio funeral home. Some of them had been "mauled by rodents. Two were found in a garage at Sherill-Hareden Funeral Home [in Toledo]. . . . Officials said four were in cremation boxes."[11]

The article quoted Kimberly Lampkin, who had contracted with the funeral home to cremate her mother. According to the article, "Lampkin said the funeral home told her they didn't cremate and bury her mother's ashes as planned until almost four months after she died in September 2001. 'It hurts to know that your mama might not be cremated and that she might be in the basement,'" Lampkin said.[12]

It sounds like the plot of a 1960s Bette Davis movie. But it's real. Who's responsible? The law is. Be it this case, those in Georgia, California, or anywhere else, it is clear that to prevent further abuses, government needs to act to protect the rights of the dead, and the living, who are paying the price with their grief.

Epilogue

On March 8, 2004, John Henry Williams, who produced the "napkin will" that brought his father, Ted, into the deep freeze in Arizona, succumbed to leukemia at the age of thirty-five. With him died any hope that the Splendid Splinter would get his last wish of being cremated and his ashes scattered in his beloved Florida waters. Wire reports have it that John Henry is being frozen in Arizona alongside his father.

Cemeteries make me uncomfortable. I don't care how they try to sell them with statuaries, great views of lakes, golf courses, whatever—*IT DOESN'T MAKE ANY DIFFERENCE*. Dead is dead. There are bodies in those graves in various states of disintegration. I just don't happen to find that a very healthy image, though I respect the religious and other reasons for burial.

When my mother came home from burying her father many years ago when I was a child, she would not enter the house until presented outside with a basin of water, in which she washed her hands. It was a ritual I would see many times in the future, a way of literally washing off your hands the stink of the dead and the graves recently visited.

That I go back naturally to the dust from whence I came is a core part of Jewish religious belief. Choosing cremation would be violating that belief. And yet, there is much attraction in the embrace of Sam McGee's smiling face.

Appendix A

Celebrities Whose Ashes Were Scattered on Land

It says a lot about a person's life how they want their ashes to be handled in death. There are more options than earth burial. But most people live anonymous lives.

Celebrities are different. We know celebrities. If they are TV stars, we let them come into our living rooms every week. Film stars we save for those special times we go to the movies. Writers, artists, photographers whom we admire touch our souls. For some, celebrities mean very little. For others, they are objects of particular curiosity. One question is: How have they chosen to dispose of their remains?

What follows is one of the most complete lists ever published of celebrities whose ashes have been scattered. This isn't so much a list as it is some basic facts about people of various generations: baby boomers, Generation X'ers, and depression-era babies. The entries are bittersweet, providing insights into the dead who were part of our extended family.

I thank Jim Tipton at findagrave.com for his assistance in compiling this list.

Adams, Ansel   b. February 20, 1902   d. April 22, 1984
No one photographed nature better with a large-format camera than this poet of the lens. Cause of death: Cancer. Ashes scattered off Mount Ansel Adams, Sierra Nevadas.

Allen, Rex   b. December 31, 1920   d. December 17, 1999
Known as "The Arizona Cowboy," he was a popular country singer and songwriter. Cause of death: Injuries suffered in an accident. Ashes scattered near the Rex Allen Museum.

Arnaz, Desi (Desiderio Alberto Arnaz y De Acha III)
    b. March 2, 1917   d. December 2, 1986
Brilliant producer, he created and starred in the TV sitcom *I Love Lucy* with his wife Lucille Ball and later built their business interests into Desilu Studios. *Star Trek* and *The Untouchables* are among the classic series that Desilu produced. Cause of death: Lung cancer. Ashes scattered.

Arthur, Jean   b. October 17, 1900   d. June 19, 1991
Feisty, likable actress who scored big in her collaboration with director Frank Capra in *Mr. Deeds Goes to Town, Mr. Smith Goes to Washington,* and *A Foreign Affair.* She was memorable as the frontier wife and mother caught in a love triangle with Van Heflin and Alan Ladd in *Shane.* Cause of death: Heart failure. Ashes scattered off Point Lobos, California.

Asimov, Isaac   b. January 2, 1920   d. April 6, 1992
One of the twentieth century's preeminent and most prolific authors. Ashes scattered.

Barber, Walter "Red"   b. February 17, 1908   d. October 22, 1992
Hall of Fame baseball broadcaster, the voice of the Brooklyn Dodgers. Late in his career, he broadcast for the New York Yankees, teaming with Hall of Fame broadcasters Phil Rizzuto and Mel Allen. Ashes scattered on his property in Tallahassee, Florida.

Beaumont, Hugh   b. February 16, 1909   d. May 3, 1982
He played wise father Ward Cleaver on the classic 1950s–60s TV series *Leave It to Beaver*. Also played Alan Ladd's sidekick in *The Blue Dahlia*. Cause of death: Heart attack. Ashes scattered at his Minnesota summer retreat.

Bixby, Bill (Wilfred Bailey)   b. January 22, 1934   d. November 21, 1993
Likeable, boyish actor best known as Tim on TV sitcom *My Favorite Martian*, the father on *The Courtship of Eddie's Father*, and Bruce Banner on TV's *The Incredible Hulk*. Cause of death: Prostate cancer. Ashes scattered at his Hana, Hawaii, estate.

Blake, Amanda (Beverly Louise Neill)   b. February 20, 1929   d. August 16, 1989
B-movie actress who hit the big time when she starred as Miss Kitty, the saloon owner with a crush on Marshal Dillon, in the television series *Gunsmoke*. Cause of death: AIDS. Her ashes were spread over an animal preserve she helped form.

Blue, Betty   b. August 14, 1931   d. August 23, 2000
Playboy Playmate of the Month, November 1956. Acted in a few movies. Ashes scattered on the property of the Playboy Mansion.

Boone, Richard   b. June 18, 1917   d. January 10, 1981.
Starred as Paladin on the unique 1960 TV series *Have Gun Will Travel*. Paladin was a West Point–trained mercenary who quoted Shakespeare as quickly as he drew his gun. Cause of death: Throat cancer. Ashes scattered in Hawaii.

Bray, Robert   b. October 23, 1917   d. March 7, 1983
Lassie's last owner. He played the bus driver in *Bus Stop* who punches out Don Murray. Cause of death: Heart attack. Ashes scattered at Zuma Beach, California.

Browne, Coral   b. July 23, 1913   d. May 29, 1991
Brilliant actress, wife of Vincent Price, she played the grown-up Alice in the 1985 film *Dreamchild*. Cause of death: Breast cancer. Ashes scattered in Rose Garden of Hollywood Forever cemetery.

Carson, Rachel   b. 1907   d. April 14, 1964
Author of the classic book on health and the environment *Silent Spring*. Ashes scattered along the coast near Sheepscott, Maine.

Caselotti, Adriana   b. May 16, 1916   d. January 19, 1997
The uncredited voice of Snow White in Walt Disney's 1939 first feature-length animated film. Sang the showstopper "Someday My Prince Will Come." According to studio history, Disney had been searching for a voice that was "ageless, friendly, natural and innocent."[1] Caselotti claimed in a 1993 interview that she received a total of $970 for her work on the film. Cause of death: Cancer. Ashes scattered in Los Angeles, California.

Cassidy, Ted   b. July 31, 1932   d. January 16, 1979
Towering actor with a menacing presence, played "Lurch" on the 1960s sitcom *The Addams Family*, known to movie audiences as Harvey Logan, the man Butch Cassidy kicks in the groin in *Butch Cassidy and the Sundance Kid*. Cause of death: Complications from open heart surgery. Ashes buried in the front lawn of his home.

Cerf, Bennett   b. May 25, 1898   d. August 27, 1971
What's My Line? panelist who was the publisher, editor, and cofounder of Random House. Ashes scattered at his Mount Kisco, New York, home.

Chapman, Graham   b. January 8, 1941   d. October 4, 1989
Comedian who gained fame as part of the Monty Python comedy troupe. His ashes were kept by partner David Sherlock until New Year's Day 2000, at which time they were scattered over Wales in a fireworks display.

Cobain, Kurt   b. February 20, 1967   d. April 5, 1994
Singer/guitarist for the groundbreaking grunge band Nirvana. Cause of death: Suicide. Ashes scattered in the Wishkah River, Washington.

Coburn, Charles   b. June 19, 1877   d. August 30, 1961
Character actor who cut off Ronald Reagan's leg in *Kings Row* and won an Oscar for Best Supporting Actor for *The More the Merrier* in 1943. Ashes scattered in his home state of Georgia, as well as in Massachusetts and New York. Even in death, Coburn was an independent.

Coca, Imogene   b. November 18, 1908   d. June 2, 2001
Sid Caesar's hilarious comedy partner on *Your Show of Shows*. Her comic takes on opera divas and ballerinas are classic bits of American comedy. She spent her last years in a New Jersey home for senior citizens. Cause of death: Natural causes. Ashes scattered.

Copland, Aaron   b. November 14, 1900   d. December 2, 1990
One of America's greatest composers, his ballet "Appalachian Spring" won the 1945 Pulitzer prize. Ashes scattered throughout Tanglewood Music Center in the Berkshire Mountains of Massachusetts.

Curtis, Ken   b. July 2, 1916   d. April 29, 1991
As Deputy Festus Hagan, he was known for drawling the name "Matthew" whenever addressing his boss Marshal Dillon on TV's longest-running western, *Gunsmoke*. Member of the Sons of the Pioneers, a popular singing group composed of silver screen cowboy actors/performers. Also a member of the stock company of actors John Ford used in various films, including *The Searchers*, in which he provided comic relief in a film about prejudice and murder. Ashes scattered, Colorado flatlands.

Denver, John   b. December 31, 1943   d. October 12, 1997
1970s folk/country singer wrote and recorded such top-ten hits as "Rocky Mountain High," "Take Me Home, Country Roads," and "Leaving on a Jet Plane." Cause of death: Plane crash. Ashes scattered across the Rocky Mountains.

Einstein, Albert   b. March 14, 1879   d. April 18, 1955
Physicist whose famous formula $E=mc^2$ changed history. While his brain was preserved, his ashes were scattered in an unknown river in New Jersey.

Fonda, Henry   b. May 16, 1905   d. August 12, 1982
Though he won his only Best Actor Oscar literally on his deathbed for *On Golden Pond* (1981), Fonda had been a consummate actor from the early 1930s. He became a movie star later in that decade. Over a fifty-year career, he appeared in such classic films as 1943's *The Ox-Bow Incident*, 1957's *12 Angry Men*, which he also produced, and the 1968 Western classic *Once Upon a Time in the West*, in which Fonda played the heavy for one of the few times in his career. Stage trained, he was lifelong friends with former roommate Jimmy Stewart. Cause of death: Heart failure. Ashes scattered.

Frisella, Daniel Vincent "Danny"   b. March 4, 1946   d. January 1, 1977
The right-handed relief specialist for the World Champion 1969 New York Mets. Born in San Francisco, California, in 1946, Frisella had fifty-seven saves and a very respectable ERA of 3.32 in his nine-year career. Cause of death: Accident (when a dune buggy he was driving overturned near Phoenix, Arizona). Ashes scattered on his duck-hunting property near Oroville, California.

Gardner, Erle Stanley   b. July 17, 1889   d. March 11, 1970
Author and creator of popular Perry Mason books. Cause of death: Cancer. Ashes scattered above Baja peninsula in Mexico.

Grant, Cary (Archibald Alexander Leach)   b. January 18, 1904   d. November 29, 1986
The archetypal Hollywood leading man—tall, suave, good looking, charismatic, and possessed of a dry martini wit. *Gunga Din* (1939), *Notorious* (1946), and *North by Northwest* (1959) are just some of his films. In real life, he was extremely self-effacing. Cause of death: Stroke. Ashes scattered in California.

Grizzard Jr., Lewis   b. October 20, 1946   d. March 20, 1994
Author and humorist, his ashes were scattered at the fifty-yard line
of Sanford Stadium at the University of Georgia.

Hamilton, Margaret   b. December 9, 1902   d. May 16, 1985
The wonderful, kind character actress played the Wicked Witch of
the West in the 1939 classic *The Wizard of Oz*. Later played Cora in
a series of well-received coffee commercials. Cause of death: Heart
attack. Ashes scattered over her property in Dutchess County,
Amenia, New York.

Harris, Richard   b. October 1, 1930   d. October 25, 2002
Irish-born stage and motion picture actor who scored his first tri-
umph as a rugby player in the 1963 film *This Sporting Life*. Later went
on to play a variety of lead and character roles, including his last as
Professor Albus Dumbledore in the first two Harry Potter films. His
1968 recording of Jimmy Webb's "MacArthur Park" was a top-ten
hit. Cause of death: Hodgkin's disease. Ashes scattered at his home
in the Bahamas.

Harrison, George   b. February 25, 1943   d. November 29, 2001
Known as "the quiet Beatle," he was only sixteen when he joined
Ringo Starr, John Lennon, and Paul McCartney to form The Beatles,
history's greatest rock band. A prolific composer, he came into his
own after the group disbanded in 1970. Under the banner of his
Handmade Films company he produced such hits as *Life of Brian*
(1979) and *Time Bandits* (1981). Cause of death: Cancer. Ashes scattered in the Ganges River in India.

Harrison, Rex (Reginald Carey)   b. March 5, 1908   d. June 2, 1990
English leading man of impeccable manners, best known as Pro-
fessor Henry Higgins in 1964's *My Fair Lady*. Cause of death: Cancer.
Some of his ashes scattered in Portofino, Italy, the rest on the grave
of second wife Lilli Palmer in Forest Lawn Cemetery, Los Angeles,
California.

Hawks, Howard   b. May 30, 1896   d. December 26, 1977
Legendary movie director. Work includes 1938's *Bringing Up Baby*, 1946's *The Big Sleep*, 1948's *Red River*, and 1959's *Rio Bravo*. Ashes scattered in desert near Calimesa, California.

Jones, Buck (Charles Frederick Gebhard)   b. December 4, 1889
    d. November 30, 1942
Popular star of 1920s and 1930s B-movie westerns. Died during a fire at Boston's Coconut Grove nightclub that killed almost five hundred people. Reportedly, he died a hero, reentering the flaming building to help rescue others. Ashes spread near Catalina Island off the southern California coast.

Kaufman, George Simon   b. November 16, 1889   d. June 2, 1961
Playwright who wrote the Marx Brothers comedies *The Cocoanuts* and *A Night at the Opera*. Also wrote *The Man Who Came to Dinner* and *You Can't Take It with You*. Ashes scattered.

Koch, Howard   b. December 2, 1902   d. August 17, 1995
Cowriter of 1942's *Casablanca*, the greatest movie of all time. Also wrote 1940's *The Sea Hawk* starring Errol Flynn. Ashes scattered in Utah.

Lindbergh, Anne Morrow   b. June 22, 1906   d. February 7, 2001
Author, aviator, and wife of Charles Lindbergh. Their son Charles III was kidnapped and killed by Bruno Richard Hauptmann in 1934. Ashes scattered.

Marx, Harpo (Adolph Arthur)   b. November 23, 1888   d. September 28, 1964
One of the five legendary Marx Brothers, arguably film history's greatest comedy team. His onstage persona was a mute clown with curly blond hair sticking out from his hat. Cause of death: Complications from heart surgery. His ashes were supposedly sprinkled into the sand trap at the seventh hole of the Rancho Mirage golf course in California.

McCartney, Linda   b. September 24, 1941   d. April 17, 1998
Photographer, animal rights activist, and wife of Paul McCartney.
Cause of death: Breast cancer. Half of her ashes scattered in the pastures and woodlands of the family farm in southern England, half
scattered on the family ranch in Tucson, Arizona.

McCorkle, Susannah   b. 1946   d. May 19, 2001
New York–based jazz and cabaret singer with a passionate following. Cause of death: Suicide. Ashes supposedly scattered near the
Conservatory Garden in Central Park, New York City.

McIntire, Tim   b. July 19, 1944   d. April 15, 1986
Talented composer, he wrote the haunting score for the 1972 Robert
Redford film *Jeremiah Johnson*. Also worked as a character actor, usually playing a blustery villain in such films as *Brubaker* (1980) (also
with Redford). Son of actors John McIntire and Jeanette Nolan.
Cause of death: Congestive heart failure. Ashes scattered on the Yaak
River in Montana.

Mercury, Freddie (Frederick Bulsara)   b. September 5, 1946
    d. November 24, 1991
Lead singer for rock group Queen, born in Zanzibar, Tanzania. A
flamboyant singer and showman, he helped propel Queen to the
top of the charts. Cause of death: Pneumonia as a result of AIDS.
Ashes scattered on the shores of Lake Geneva, Switzerland.

Merman (Zimmerman), Ethel   b. January 16, 1908   d. February
    15, 1984
Broadway star of *Annie Get Your Gun* and other musicals, she had a
voice she belted out to the rafters. She parodied her own image in
the comedy *Airplane* (1980). Ashes scattered down Broadway in
New York City.

Miller, Henry   b. December 26, 1891   d. June 7, 1980
Controversial author of *Tropic of Cancer*, *Tropic of Capricorn*, and
Daisy Miller. Ashes scattered off Big Sur, California.

Mingus, Charles   b. April 22, 1922   d. January 5, 1979
Legendary jazz musician. Ashes scattered in the Ganges River, India.

Morris, Chester (John Chester Brooks)   b. February 16, 1901
     d. September 11, 1970
A square-jawed, quirky leading man, played suave former thief
Boston Blackie in a series of wonderful 1930s and 1940s B movies.
Cause of death: Barbiturate overdose. Ashes scattered in an
unknown German river.

Murphy, George Lloyd   b. July 4, 1902   d. May 3, 1992
Actor/dancer in films from the 1930s through the 1950s. One-term
California U.S. senator, 1965–1971. Ashes scattered.

Murrow, Edward R.   b. April 25, 1908   d. April 27, 1965
The twentieth century's preeminent journalist. His radio reports of
the Battle of Britain are legendary. Cause of death: Lung cancer.
Ashes scattered in the glen at Glen Arden Farm, Pawling, New York.

Oates, Warren   b. July 5, 1928   d. April 3, 1982
Fine character actor who appeared in two seminal westerns: *Ride the
High Country* (1962) and *The Wild Bunch* (1969), both directed by
his friend Sam Peckinpah. Cause of death: Heart attack. Ashes scattered in Montana.

O'Grady, Lani   b. October 2, 1954   d. September 25, 2001
Played the role of Dick Van Patten's oldest daughter on the 1970s TV
show *Eight Is Enough*. Cause of death: Drug overdose. Ashes scattered
in Hawaii.

O'Keeffe, Georgia   b. November 15, 1887   d. March 6, 1986
One of America's premier abstractionists of the twentieth century,
famous for the southwestern influence in her work. Ashes scattered
at the Pedernal Mountain in Abiquiu, New Mexico

Parker, Dorothy   b. August 22, 1893   d. June 7, 1967
A member of the famous writers group the Algonquin Round Table.

Known for her sharp wit and keen intelligence. Attempted suicide several times. Left her estate to Dr. Martin Luther King Jr. When King was assassinated, the Parker estate was given to the NAACP. Cause of death: Heart attack. Ashes scattered at a specially designed memorial, Baltimore, Maryland.

Phoenix, River (River Jude Bottom)   b. August 23, 1970   d. October 31, 1993
Like James Dean before him, Phoenix died tragically young, before his full talent was close to being realized. Cause of death: Drug overdose. Died on the pavement outside actor Johnny Depp's Viper Club in Los Angeles. His brother, actor Joaquin Phoenix, was by his side. Ashes scattered at family's Florida ranch.

Rayburn, Gene   b. December 22, 1917   d. November 29, 1999
The archetypal game show host, complete with toothy grin and obnoxiously patterned sports jackets, Rayburn hosted *The Match Game* and served as announcer for *The Tonight Show* in 1954. Cause of death: Congestive heart failure. His cremains were spread over his daughter's garden.

Reeves, Steve   b. January 21, 1926   d. May 1, 2000
Bodybuilder who won the titles Mr. World in 1948 and Mr. Universe in 1950, considered the world's best built man. Well before Arnold Schwarzenegger, Reeves parlayed his body into a string of successful "sword and sandal" epics, playing the role of Hercules. He had a distinct physical presence that outweighed his acting ability. Ashes scattered in Montana.

Reuther, Walter Philip   b. September 1, 1907   d. May 9, 1970
Leader of the United Auto Workers (UAW) union. Cause of death: Plane crash. Ashes scattered over UAW property, Onaway, Michigan.

Rodgers, Richard   b. June 28, 1902   d. December 30, 1979
Teamed with Oscar Hammerstein II and Lorenz Hart to write some of the twentieth century's greatest stage musicals. Also wrote music to many films, including *Oklahoma!*, *Carousel*, *The King and I*, *South*

Pacific, and *The Sound of Music.* For *The King and I,* he and his partner Hammerstein cast an unknown TV director named Yul Brynner in the lead. Ashes scattered.

Silver, Joe   b. September 28, 1922   d. February 27, 1989
Stage-trained character actor in movies and TV. Was a regular on the 1967 cult TV series *Coronet Blue.* Cause of death: Liver cancer. Ashes scattered along Broadway in New York City.

Silverheels, Jay (Harold J. Smith)   b. June 26, 1912   d. March 5, 1980
Television's Tonto on *The Lone Ranger.* Silverheels played second fiddle to Clayton Moore's Ranger, but managed to invest the role with the intelligence and dignity it deserved. Ashes spread on his homestead on Six Nations Reservation, Brantford, Ontario, Canada.

Slayton, Donald K. "Deke"   b. March 1, 1924   d. June 13, 1993
One of the seven original servicemen picked to become *Mercury* astronauts. Grounded in 1962 because of a minor heart problem, Slayton finally went into space in 1975 aboard an *Apollo* spacecraft that linked up, for the first time, with a Soviet spacecraft. Cause of death: Brain cancer. Ashes scattered over family farm, Sparta, Wisconsin.

Stanwyck, Barbara   b. July 16, 1907   d. January 20, 1990
In 1933's Frank Capra film, *The Bitter Tea of General Yen,* she made screen history as part of an onscreen interracial romance. The femme fatale in Billy Wilder's 1944 *Double Indemnity,* she was married in real life to matinee idol Robert Taylor. She made a comeback in her sixties when she became the matriarch of one of TV's most dysfunctional families on 1960's *The Big Valley.* Cause of death: Congestive heart failure. Ashes scattered somewhere in California.

Starrett, Charles   b. March 28, 1903   d. March 22, 1986
Famous B-movie cowboy star from the 1940s, best known for his role as Durango Kid. He was in over one hundred movies and was one of the top ten highest paid stars of his time. He died in Borrego

Springs, California. Cause of death: Cancer. Ashes scattered via air over Dartmouth College, Hanover, New Hampshire.

Stout, Rex Todhunter   b. December 1, 1886   d. October 27, 1975
Author, creator of the Nero Wolfe series of mysteries. The latest TV incarnation of his hero was brought to the small screen in 2000 with Maury Chaykin playing the title role and Tim Hutton as Wolfe's legman Archie Goodwin. Ashes scattered.

Taylor II, Walter Clarence "Dub"   b. February 26, 1907
    d. October 3, 1994
With his toothless grin and tufts of white hair sticking out from the sides of his weathered bowler hat, Taylor was a welcome and endearing presence in hundreds of film and television westerns. Cause of death: Congestive heart failure. Ashes scattered near Westlake Village, California.

Tone, Franchot   b. February 27, 1905   d. September 18, 1968
Motion picture and television actor. He appeared in the films *The Lives of a Bengal Lancer* (1935), *Mutiny on the Bounty* (1935), *Dangerous* (1935), *Five Graves to Cairo* (1943), and *Advise and Consent* (1962), among many others. Married for a time to legendary screen actress Joan Crawford. Cause of death: Lung cancer. Ashes scattered.

Truex, Ernest   b. September 19, 1889   d. June 27, 1973
Terrific character actor who specialized in "grandpa" roles, especially in *The Twilight Zone* episodes "What You Need" (1959) and "Kick the Can" (1962). Cause of death: Heart attack. Ashes scattered in central California.

Vance, Vivian (Vivian Roberta Jones)   b. July 26, 1909
    d. August 17, 1979
I Love Lucy's Ethel Mertz. 'Nuff said. Cause of death: Cancer. Ashes scattered.

Villechaize, Hervé   b. April 23, 1943   d. September 4, 1993
"The plane, boss, the plane," he cried at the beginning of every

episode of *Fantasy Island* as sidekick Tattoo. Ashes scattered off Point Fermin, Los Angeles, California.

Waller, Thomas 'Fats'   b. May 21, 1904   d. December 15, 1943
Jazz innovator, musician, pianist. Cause of death: pneumonia. Ashes scattered over Harlem, New York, by the "Black Ace," a World War I aviator.

Wood, Ed   b. October 10, 1924   d. December 10, 1978
Ignored until the 1980s, when promoters dubbed him "the worst director of all time," Ed Wood's *Plan 9 from Outer Space* is unofficially the worst movie ever made. *Glen or Glenda*, about a transvestite—played by Wood, who was one—provided insight into Wood's personality. He helped revive Bela Lugosi's career late in the actor's life. Ashes scattered.

Woolf, Virginia (Adeline Virginia)   b. January 25, 1882
    d. March 28, 1941
Writer who had an indelible effect on twentieth-century literature. Novels include *Mrs. Dalloway*, *To the Lighthouse*, and *Orlando*. A member of a group of Paris expatriates of the 1920s that included Ernest Hemingway and F. Scott Fitzgerald. Cause of death: Suicide by drowning in a river near her home. Ashes buried on the grounds of Monks' House, England.

Yawkey, Thomas   b. February 21, 1903   d. July 9, 1976
Beloved owner of the Boston Red Sox, always close to his players. Elected to the executive wing of the Baseball Hall of Fame in 1980. Ashes scattered over Winyah Bay, South Carolina.

Young, Faron   b. February 25, 1932   d. December 10, 1996
Country singer, member of the Country Music Hall of Fame and star of the Grand Ole Opry from 1952 to 1964. In 1970, he sang "The Guns of Johnny Rondo" in an episode of *The High Chaparral* TV series. Cause of death: Suicide by gunshot to the head. Ashes scattered over Old Hickory Lake in Tennessee.[2]

Appendix B

Celebrities Whose Ashes Were Scattered on Water

A scattering of ashes on the sea is a procedure more complicated than done on land because of federal requirements that have to be met (see Appendix C). But for the family or friend who performs this service, it offers a sense of tranquility and peace that nothing else can.

Those who request this option usually have a special affinity for the ocean, an identity with it, a real connection. In most cases, this spiritual side of the celebrity was kept private, which makes it that much more interesting to find out who wanted their ashes scattered at sea.

Abbott, Bud   b. October 2, 1895   d. April 24, 1974
Half of the comedy team Abbott and Costello, Abbott was the greatest straight man in film history. Cause of death: Cancer. Ashes scattered in the Pacific Ocean.

Adams, Stanley   b. April 7, 1915   d. April 27, 1977
Remembered by every "Trekkie" for his notable role as Cyrano Jones in the *Star Trek* episode "The Trouble with Tribbles." Cause of death: Suicide by gunshot. Ashes scattered at sea.

Andrews, Edward   b. October 9, 1914   d. March 8, 1985
Character actor with a background in stage, screen, and television from the 1930s to the 1980s. The *Twilight Zone, Route 66,* and *Bonanza* are just three of the classic TV series in which he had featured guest roles. Cause of death: Heart attack. Ashes scattered at sea

Arbuckle, Roscoe Conkling "Fatty"   b. March 24, 1887   d. June 29, 1933
Actor/comedian, married to actress Minta Durfee. His career was destroyed by a fabricated rape and murder charge that led to a sensational trial. By the time Arbuckle was acquitted—and the jury actually apologized for the proceeding in the first place—the comedian's career was ruined. He died of a heart attack, but his fellow comedian and friend Buster Keaton said he died from a broken heart. Ashes scattered in the Pacific Ocean.

Bailey, Raymond   b. May 6, 1904   d. April 15, 1980
He played banker Milburn Drysdale on the 1960s TV series *The Beverly Hillbillies.* Cause of death: Heart attack. Ashes scattered at sea off Redondo Beach, California.

Banky, Vilma   b. January 9, 1898   d. March 18, 1991
Silent screen actress, best remembered for her work with Rudolf Valentino in *The Eagle* (1925) and *The Son of the Sheik* (1926). She was married to silent movie actor Rod La Rocque from 1927 to 1969. Ashes scattered at sea.

Bond, Ward   b. April 9, 1903   d. November 5, 1960
A member of director John Ford's movie stock company, Bond was frequently the butt of Ford's on-set jokes, despite his stalwart support in films that include *My Darling Clementine* and *The Searchers.* Later played Major Seth Adams on TV's long-running western hit *Wagon Train.* After his death in 1960, he was replaced by John McIntyre for the rest of *Wagon Train's* run. Cause of death: Heart attack. Ashes spread in the Pacific Ocean somewhere between Newport Beach and Catalina Island.

Bondi, Beulah   b. May 3, 1888   d. January 11, 1981
Character actress who created the role of Ma Bailey, Jimmy Stewart's mother in 1946's *It's a Wonderful Life*. Cause of death: Injuries sustained after tripping over her cat. Ashes scattered at sea.

Carradine, John   b. February 5, 1906   d. November 27, 1988
Another of John Ford's favorite actors, the gaunt Carradine was a classically trained Shakespearean actor who brought his considerable talent and presence to such disparate films as *Bride of Frankenstein*, *The Grapes of Wrath*, and *Billy the Kid versus Dracula*. He is the father of actors David, Keith, and Robert Carradine. Ashes scattered at sea.

Caulfield, Joan   b. June 1, 1922   d. June 18, 1991
Starred in two romantic comedies with William Holden—*Dear Ruth* (1947) and *Dear Wife* (1949). After that, she drifted into B films where she specialized in playing glamorous women. Starred opposite Barry Nelson in the 1950s TV series *My Favorite Husband*. Cause of death: Cancer. Ashes scattered in the Pacific Ocean

Chaney Jr., Lon (Creighton Tull Chaney)   b. February 10, 1906   d. July 12, 1973
Son of Lon Chaney, the silent screen's "Man of a Thousand Faces," Creighton later adopted his father's first name to help with his career. As Lon Chaney Jr., he was among the foremost horror movie actors in film history. His sympathetic portrayal of Larry Talbot in *The Wolf Man* (1941) helped to define the horror genre. He also put in fine character turns in *Of Mice and Men* (1939), *The Defiant Ones* (1958), and *High Noon* (1952). Cause of death: Liver failure (he was an alcoholic). Ashes scattered at sea.

Clark, Fred   b. March 9, 1914   d. December 5, 1968
Solid character actor in many films from the 1940s through the 1960s, including *White Heat* (1949) and *Sunset Boulevard* (1950). Cause of death: Liver ailment. Ashes scattered at sea.

Cox, Wally   b. December 6, 1924   d. February 15, 1973
Marlon Brando was so shaken up when his childhood friend Cox died that he couldn't go to the funeral. Cox made his reputation as a mild-mannered teacher in the 1950s TV series *Mr. Peepers*. Later went on to be a fellow panelist of "Vinnie" Price on *The Hollywood Squares*. Cause of death: Unknown. Ashes scattered at sea.

Devine, Andy (Jeremiah Schwartz)   b. October 7, 1905   d. February 18, 1977
A character actor in numerous films, his two TV claims to fame are as host of the popular 1950s Saturday-morning kid show *Andy's Gang*, and Guy Madison's sidekick Jingles on *The Adventures of Wild Bill Hickok*. Cause of death: Leukemia. Ashes scattered at sea.

Donlevy, (Waldo) Brian   b. February 9, 1901   d. April 5, 1972
Stalwart tough guy with the heart of gold, he showed his comic abilities in Preston Sturges's 1940 film *The Great McGinty*. As a soldier, served with General Pershing in the 1916 Mexican expedition to capture Pancho Villa. Cause of death: Cancer. Ashes scattered at sea.

Dru, Joanne   b. January 31, 1923   d. September 10, 1996
Sister of actor/game show host Peter Marshall, she had a believability that convinced audiences that she could be the durable women she portrayed in such classics as *She Wore a Yellow Ribbon* (1949) and *All the King's Men* (1949). Later went on to star in the 1960s TV series *Guestward Ho!* Cause of death: Lymphedema. Ashes scattered at sea, Monterey County, California.

Duchin, Eddy   b. April 10, 1910   d. February 9, 1951
Talented pianist and bandleader who took occasional acting forays. Recorded on Columbia, Brunswick, Take Two, and RCA Victor labels, he was extremely popular in the 1930s, during which time his movies included *Hit Parade of 1937* (1937) and *Mr. Broadway* (1933). His song hits included "Stardust," "Just One of Those Things," "How About You?" "Shine on Harvest Moon," "September Song," "What Is This Thing Called Love?" "My Blue Heaven,"

"Embraceable You," and "Down Argentina Way." *The Eddy Duchin Story* (1956) featured Tyrone Power in the title role. Cause of death: Leukemia. Ashes scattered in the Atlantic Ocean.

Fleming, Art   b. May 1, 1924   d. April 25, 1995
Beloved TV personality, the original host of TV's *Jeopardy!*, from 1964 to 1975, when the program was still taped in New York. Cause of death: Cancer. Ashes scattered at sea.

French, Victor   b. December 4, 1934   d. June 15, 1989
It was French's grizzled portrayal of Mark, an ex-cop on *Highway to Heaven*, that gave the Michael Landon TV series about a do-gooding angel its edge. Ashes scattered in the water near Santa Barbara, California.

Hale Jr., Alan   b. March 18, 1918   d. January 2, 1990
It makes sense that the man who played a character called "The Skipper" would have his ashes scattered at sea. Alan Hale Jr. was never one to disappoint his fans. He had a big set of shoes to fill. Alan Hale Sr. was one of Hollywood's most revered character actors. Hale Jr. followed the same career path, except where senior acted mostly in A films, the Bs made Junior his living. He found his calling in television, where in the 1950s he starred as TV's Casey Jones. But it was his role in one of the 1960s most loved and reviled sitcoms, *Gilligan's Island*, that made him a star. After that, wherever he went, people called him by his character's name, Skipper, and Hale loved it. Cause of death: Respiratory failure due to cancer. Ashes scattered at sea.

Hamer, Rusty   b. February 15, 1947   d. January 18, 1990
He is best remembered for his character Rusty Williams, Danny Thomas's TV son on *Make Room for Daddy*, later retitled *The Danny Thomas Show*. Cause of death: Suicide. Ashes scattered at sea.

Hartman, Phil   b. September 24, 1948   d. May 28, 1998
An interesting murder case. Phil Hartman, who gained fame on NBC's *Saturday Night Live* and the sitcom *NewsRadio*, was killed in his bed by his wife, Brynn, who then took her own life. Their chil-

dren, Sean and Birgen, were in the house at the time. Ashes scattered over Santa Catalina's Emerald Bay, California.

Hayden, Sterling Walter (Sterling Relyea Walter)   b. March 26, 1916   d. May 23, 1986
When his father died in 1925, his stepfather renamed him. He was a ship's captain and sailed around the world. In 1940 he signed a contract with Paramount, but before he could become a big star, Word War II began and he joined the U.S. Marines. He was decorated with the Silver Star for his heroism. His flourishing movie career after the war was interrupted by testimony before the House Un-American Activities Committee regarding his brief flirtation with communism during his wartime service in Yugoslavia. Best remembered for playing the sensitive killer in *The Asphalt Jungle* (1950), the title role in *Johnny Guitar* (1954), and the police captain who breaks Al Pacino's cheek bone in *The Godfather* (1972) (and later gets shot in the throat as retribution). Cause of death: Cancer. Not surprisingly, this lifelong sailor's ashes were scattered in San Francisco Bay.

Heflin, Van (Emmett Evan Heflin, Jr.)   b. December 13, 1910   d. July 23, 1971
Fine character actor and later leading man, won the Oscar for Best Supporting Actor in 1942's *Johnny Eager*. Later played in two classic westerns: 1953's *Shane* opposite Jean Arthur (who was also cremated) and *3:10 to Yuma*, opposite Glenn Ford. Cause of death: Heart attack. Ashes scattered at sea.

Holden, William   b. April 17, 1918   d. November 16, 1981
One of the greatest screen actors in history, he won a well-deserved Oscar for Best Actor for 1953's *Stalag 17* as the cynical POW Sefton. A wildlife activist, he later had a long relationship with actress Stephanie Powers. Cause of death: Injuries from a fall. Ashes scattered in the Pacific Ocean.

Hudson, Rock (Roy Harold Scherer Jr.)   b. November 17, 1925   d. October 2, 1985
From the late 1950s to the late 1960s, there was no more popular

leading man than Rock Hudson. Some of his films with Doris Day are considered comic comments on the battle of the sexes. But he led a double life—raging heterosexual matinee idol by day, a closeted gay man by night. He did not reveal his sexuality for fear of what it would do to his career. Cause of death: AIDS. Hudson was the first prominent member of the movie business to announce that he had the disease. Ashes scattered at sea.

Kelley, DeForest   b. January 20, 1920   d. June 11, 1999
Until 1964, he was a relatively unknown character actor. But when Gene Roddenberry cast him as Dr. Leonard "Bones" McCoy on the original *Star Trek*, television history was made. His classic line, "He's dead, Jim," was repeated to the point of parody. The kindhearted Kelley brought humanity to his role of the beleaguered outer-space physician constantly at odds with the logical Mr. Spock. Cause of death: Stomach cancer. Ashes scattered in the Pacific Ocean.

Klemperer, Werner   b. March 22, 1920   d. December 6, 2000
Wonderful film character actor who is best known for playing Colonel Klink on the classic 1960s sitcom *Hogan's Heroes*. Cause of death: Cancer. Ashes scattered at sea.

La Rocque, Rod   b. November 20, 1898   d. October 15, 1969
Silent movie star, he made his screen debut in 1914. Married to actress Vilma Banky. Best remembered for his films *The Ten Commandments* (1923), *The Coming of Amos* (1925), and *Braveheart* (1925). Also had a role in Frank Capra's *Meet John Doe* (1942) opposite Barbara Stanwyck (who was also cremated). Cause of death: Unknown. Ashes scattered at sea.

Lawford, Peter Sydney   b. September 7, 1923   d. December 24, 1984
A member of the fabled 1960s Sinatra "Rat Pack," Lawford was a British actor of limited ability but boundless charm. Beginning as a contract player with MGM, he went on to become not only a reliable supporting actor in numerous films but also the brother-in-law of

John F. Kennedy. A good friend of Marilyn Monroe's, he talked to her the day she died. Cause of death: Cardiac arrest complicated by kidney and liver failure. Ashes scattered in the Pacific Ocean.

Mahoney, Jock   b. February 7, 1919   d. December 14, 1989
Starred in TV westerns, *Yancy Derringer* and *The Range Rider*, later in the big-screen *Tarzan* of the 1960s. Stepfather of actress Sally Field. Ashes scattered at sea, Kitsap County, Washington.

McCrea, Joel   b. November 5, 1905   d. October 20, 1990
Regarded primarily as a star of westerns, he was originally a leading man in a slew of 1930s comedies, most memorably Preston Sturges's *The Palm Beach Story* (1942) and the classic *Sullivan's Travels* (1941). As he aged, he switched gears and acted in westerns, most notably in Sam Peckinpah's 1962 classic, *Ride the High Country* (his last film). Also starred in Alfred Hitchcock's *Foreign Correspondent* (1940). Married to actress Frances Dee and father of *Beach Party* movie actor Jody McCrea. Cause of death: Pulmonary complications. Ashes scattered off the coast of Long Beach, California.

Morrow, Jeff Irving   b. January 13, 1907   d. December 26, 1993
He was the friendly alien Exeter in the 1955 sci-fi classic *This Island Earth*. Cause of death: Alzheimer's disease. Ashes scattered off the coast of Palos Verdes, California.

Nader, George   b. October 19, 1921   d. February 4, 2002
Star of the offbeat 1958 syndicated series *The Man and the Challenge*. Cause of death: Cardiac failure. Ashes scattered at sea.

Payne, John   b. May 23, 1912   d. December 6, 1989
A popular lead in 1940s light musicals, he later became a television idol as peripatetic gunman Vint Bonner on *The Restless Gun*. Married to actress Anne Shirley and later to actress Gloria DeHaven. Cause of death: Heart ailment. Ashes scattered at sea.

Platt, Edward   b. February 14, 1916   d. March 19, 1974
He played The Chief on the 1960s comedy series *Get Smart*, who had

to put up with Maxwell Smart's antics. Cause of death: Heart attack. Ashes scattered at sea.

Preston, Robert b. June 8, 1918   d. March 21, 1987
Few actors have had more fascinating careers than Preston's. While just twenty years old, he signed a contract with Paramount to star as second lead in a string of 1930s pictures, usually with Alan Ladd top lining. Preston, who looked as young as his age, had to grow a mustache to appear older. By the 1940s, he tired of supporting roles and went east to the New York stage. There he scored the role of his life in 1957's *The Music Man*, for which he won a Tony Award. Repeating the role onscreen in 1962, Preston launched the second phase of his career as leading man/Broadway star, culminating with his Best Supporting Actor Oscar nomination for his portrayal of the gay entertainer in 1982's *Victor/Victoria*. Cause of death: Lung cancer. Ashes scattered at sea.

Price, Vincent   b. May 27, 1911   d. October 25, 1993
Like Lon Chaney Jr., one of filmdom's best-loved horror actors, Price managed to infuse all his characters with humor and humanity. He had a deep, penetrating voice and a magnetic screen presence. Self-deprecating, he was a respected art critic and collector. Some of his best-known films are *The Fly* (1958), the 1953 3-D *House of Wax* with Charles Bronson, and 1944's haunting *Laura*. In the latter part of his career, he was a regular on TV's *The Hollywood Squares*, where host Peter Marshall always referred to him affectionately as "Vinnie." Cause of death: Lung cancer. Ashes scattered at sea.

Rettig, Tommy   b. December 10, 1941   d. February 15, 1996
Rettig was a well-known child actor of the 1950s and appeared in many films. But he shot to real fame when he played Jeff, Lassie's first owner, in the 1950s *Lassie* TV series. Like many child actors, he was unable to make the transition to adult roles. Cause of death: Natural causes. Ashes scattered at sea.

Sanders, George   b. July 3, 1906   d. April 25, 1972
Perhaps the suavest actor in the history of motion pictures, the British-born Sanders appeared in 124 films between 1934 and 1972,

including *Lloyd's of London* (1936) and *All About Eve* (1950), for which he won an Oscar as Best Supporting Actor. Besides his work in A films, he had a thriving career in the B's as Simon Templar in the *Saint* movies and Guy Lawrence in the *Falcon*. His actor brother Tom Conway replaced him in the latter role. Cause of death: Suicide. (His suicide note read, "I am bored.") Ashes scattered in the English Channel.

Smith, Kent   b. March 19, 1907   d. April 23, 1985
Stalwart American motion picture and television actor of the 1930s through 1970s. Appeared in several classic TV series such as *The Defenders*, *Perry Mason*, *The Outer Limits*, and *Peyton Place*, among others. Married for a time to actress Betty Gillette, and later to actress Edith Atwater. Ashes scattered at sea.

Stevens, Craig   b. July 8, 1918   d. May 10, 2000
He played TV's coolest private eye in *Peter Gunn*. The landmark 1950s series used a jazzy Henry Mancini score. Stevens had a look in his eye of a guy who really would carry a gun under those well-tailored single-breasted suits. Cause of death: Cancer. Ashes scattered at sea.

Tryon, Thomas (Tom)   b. January 14, 1926   d. September 4, 1991
Actor and novelist, he shot to fame in Walt Disney's 1950s TV series *Texas John Slaughter*. After appearing in a string of forgettable 1960s films, he turned to writing. Inspired by Ira Levin's horror novel *Rosemary's Baby*, he wrote *The Other* in 1971, which became a best-seller. He wrote a string of successful novels after that. Cause of death: Stomach cancer. Ashes scattered at sea.

Williams, Guy (Armand Catalano)   b. January 14, 1924   d. May 7, 1989
Actor of great panache and likability, played Don Diego/Zorro on the classic Disney TV series *Zorro*. His dueling scenes leave the viewer breathless. Also played Professor John Robinson in the *Lost in Space* TV series. He made guest appearances on *Bonanza* as Will Cartwright, the long-lost fourth Cartwright. Cause of death: Brain aneurysm. Ashes scattered off the coast of Malibu, California.[1]

Appendix C

Forms Needed for Arranging a Cremation

KEY TO FORMS

Form A: the complete federal requirements for burial at sea of cremated human remains.

Form B: an example of the type of form needed to authorize the scattering of the ashes at sea.

Form C: Seattle's People's Memorial Association (PMA) uses this letter as a way of expediting and clarifying the wishes of those who become disabled or die and cannot speak for themselves.

Form D: Excerpt from Publication 52, 1999, of the U.S. Postal Service's regulations regarding the mailing of cremated remains.

Form E: Type of form a funeral home might provide to gather information about religious preference.

FORM A

Title 40, Volume 17, Parts 190 to 259
Revised as of July 1, 1999
From the U.S. Government Printing Office via GPO Access
CITE: 40CFR229.1, Page 240–241
Title 40—Protection of the Environment
Environmental Protection Agency
PART 229—General Permits—Table of Contents
Sec. 229.1—Burial at sea

(a) All persons subject to title I of the Act are hereby granted a general permit to transport human remains from the United States and all persons owning or operating a vessel or aircraft registered in the United States or flying the United States flag and all departments, agencies, or instrumentalities of the United States are hereby granted a general permit to transport human remains from any location for the purpose of burial at sea and to bury such remains at sea subject to the following conditions:

(1) Except as herein otherwise provided, human remains shall be prepared for burial at sea and shall be buried in accordance with accepted practices and requirements as may be deemed appropriate and desirable by the United States Navy, United States Coast Guard, or civil authority charged with the responsibility for making such arrangements;

(2) Burial at sea of human remains which are not cremated shall take place no closer than 3 nautical miles from land and in water no less than one hundred fathoms (six hundred feet) deep and in no less than three hundred fathoms (eighteen hundred feet) from (i) 27 deg.30'00" to 31 deg.00'00" North Latitude off St. Augustine and Cape Canaveral, Florida; (ii) 82 deg.20'00" to 84 deg.00'00" West Longitude off Dry Tortugas, Florida; and (iii) 87 deg.15'00" to 89 deg.50'00" West Longitude off the Mississippi River Delta, Louisiana, to Pensacola, Florida. All necessary meas-

ures shall be taken to ensure that the remains sink to the bottom rapidly and permanently; and

(3) Cremated remains shall be buried in or on ocean waters without regard to the depth limitations specified in paragraph (a)(2) of this section provided that such burial shall take place no closer than 3 nautical miles from land.

(b) For purposes of this section and Secs. 229.2 and 229.3, land means that portion of the baseline from which the territorial sea is measured, as provided for in the Convention on the Territorial Sea and the Contiguous Zone, which is in closest proximity to the proposed disposal site.

(c) Flowers and wreaths consisting of materials which are readily decomposable in the marine environment may be disposed of under the general permit set forth in this section at the site at which disposal of human remains is authorized.

(d) All burials conducted under this general permit shall be reported within 30 days to the Regional Administrator of the Region from which the vessel carrying the remains departed.

FORM B
SHEEPSHEAD BAY ASHES AT SEA
Authorization for the Scattering of Cremated Remains at Sea

I hereby authorize SHEEPSHEAD BAY ASHES AT SEA to take possession of and make arrangements for, the disposition of the cremated remains of

_____ ("Deceased") in accordance with and subject to the terms and conditions set forth in this Authorization; the company's Rules and Regulations; and any applicable federal, state, provincial or local laws and regulations.

I certify that I have the full legal right and authority to authorize the disposition of the remains of the Deceased.

I hereby authorize SHEEPSHEAD BAY ASHES AT SEA to make disposition of cremated remains of the Deceased at sea in:

__ Atlantic Ocean, East Coast, USA, __ Atlantic Ocean, SC
__ Atlantic Ocean, FL

I hereby direct SHEEPSHEAD BAY ASHES AT SEA to scatter said cremated remains
at sea, in accordance with State and Federal Law.

Special Instructions:

_____

_____

If no specific instructions are provided herein, scattering will be performed by
SHEEPSHEAD BAY ASHES AT SEA, in a timely manner, weather permitting.

"Scattering" consists of the scattering of cremated remains at sea. I understand that
once the cremated remains of the Deceased are scattered, they are unrecoverable.
Unless otherwise specifically provided for herein, once scattering of cremated
remains of the Deceased has been performed, SHEEPSHEAD BAY ASHES AT SEA
will dispose of the container which contained said cremated remains.

The obligation of SHEEPSHEAD BAY ASHES AT SEA shall be limited to the disposition of the cremated remains as directed herein. I agree to release and hold harm-
less SHEEPSHEAD BAY ASHES AT SEA, its affiliates and their agents, employees,
successors and assigns from any and all loss, damage, liability or causes of action
(including attorney's fee and expenses of litigation) in connection with the disposition of the cremated remains of the Deceased as authorized herein or respect to
the identification of said cremated remains as being those of the Deceased.

Date of authorization

_____EMAIL:_____

_____   _____   _____
Signature   Print Name   Relationship to Deceased

_____, _____, ___ _____
Address   City,   State   Zip Code

_____
Telephone Number

FORM C

Dear Family:

Because we all know that any of us could become disabled or die at any time of our lives, I feel it is important to provide you with information you may need in the event you get an unexpected call telling you there has been a medical emergency or death. I am trying to keep this letter simple and easy to update, while also giving you a roadmap of how to get further information when it is needed.

My full legal name:_____ _____Date of birth: _____

Mailing address:_____Phone: _____

City:_____State: ___ Zip: _____SS #:_____

Place of birth: _____ Date of birth: _____

Citizenship:_____Military Service: _____

Military discharge papers location:

_____

Spouse: _____Spouse SS#: _____

Former spouses and years of marriage:

_____

Location of paperwork regarding marriage dissolution or estate of former spouse:

_____

Health Insurance Co.: _____ Policy No. _____

Medicare Claim No.:_____Primary Doctor: _____

Address of doctor: _____

Doctor's Phone: _____

Life insurance company: _____ Policy no.: _____

Other insurance:_____

Attorney: Name:_____

Address: _____

Phone: _____

I ____ have/ ____ have not/ executed a will dated: _____.
The original of this will is located: _____.
A copy is at: _____.

The person named as **Personal Representative** in the will is:
_____.

Bank: Name:_____

Address: _____

Phone: _____

Types of accounts: _____

Safe deposit box? ___ yes/ ___no. Contents: _____

Accountant: Name:_____

Address: _____

Phone:_____

Location of tax returns & records: _____

Investment Advisor: Name:_____

Address: _____

Phone: _____

Location of investment records: _____

Real Estate Owned: Description: _____

Address: _____

Contact Person:_____ Phone:_____

Location of records: _____

Disability: I _____ have/ _____have not/ executed a **Durable Power of Attorney for Healthcare.** I have named _____ (Ph: _____) to be my healthcare decision-maker and selected _____ (Ph: _____) as the alternate. A copy of this document can be found:

_____

    I ____ have/ ____ have not/ executed an **Advance Directive** (Living Will). A copy of this document is located: _____. I ___ have/ ____ have not/ executed a **General and Durable Power of Attorney** naming _____ to act on my behalf regarding my personal and financial affairs. A copy of this document can be found: _____

End of Life: I _____ am/ _____ am not/ a member of **People's Memorial Association** (Ph: 206-325-0489), which is affiliated with the **Funeral Consumers Alliance** (Ph: 1-800-765-0107). Members of People's Memorial are entitled to reduced fees for cremation and funeral expenses. My membership number is: _____. In the event of death, have my body picked up by: _____. Phone _____ to make these arrangements. Instructions regarding my wishes for mortuary arrangements have been provided to:

_____

    In general, my wishes are for ____ cremation; ____ burial; or _____ entombment. My remains should be: _____ disposed of at sea; _____ placed in a Veteran's Cemetery; _____ buried or entombed at:_____ or

_____

    I have pre-paid for the following services:

_____

    The documents regarding this prepayment are located:

_____

I ____ am/ ____ am not/ an **organ donor** and would like appropriate arrangements made at my death.

Signed: _____ Date:_____

PMA 11-26-02

FORM D

HAZARDOUS, RESTRICTED AND PERISHABLE MAIL
46 LIQUIDS AND POWDERS
462.2 CREMATED REMAINS

Human ashes are permitted to be mailed provided they are packaged as required in 463b. The identity of the contents should be marked on the address label. Mailpieces must be sent registered mail with return receipt service.

463 PACKAGING AND MARKING

b. *Powders.* Dry materials that could cause damage, discomfort, destruction, or soiling upon escape (i.e., leakage) must be packed in siftproof containers or other containers that are sealed in durable siftproof outer containers.[1]

1. Biographical Information

Full Name: _____

Hebrew Name (in Hebrew or English letters): _____

Street/Mailing Address: _____

City: _____   State: _____   Zip Code: _____

Telephone Number: (_____) _____ - _____

Length of Residence at Present Address: _____

Formerly of _____

Place of Birth: _____   Date of Birth: _____

Your Father's English Name: _____

Your Father's Hebrew Name: _____

Is/was your Father:

    Kohen ____, Levi ____, Israelite ____, Information Unavailable ____

Your Mother's English Name: _____

Your Mother's Hebrew Name: _____

Of what country are you a citizen: _____

Veteran of US: yes - no; War or Dates Served: _____

    Branch: _____; Where: _____
    (A copy of your discharge should be attached to this booklet)

Social Security #: _____ - _____ - _____

Occupation when Employed: _____

Name and Locality of Employ: _____

Length of Employ: _____; Retired in: _____

Marital Status: Never Married ____; Married (when?) _____;
               Divorced _____; Widowed (when?) _____.

Organizations, Memberships & Accomplishments (include full names, dates, offices held, etc.):

_____

_____

_____

_____

II.· Family Record

Spouse (include maiden name):

_____

Children (living & deceased):

_____   _____

_____   _____

_____   _____

_____   _____

Brothers & Sisters (living & deceased):

_____   _____

_____   _____

_____   _____

_____   _____

Grandchildren (living & deceased):

_____   _____

_____   _____

_____   _____

_____   _____

Great Grandchildren (living & deceased):

_____   _____

_____   _____

_____   _____

_____   _____

Other Family:

_____   _____

_____   _____

_____   _____

_____   _____

III. Funeral Instructions

What care should be performed prior to interment (please check):

_____ Taharah (Washing of the body)

_____ Tachrichim (Traditional shroud)

_____ Tallit (Prayer shawl)

_____ Traditional Jewish Casket

List any other personal requests: _____

_____

_____.

Do you wish the funeral service to be held:

_____ at the _____ Funeral Home, and at the graveside for burial

_____ at the graveside only

State other preference: _____

By whom would you like religious services to be conducted: _____

_____.

Whom would you like to serve as pallbearers (suggest 6 or 8):

1. _____   2. _____

3. _____   4. _____

5. _____   6. _____

7. _____   8. _____

Newspaper Obituaries should be placed in which Newspapers or Cities:

1. _____ (city) _____

2. _____ (city) _____

3. _____ (city) _____

4. _____ (city) _____

IV. Cemetery Arrangements

Name of Cemetery: _____

City and State: _____

Location of Plot/Grave: _____

Where can the Cemetery Deed be found: _____

Do you wish a concrete outer container in the grave: yes – no

Should a society, organization or individual be notified to grant permission to open the grave, list the name, address and telephone #

_____

_____

V. Optional Arrangements

If donations are made in your memory, which charity or organization(s) do you prefer to be the recipient(s)?

1. _____   2. _____

3. _____   4. _____

How should funeral expenses be paid:

____ My estate

____ A pre-financed funeral account which I have established in trust
       for the   Funeral Home, Inc.:

        Name of Bank: _____

        Account Number: _____

____ Other: _____

Listed below are several options. Although not in line with traditional Jewish funeral customs, check any (or add any) special considerations:

____ Embalming
____ Viewing of the body
____ Flowers
____ Cremation (information available from funeral home)
____ Anatomical Donation (information available from funeral home)

____ _____

____ _____

Appendix D

Cremation Statistics

The Cremation Association of North America (www.cremationassociation.org) maintains a database of cremation statistics that goes back to 1876, the year the Baron De Palm was cremated at Julius LeMoyne's crematory in Washington, Pennsylvania. A few things become clear after even casual examination.

In LeMoyne's time, from 1876 to 1884, forty-one people found their way into the retort. By 1886 that figure had more than doubled to one hundred fourteen. By 1900, when over forty crematories dotted the U.S. landscape, 2,414 cremations took place.

The startling rise in popularity from 9.72 percent in 1980 to 27.25 percent in 2001 is staggering. Put into human terms, 193,343 people were cremated in 1980. Twenty-one years later, in 2001, that figure was up to 651,176.

The data also allows the United States to compare the popularity of cremation with our Canadian cousins. It is clear that the practice is much more accepted there. For example, in 1999, the last year in which cremation statistics and percentages were available for both countries, 25.04 percent of Americans opted for cremation. Canada trumped that figure with 46.15 percent, almost double.

Maybe it's that baby boomer thing, but I was interested in the cremation stats for the year I was born. Exact statistics weren't available; the years 1949–53 are grouped together. But only 4.05 percent of the dead were cremated during those years, which meant an awful lot of people trekked to the cemetery in all kinds of weather.

HISTORICAL CREMATION DATA

	UNITED STATES			CANADA		
YEAR	Deaths	Cremations	%	Deaths	Cremations	%
1876-84		41				
1885		47				
1886		114				
1887		127				
1888		190				
1889		253				
1890		373				
1891		471				
1892		562				
1893		668				
1894		824				
1895		1,017				
1896		1,101				
1897		1,390				
1898		1,693				
1899		1,996				
1900		2,414				
1901		2,713				
1902		3,197			3	
1903		3,526			6	
1904		4,077			16	
1905		4,309			19	
1906		4,518			19	
1907		5,409			27	
1908		6,100			52	
1909		5,602			88	
1910		6,369			97	
1911		7,450			74	
1912		7,379			71	
1913		10,119			64	
1914-18		65,571				
1919-21		40,568				
1922		15,563		106,100	141	0.13%
1923		16,516		108,900	152	0.14%
1924-28		101,467		538,700		
1929-33		142,346		553,100	3,044	0.55%
1934-38	7,100,000	182,054	2.56%	554,800	4,160	0.75%
1939-43	7,048,000	226,227	3.21%	586,000	6,319	1.08%
1944-48	7,098,000	264,002	3.72%	601,000	8,375	1.39%
1949-53	7,393,000	299,202	4.05%	628,800	12,225	1.94%
1954	1,481,000			124,900		
1955	1,529,000			128,500		
1956	1,564,000			132,000		
1957	1,633,000			136,600		(Continued)

HISTORICAL CREMATION DATA (continued)

HISTORICAL CREMATION DATA – United States vs. Canada

| YEAR | UNITED STATES | | | CANADA | | |
	Deaths	Cremations	%	Deaths	Cremations	%
1958	1,648,000	58,760	3.57%	135,200	3,724	2.75%
1959	1,657,000	59,376	3.58%	139,900	4,096	2.93%
1960	1,712,000	60,987	3.56%	139,700	4,537	3.25%
1961	1,702,000	61,595	3.62%	141,000	4,891	3.47%
1962	1,757,000	63,435	3.61%	143,700	5,138	3.58%
1963	1,814,000	67,330	3.71%	147,400	5,792	3.93%
1964	1,798,000	67,658	3.76%	145,900	6,382	4.37%
1965	1,828,000	70,796	3.87%	148,900	6,906	4.64%
1966	1,863,000	73,339	3.94%	149,900	7,388	4.93%
1967	1,851,000	77,375	4.18%	150,300	7,991	5.32%
1968	1,930,000	83,977	4.35%	153,200	8,081	5.27%
1969	1,922,000	85,683	4.46%	154,500	8,408	5.44%
1970	1,921,000	88,096	4.59%	156,000	9,188	5.89%
1971	1,928,000	92,251	4.78%	157,300	9,406	5.98%
1972	1,964,000	97,067	4.94%	162,400	11,717	7.21%
1973	1,973,000	112,298	5.69%	164,000	15,880	9.68%
1974	1,934,400	119,480	6.18%	166,800	17,415	10.44%
1975	1,892,900	123,918	6.55%	167,400	20,694	12.36%
1976	1,910,900	140,052	7.33%	171,000	22,615	13.23%
1977	1,902,100	145,733	7.66%	167,500	24,713	14.75%
1978	1,924,100	163,260	8.49%	171,000	28,456	16.64%
1979	1,905,000	179,393	9.42%	170,600	30,274	17.75%
1980	1,989,841	193,343	9.72%	172,000	32,423	18.85%
1981	1,977,981	217,770	11.01%	173,000	34,884	20.16%
1982	1,974,797	232,789	11.79%	183,700	37,222	20.26%
1983	2,019,201	249,182	12.34%	184,000	41,887	22.76%
1984	2,039,369	266,441	13.06%	185,500	44,630	24.06%
1985	2,086,440	289,091	13.86%	190,500	49,216	25.84%
1986	2,105,361	300,587	14.28%	195,000	54,482	27.94%
1987	2,123,323	323,371	15.23%	197,000	53,867	27.34%
1988	2,167,999	332,183	15.32%	186,600	57,568	30.85%
1989	2,150,466	352,370	16.39%	195,500	60,087	30.74%
1990	2,148,463	367,975	17.13%	193,000	62,797	32.54%
1991	2,169,518	400,465	18.46%	195,000	66,087	33.89%
1992	2,175,613	415,966	19.12%	185,211	64,557	34.86%
1993	2,268,553	448,532	19.77%	193,557	70,017	36.17%
1994	2,278,994	470,915	20.66%	195,331	75,489	38.65%
1995	2,312,132	488,224	21.11%	210,545	79,206	37.62%
1996	2,314,690	492,434	21.27%	207,772	81,960	39.45%
1997	2,314,245	533,773	23.06%	209,395	85,196	40.69%
1998	2,337,256	563,384	24.10%	213,004	90,200	42.35%
1999	2,391,399	598,721	25.04%	222,538	102,702	46.15%
2000	2,403,351*	629,362	26.19%	229,138	N/A	N/A
2001	2,409,000*	651,176**	27.25%**	N/A	N/A	N/A

*Figure from the National Vital Statistics Report, Vol. 50, No. 15.

**Preliminary figure.   N/A = Not Available.

HISTORICAL CREMATION DATA (continued)

	Number of Crematories	Confirmed 2000 Cremations	2000 Deaths	Actuals 1996 % of deaths cremated	Confirmed 2000 % of deaths cremated	Projections 2010 % of deaths cremated	2025 % of deaths cremated
***United States	1,601	629,362	2,403,351	21.20%	26.19%	38.98%	47.55%
(5-year average compounded)							
Alabama*	21	2,141	44,392	3.23%	4.82%	12.34%	19.75%
Alaska*	7	1,509	2,863	47.81%	52.71%	64.57%	65+%
Arizona*	43	22,299	41,507	48.77%	53.72%	65+%	65+%
Arkansas*	15	3,941	28,187	10.40%	13.98%	27.18%	37.91%
California****	167	108,938	230,505	39.93%	47.26%	65+%	65+%
Colorado*	38	13,324	27,666	41.33%	48.16%	65+%	65+%
Connecticut*	25	9,002	31,177	21.62%	28.87%	55.27%	65+%
Delaware**	13	1,740	6,731	20.93%	25.85%	40.91%	51.46%
District of Columbia*	0	1,689	7,174	19.73%	23.54%	34.40%	41.58%
Florida*	148	75,634	165,524	41.15%	45.69%	56.84%	63.39%
Georgia*	30	9,910	54,431	10.67%	18.21%	65+%	65+%
Hawaii*	10	5,096	8,515	57.31%	59.85%	65+%	65+%
Idaho*	19	3,709	9,355	32.65%	39.65%	60.31%	65+%
Illinois**	69	20,950	108,201	17.61%	19.36%	NA	NA
Indiana*	39	5,474	53,573	11.03%	10.22%	8.81%	8.18%
Iowa*	30	4,548	27,727	12.89%	16.40%	27.88%	36.34%
Kansas*	16	4,451	24,676	13.59%	18.04%	34.03%	46.73%
Kentucky*	22	3,013	38,797	5.74%	7.77%	15.38%	21.64%
Louisiana*	10	4,320	41,564	7.55%	10.39%	21.45%	30.82%
Maine*	12	5,413	12,280	35.80%	44.08%	65+%	65+%
Maryland*	26	9,903	43,619	17.77%	22.70%	38.99%	51.09%
Massachusetts*	15	13,629	57,510	19.99%	23.70%	34.10%	40.90%
Michigan*	49	25,657	85,764	24.29%	29.92%	47.04%	58.99%
Minnesota*	35	11,464	37,780	24.02%	30.34%	50.67%	65+%
Mississippi*	11	1,739	27,893	4.18%	6.23%	15.92%	25.43%
Missouri*	37	8,983	54,602	9.50%	16.45%	64.56%	65+%
Montana*	18	4,058	8,042	44.26%	50.46%	65+%	65+%
Nebraska*	9	2,872	15,185	13.77%	18.91%	38.85%	55.69%
Nevada*	11	9,447	16,081	53.89%	58.75%	65+%	65+%
New Hampshire*	16	4,446	9,621	38.04%	46.21%	65+%	65+%
New Jersey*	23	17,703	75,701	19.92%	23.39%	32.92%	39.05%
New Mexico*	13	5,081	13,384	31.96%	37.96%	54.89%	65+%
New York*	43	31,998	157,484	16.12%	20.32%	33.77%	43.53%
North Carolina*	57	11,898	72,541	12.80%	16.40%	28.34%	37.26%
North Dakota*	3	718	6,241	7.35%	11.50%	33.52%	57.21%
Ohio*	64	21,921	108,054	16.67%	20.29%	31.04%	38.40%
Oklahoma*	15	4,863	34,707	8.47%	14.01%	47.99%	65+%
Oregon*	59	16,580	29,567	48.00%	56.08%	65+%	65+%
Pennsylvania*	65	27,643	130,092	16.67%	21.25%	36.25%	47.35%
Rhode Island**	6	2,458	10,142	25.63%	24.23%	NA	NA
South Carolina*	19	5,164	36,117	9.70%	14.30%	35.41%	55.73%
South Dakota*	4	1,080	7,229	10.60%	14.94%	32.83%	48.66%
Tennessee**	11	3,525	58,468	6.40%	6.03%	NA	NA
Texas*	59	24,435	151,977	12.33%	16.08%	29.02%	38.99%
Utah*	10	2,208	12,692	13.50%	17.40%	30.52%	40.42%
Vermont*	7	2,130	5,100	35.18%	41.76%	60.30%	65+%
Virginia*	50	11,057	55,689	18.13%	19.85%	23.98%	26.35%
Washington*	66	25,246	43,934	51.99%	57.46%	65+%	65+%
West Virginia*	11	1,217	21,063	5.25%	5.78%	7.04%	7.78%
Wisconsin*	47	12,108	44,844	20.83%	27.00%	48.02%	64.05%
Wyoming*	8	1,030	3,746	20.50%	27.50%	53.20%	65+%

Data shown for the "Number of Crematories" was collected from surveys distributed to leading crematory manufacturers.
*Official 2000 figure from State Health Department or similar entity.
**Estimated using official 95-99 state data and 2000 confirmed death count from National Vital Statistics.
***2000 United States death total from the National Vital Statistics Report, Volume 50, Number 15.
****California cremation total collected from the Association of California Cremationists.
NA – Cremation data is not supplied by Illinois, Rhode Island or Tennessee's State Health Departments. Projections to 2010 and 2025 are not included.

Sir Thomas Browne's "Hydriotaphia"

I find Sir Thomas Browne's "Hydriotaphia" to be the most moving meditation on death that I have ever read. Here, at the end of an existential journey, I find it a tremendous comfort to read his words.

Since it is in the public domain, I am including the entire text here for the reader's leisurely perusal.

HYDRIOTAPHIA.
URN BURIAL; OR, A DISCOURSE OF THE SEPUL-
CHRAL URNS
LATELY FOUND IN NORFOLK.

TO MY WORTHY AND HONOURED FRIEND,

THOMAS LE GROS, OF CROSTWICK, ESQUIRE.

WHEN the general pyre was out, and the last valediction over, men took a lasting adieu of their interred friends, little expecting the curiosity of future ages should comment upon their ashes; and, having no old experience of the duration of their relicks, held no opinion of such after-considerations.

But who knows the fate of his bones, or how often he is to be buried? Who hath the oracle of his ashes, or whither they are to be scattered? The relicks of many lie like the ruins of Pompey's,* in all parts of the earth; and when they arrive at your hands these may seem to have wandered far, who, in a direct and meridian travel,† have but few miles of known earth between yourself and the pole.

That the bones of Theseus should be seen again in Athens‡ was not beyond conjecture and hopeful expectation: but that these should arise so opportunely to serve yourself was an hit of fate, and honour beyond prediction.

We cannot but wish these urns might have the effect of theatrical vessels and great Hippodrome urns§ in Rome, to resound the acclamations and honour due unto you. But these are sad and sepulchral pitchers, which have no joyful voices; silently expressing old mortality, the ruins of forgotten times, and can only speak with life, how long in this corruptible frame some parts may be uncorrupted; yet able to outlast bones long unborn, and noblest pile among us.

We present not these as any strange sight or spectacle unknown

---

* "Pompeios juvenes Asia atque Europa, sed ipsum terra tegit Libyos."

† Little directly but sea, between your house and Greenland.

‡ Brought back by Cimon Plutarch.

§ The great urns at the Hippodrome at Rome, conceived to resound the voices of people at their shows.

to your eyes, who have beheld the best of urns and noblest variety of ashes; who are yourself no slender master of antiquities, and can daily command the view of so many imperial faces; which raiseth your thoughts unto old things and consideration of times before you, when even living men were antiquities; when the living might exceed the dead, and to depart this world could not be properly said to go unto the greater number.* And so run up your thoughts upon the ancient of days, the antiquary's truest object, unto whom the eldest parcels are young, and earth itself an infant, and without Egyptian† account makes but small noise in thousands.

We were hinted by the occasion, not catched the opportunity to write of old things, or intrude upon the antiquary. We are coldly drawn unto discourses of antiquities, who have scarce time before us to comprehend new things, or make out learned novelties. But seeing they arose, as they lay almost in silence among us, at least in short account suddenly passed over, we were very unwilling they should die again, and be buried twice among us.

Beside, to preserve the living, and make the dead to live, to keep men out of their urns, and discourse of human fragments in them, is not impertinent unto our profession; whose study is life and death, who daily behold examples of mortality, and of all men least need artificial *mementos*, or coffins by our bedside, to mind us of our graves.

'Tis time to observe occurrences, and let nothing remarkable escape us: the supinity of elder days hath left so much in silence, or time hath so martyred the records, that the most industrious heads do find no easy work to erect a new Britannia.

'Tis opportune to look back upon old times, and contemplate our forefathers. Great examples grow thin, and to be fetched from the passed world. Simplicity flies away, and iniquity comes at long strides upon us. We have enough to do to make up ourselves from present and passed times, and the whole stage of things scarce serveth for our instruction. A complete piece of virtue must be made from the Centos of all ages, as all the beauties of Greece could make but one handsome Venus.

---

* "Abiit ad plures."
† Which makes the world so many years old.

When the bones of King Arthur were digged up,* the old race might think they beheld therein some originals of themselves; unto these of our urns none here can pretend relation, and can only behold the relicks of those persons who, in their life giving the laws unto their predecessors, after long obscurity, now lie at their mercies. But, remembering the early civility they brought upon these countries, and forgetting long-passed mischiefs, we mercifully preserve their bones, and piss not upon their ashes.

In the offer of these antiquities we drive not at ancient families, so long outlasted by them. We are far from erecting your worth upon the pillars of your forefathers, whose merits you illustrate. We honour your old virtues, conformable unto times before you, which are the noblest armoury. And, having long experience of your friendly conversation, void of empty formality, full of freedom, constant and generous honesty, I look upon you as a gem of the old rock,† and must profess myself even to urn and ashes.—Your ever faithful Friend and Servant,

THOMAS BROWNE. NORWICH, *May 1st.*

HYDRIOTAPHIA.

CHAPTER I.

IN the deep discovery of the subterranean world a shallow part would satisfy some inquirers; who, if two or three yards were open about the surface, would not care to rake the bowels of Potosi,‡ and regions toward the centre. Nature hath furnished one part of the earth, and man another. The treasures of time lie high, in urns, coins, and monuments, scarce below the roots of some vegetables. Time hath endless rarities, and shows of all varieties; which reveals old things in heaven, makes new discoveries in earth, and even earth itself a discovery. That great antiquity America lay buried for thousands of years, and a large part of the earth is still in the urn unto us.

---

* In the time of Henry the Second.
† "Adamas de rupe veteri præstantissimus."
‡ The mountains of Peru.

Though if Adam were made out of an extract of the earth, all parts might challenge a restitution, yet few have returned their bones far lower than they might receive them; not affecting the graves of giants, under hilly and heavy coverings, but content with less than their own depth, have wished their bones might lie soft, and the earth be light upon them. Even such as hope to rise again, would not be content with central interment, or so desperately to place their relicks as to lie beyond discovery; and in no way to be seen again; which happy contrivance hath made communication with our fore-fathers, and left unto our view some parts, which they never beheld themselves.

Though earth hath engrossed the name, yet water hath proved the smartest grave; which in forty days swallowed almost mankind, and the living creation; fishes not wholly escaping, except the salt ocean were handsomely contempered by a mixture of the fresh element.

Many have taken voluminous pains to determine the state of the soul upon disunion; but men have been most phantastical in the singular contrivances of their corporal dissolution: whilst the soberest nations have rested in two ways, of simple inhumation and burning.

That carnal interment or burying was of the elder date, the old examples of Abraham and the patriarchs are sufficient to illustrate; and were without competition, if it could be made out that Adam was buried near Damascus, or Mount Calvary, according to some tradition. God himself, that buried but one, was pleased to make choice of this way, collectible from Scripture expression, and the hot contest between Satan and the archangel about discovering the body of Moses. But the practice of burning was also of great antiquity, and of no slender extent. For (not to derive the same from Hercules) noble descriptions there are hereof in the Grecian funerals of Homer, in the formal obsequies of Patroclus and Achilles; and somewhat elder in the Theban war, and solemn combustion of Meneceus, and Archemorus, contemporary unto Jair the eighth judge of Israel. Confirmable also among the Trojans, from the funeral pyre of Hector, burnt before the gates of Troy: and the burning of Penthesilea the Amazonian queen: and long continuance of that practice, in the inward countries of Asia; while as low as the reign of Julian, we find that the king of Chionia* burnt the body of his son, and interred the ashes in a silver urn.

The same practice extended also far west; and besides Herulians, Getes, and Thracians, was in use with most of the Celtæ, Sarmatians, Germans, Gauls, Danes, Swedes, Norwegians; not to omit some use thereof among Carthaginians and Americans. Of greater antiquity among the Romans than most opinion, or Pliny seems to allow: for (besides the old table laws† of burning or burying within the city, of making the funeral fire with planed wood, or quenching the fire with wine), Manlius the consul burnt the body of his son: Numa, by special clause of his will, was not burnt but buried; and Remus was solemnly burned, according to the description of Ovid.‡

Cornelius Sylla was not the first whose body was burned in Rome, but the first of the Cornelian family; which being indifferently, not frequently used before; from that time spread, and became the prevalent practice. Not totally pursued in the highest run of cremation; for when even crows were funerally burnt, Poppæa the wife of Nero found a peculiar grave interment. Now as all customs were founded upon some bottom of reason, so there wanted not grounds for this; according to several apprehensions of the most rational dissolution. Some being of the opinion of Thales, that water was the original of all things, thought it most equal[1] to submit unto the principle of putrefaction, and conclude in a moist relentment.[2] Others conceived it most natural to end in fire, as due unto the master principle in the composition, according to the doctrine of Heraclitus; and therefore heaped up large piles, more actively to waft them toward that element, whereby they also declined a visible degeneration into worms, and left a lasting parcel of their composition.

Some apprehended a purifying virtue in fire, refining the grosser commixture, and firing out the æthereal particles so deeply immersed in it. And such as by tradition or rational conjecture held

---

* Gumbrates, king of Chionia, a country near Persia.

† XII. Tabulæ, part i., de jure sacro, " Hominem mortuum in urbe ne sepelito neve urito."

‡ "Ultima prolata subdita flamma rogo," &c. *Fast.* , lib. iv., 856.

any hint of the final pyre of all things; or that this element at last must be too hard for all the rest; might conceive most naturally of the fiery dissolution. Others pretending no natural grounds, politickly declined the malice of enemies upon their buried bodies. Which consideration led Sylla unto this practice; who having thus served the body of Marius, could not but fear a retaliation upon his own; entertained after in the civil wars, and revengeful contentions of Rome.

But as many nations embraced, and many left it indifferent, so others too much affected, or strictly declined this practice. The Indian Brachmans seemed too great friends unto fire, who burnt themselves alive and thought it the noblest way to end their days in fire; according to the expression of the Indian, burning himself at Athens, in his last words upon the pyre unto the amazed spectators, " thus I make myself immortal."*

But the Chaldeans, the great idolaters of fire, abhorred the burning of their carcases, as a pollution of that deity. The Persian magi declined it upon the like scruples, and being only solicitous about their bones, exposed their flesh to the prey of birds and dogs. And the Persees now in India, which expose their bodies unto vultures, and endure not so much as *feretra* or biers of wood, the proper fuel of fire, are led on with such niceties. But whether the ancient Germans, who burned their dead, held any such fear to pollute their deity of Herthus, or the earth, we have no authentic conjecture.

The Egyptians were afraid of fire, not as a deity, but a devouring element, mercilessly consuming their bodies, and leaving too little of them; and therefore by precious embalmments, depositure in dry earths, or handsome inclosure in glasses, contrived the notablest ways of integral conservation. And from such Egyptian scruples, imbibed by Pythagoras, it may be conjectured that Numa and the Pythagorical sect first waived the fiery solution.

The Scythians, who swore by wind and sword, that is, by life and death, were so far from burning their bodies, that they declined all interment, and made their graves in the air: and the Ichthyophagi, or fish-eating nations about Egypt, affected the sea for their grave;

---

* And therefore the inscription on his tomb was made accordingly, " Hic Damase."

thereby declining visible corruption, and restoring the debt of their bodies. Whereas the old heroes, in Homer, dreaded nothing more than water or drowning; probably upon the old opinion of the fiery substance of the soul, only extinguishable by that element; and therefore the poet emphatically implieth* the total destruction in this kind of death, which happened to Ajax Oileus.

The old Balearians had a peculiar mode, for they used great urns and much wood, but no fire in their burials, while they bruised the flesh and bones of the dead, crowded them into urns, and laid heaps of wood upon them. And the Chinese without cremation or urnal interment of their bodies, make use of trees and much burning, while they plant a pine-tree by their grave, and burn great numbers of printed draughts of slaves and horses over it, civilly content with their companies in *effigy*, which barbarous nations exact unto reality.

Christians abhorred this way of obsequies, and though they sticked not to give their bodies to be burnt in their lives, detested that mode after death: affecting rather a depositure than absumption, and properly submitting unto the sentence of God, to return not unto ashes but unto dust again, and conformable unto the practice of the patriarchs, the interment of our Saviour, of Peter, Paul, and the ancient martyrs. And so far at last declining promiscuous interment with Pagans, that some have suffered ecclesiastical censures,† for making no scruple thereof.

The Mussulman believers will never admit this fiery resolution. For they hold a present trial from their black and white angels in the grave; which they must have made so hollow, that they may rise upon their knees.

The Jewish nation, though they entertained the old way of inhumation, yet sometimes admitted this practice. For the men of Jabesh burnt the body of Saul; and by no prohibited practice, to avoid contagion or pollution, in time of pestilence, burnt the bodies of their friends.‡ And when they burnt not their dead bodies, yet sometimes used great burnings near and about them, deducible from the expressions concerning Jehoram, Zedechias, and the sumptuous

---

* Which Magius reads *exapolole*.

† Martialis the Bishop.

‡ *Amos vi. 10.

pyre of Asa. And were so little averse from Pagan burning, that the
Jews lamenting the death of Cæsar their friend, and revenger on
Pompey, frequented the place where his body was burnt for many
nights together. And as they raised noble monuments and mau-
soleums for their own nation,* so they were not scrupulous in
erecting some for others, according to the practice of Daniel, who
left that lasting sepulchral pile in Ecbatana, for the Median and Persian kings.†

But even in times of subjection and hottest use, they conformed
not unto the Roman practice of burning; whereby the prophecy was
secured concerning the body of Christ, that it should not see corruption, or a bone should not be broken; which we believe was also
providentially prevented, from the soldier's spear and nails that
passed by the little bones both in his hands and feet; not of ordinary
contrivance, that it should not corrupt on the cross, according to the
laws of Roman crucifixion, or an hair of his head perish, though
observable in Jewish customs, to cut the hair of malefactors.

Nor in their long cohabitation with Egyptians, crept into a
custom of their exact embalming, wherein deeply slashing the muscles, and taking out the brains and entrails, they had broken the subject of so entire a resurrection, nor fully answered the types of
Enoch, Elijah, or Jonah, which yet to prevent or restore, was of equal
facility unto that rising power able to break the fasciations and
bands of death, to get clear out of the cerecloth, and an hundred
pounds of ointment, and out of the sepulchre before the stone was
rolled from it.

But though they embraced not this practice of burning, yet
entertained they many ceremonies agreeable unto Greek and Roman
obsequies. And he that observeth their funeral feasts, their lamenta-
tions at the grave, their music, and weeping mourners; how they
closed the eyes of their friends, how they washed, anointed, and
kissed the dead; may easily conclude these were not mere Pagan
civilities. But whether that mournful burthen, and treble calling out
after Absalom, had any reference unto the last conclamation, and

---

* As in that magnificent sepulchral monument erected by Simon.—1 *Macc.* xiii.

† *kataskeuasma thaumasios pepoiemenon*, whereof a Jewish priest had always custody until
Josephus' days.—*Jos. Antiq.* , lib. x.

triple valediction, used by other nations, we hold but a wavering conjecture.

Civilians make sepulture but of the law of nations, others do naturally found it and discover it also in animals. They that are so thick-skinned as still to credit the story of the Phoenix, may say something for animal burning. More serious conjectures find some examples of sepulture in elephants, cranes, the sepulchral cells of pismires, and practice of bees,—which civil society carrieth out their dead, and hath exequies, if not interments.

CHAPTER II.

THE solemnities, ceremonies, rites of their cremation or interment, so solemnly delivered by authors, we shall not disparage our reader to repeat. Only the last and lasting part in their urns, collected bones and ashes, we cannot wholly omit or decline that subject, which occasion lately presented, in some discovered among us.

In a field of Old Walsingham, not many months past, were digged up between forty and fifty urns, deposited in a dry and sandy soil, not a yard deep, nor far from one another.—Not all strictly of one figure, but most answering these described; some containing two pounds of bones, and teeth, with fresh impressions of their combustion; besides the extraneous substances, like pieces of small boxes, or combs handsomely wrought, handles of small brass instruments, brazen nippers, and in one some kind of opal.

Near the same plot of ground, for about six yards compass, were digged up coals and incinerated substances, which begat conjecture that this was the *ustrina* or place of burning their bodies, or some sacrificing place unto the *Manes*, which was properly below the surface of the ground, as the *aræ* and altars unto the gods and heroes above it.

That these were the urns of Romans from the common custom and place where they were found, is no obscure conjecture, not far from a Roman garrison, and but five miles from Brancaster, set down by ancient record under the name of Branodunum. And where the adjoining town, containing seven parishes, in no very different sound, but Saxon termination, still retains the name of Burnham, which being an early station, it is not improbable the neighbour parts were filled with habitations, either of Romans themselves, or Britons Romanized, which observed the Roman customs.

Nor is it improbable, that the Romans early possessed this country. For though we meet not with such strict particulars of these parts before the new institution of Constantine and military charge of the count of the Saxon shore, and that about the Saxon invasions, the Dalmatian horsemen were in the garrison of Brancaster; yet in the time of Claudius, Vespasian, and Severus, we find no less than three legions dispersed through the province of Britain. And as high as the reign of Claudius a great overthrow was given unto the Iceni, by the Roman lieutenant Ostorius. Not long after, the country was so molested, that, in hope of a better state, Prastaagus bequeathed his kingdom unto Nero and his daughters; and Boadicea, his queen, fought the last decisive battle with Paulinus. After which time, and conquest of Agricola, the lieutenant of Vespasian, probable it is, they wholly possessed this country; ordering it into garrisons or habitations best suitable with their securities. And so some Roman habitations not improbable in these parts, as high as the time of Vespasian, where the Saxons after seated, in whose thin-filled maps we yet find the name of Walsingham. Now if the Iceni were but Gammadims, Anconians, or men that lived in an angle, wedge, or elbow of Britain, according to the original etymology, this country will challenge the emphatical appellation, as most properly making the elbow or *iken* of Icenia.

That Britain was notably populous is undeniable, from that expression of Cæsar.* That the Romans themselves were early in no small numbers—seventy thousand, with their associates, slain, by Boadicea, affords a sure account. And though not many Roman habitations are now known, yet some, by old works, rampiers, coins, and urns, do testify their possessions. Some urns have been found at Castor, some also about Southcreak, and, not many years past, no less than ten in a field at Buston, not near any recorded garrison. Nor is it strange to find Roman coins of copper and silver among us; of Vespasian, Trajan, Adrian, Commodus, Antoninus, Severus, &c.;

---

* "Hominum infinita multitudo est creberrimaque; ædificia fere Gallicis consimilia." —*Cæsar de Bello. Gal.* , lib. v.

but the greater number of Dioclesian, Constantine, Constans, Valens, with many of Victorinus Posthumius, Tetricus, and the thirty tyrants in the reign of Gallienus; and some as high as Adrianus have been found about Thetford, or Sitomagus, mentioned in the *Itinerary* of Antoninus, as the way from Venta or Castor unto London. But the most frequent discovery is made at the two Castors by Norwich and Yarmouth at Burghcastle, and Brancaster.

Besides the Norman, Saxon, and Danish pieces of Cuthred, Canutus, William, Matilda, and others, some British coins of gold have been dispersedly found, and no small number of silver pieces near Norwich, with a rude head upon the obverse, and an ill-formed horse on the reverse, with inscriptions *Ic. Duro. T.*; whether implying Iceni, Durotriges, Tascia, or Trinobantes, we leave to higher conjecture. Vulgar chronology will have Norwich Castle as old as Julius Cæsar; but his distance from these parts, and its Gothick form of structure, abridgeth such antiquity. The British coins afford conjecture of early habitation in these parts, though the city of Norwich arose from the ruins of Venta; and though, perhaps, not without some habitation before, was enlarged, builded, and nominated by the Saxons. In what bulk or populosity it stood in the old East-Angle monarchy tradition and history are silent. Considerable it was in the Danish eruptions, when Sueno burnt Thetford and Norwich, and Ulfketel, the governor thereof, was able to make some resistance, and after endeavoured to burn the Danish navy.

How the Romans left so many coins in countries of their conquests seems of hard resolution; except we consider how they buried them under ground when, upon barbarous invasions, they were fain to desert their habitations in most part of their empire, and the strictness of their laws forbidding to transfer them to any other uses: wherein the Spartans were singular, who, to make their copper money useless, contempered it with vinegar. That the Britons left any, some wonder, since their money was iron and iron rings before Cæsar; and those of after-stamp by permission, and but small in bulk and bigness. That so few of the Saxons remain, because, overcome by succeeding conquerors upon the place, their coins, by degrees, passed into other stamps and the marks of after-ages.

Than the time of these urns deposited, or precise antiquity of these relicks, nothing of more uncertainty; for since the lieutenant of Claudius seems to have made the first progress into these parts, since Boadicea was overthrown by the forces of Nero, and Agricola put a full end to these conquests, it is not probable the country was fully garrisoned or planted before; and, therefore, however these urns might be of later date, not likely of higher antiquity.

And the succeeding emperors desisted not from their conquests in these and other parts, as testified by history and medal-inscription yet extant: the province of Britain, in so divided a distance from Rome, beholding the faces of many imperial persons, and in large account; no fewer than Cæsar, Claudius, Britannicus, Vespasian, Titus, Adrian, Severus, Commodus, Geta, and Caracalla.

A great obscurity herein, because no medal or emperor's coin enclosed, which might denote the date of their interments; observable in many urns, and found in those of Spitalfields, by London, which contained the coins of Claudius, Vespasian, Commodus, Antoninus, attended with lacrymatories, lamps, bottles of liquor, and other appurtenances of affectionate superstition, which in these rural interments were wanting.

Some uncertainty there is from the period or term of burning, or the cessation of that practice. Macrobius affirmeth it was disused in his days; but most agree, though without authentic record, that it ceased with the Antonini,—most safely to be understood after the reign of those emperors which assumed the name of Antoninus, extending unto Heliogabalus. Not strictly after Marcus; for about fifty years later, we find the magnificent burning and consecration of Servus; and, if we so fix this period or cessation, these urns will challenge above thirteen hundred years.

But whether this practice was only then left by emperors and great persons, or generally about Rome, and not in other provinces, we hold no authentic account; for after Tertullian, in the days of Minucius, it was obviously objected upon Christians, that they condemned the practice of burning. * And we find a passage in Sidonius, which asserteth that practice in France unto a lower account. And,

---

* "Execrantur rogos, et damnant ignium sepulturam." —Min. in Oct.

perhaps, not fully disused till Christianity fully established, which gave the final extinction to these sepulchral bonfires.

Whether they were the bones of men, or women, or children, no authentic decision from ancient custom in distinct places of burial. Although not improbably conjectured, that the double sepulture, or burying-place of Abraham, had in it such intention. But from exility of bones, thinness of skulls, smallness of teeth, ribs, and thigh-bones, not improbable that many thereof were persons of minor age, or woman. Confirmable also from things contained in them. In most were found substances resembling combs, plates like boxes, fastened with iron pins, and handsomely overwrought like the necks or bridges of musical instruments; long brass plates overwrought like the handles of neat implements; brazen nippers, to pull away hair; and in one a kind of opal, yet maintaining a bluish colour.

Now that they accustomed to burn or bury with them, things wherein they excelled, delighted, or which were dear unto them, either as farewells unto all pleasure, or vain apprehension that they might use them in the other world, is testified by all antiquity, observable from the gem or beryl ring upon the finger of Cynthia, the mistress of Propertius, when after her funeral pyre her ghost appeared unto him; and notably illustrated from the contents of that Roman urn preserved by Cardinal Farnese, wherein besides great number of gems with heads of gods and goddesses, were found an ape of agath, a grasshopper, an elephant of amber, a crystal ball, three glasses, two spoons, and six nuts of crystal; and beyond the content of urns, in the monument of Childerek the first, and fourth king from Pharamond, casually discovered three years past at Tournay, restoring unto the world much gold richly adorning his sword, two hundred rubies, many hundred imperial coins, three hundred golden bees, the bones and horse-shoes of his horse interred with him, according to the barbarous magnificence of those days in their sepulchral obsequies. Although, if we steer by the con-jecture of many a Septuagint expression, some trace thereof may be found even with the ancient Hebrews, not only from the sepulchral treasure of David, but the circumcision knives which Joshua also buried.

Some men, considering the contents of these urns, lasting pieces and toys included in them, and the custom of burning with many other nations, might somewhat doubt whether all urns found among us, were properly Roman relicks, or some not belonging unto our British, Saxon, or Danish forefathers.

In the form of burial among the ancient Britons, the large discourses of Cæsar, Tacitus, and Strabo are silent. For the discovery whereof, with other particulars, we much deplore the loss of that letter which Cicero expected or received from his brother Quintus, as a resolution of British customs; or the account which might have been made by Scribonius Largus, the physician, accompanying the Emperor Claudius, who might have also discovered that frugal bit of the old Britons, which in the bigness of a bean could satisfy their thirst and hunger.

But that the Druids and ruling priests used to burn and bury, is expressed by Pomponius; that Bellinus, the brother of Brennus, and King of the Britons, was burnt, is acknowledged by Polydorus, as also by Amandus Zierexensis in *Historia* and Pineda in his *Universa Historia* (Spanish). That they held that practice in Gallia, Cæsar expressly delivereth. Whether the Britons (probably descended from them, of like religion, language, and manners) did not sometimes make use of burning, or whether at least such as were after civilized unto the Roman life and manners, conformed not unto this practice, we have no historical assertion or denial. But since, from the account of Tacitus, the Romans early wrought so much civility upon the British stock, that they brought them to build temples, to wear the gown, and study the Roman laws and language, that they conformed also unto their religious rites and customs in burials, seems no improbable conjecture.

That burning the dead was used in Sarmatia is affirmed by Gaguinus; that the Sueons and Gathlanders used to burn their princes and great persons, is delivered by Saxo and Olaus; that this was the old German practice, is also asserted by Tacitus. And though we are bare in historical particulars of such obsequies in this island, or that the Saxons, Jutes, and Angles burnt their dead, yet came they from parts where 'twas of ancient practice; the Germans using it, from whom they were descended. And even in Jutland and Sleswick in Anglia Cymbrica, urns with bones were found not many years before us.

But the Danish and northern nations have raised an era or point of compute from their custom of burning their dead: some deriving it from Unguinus, some from Frotho the great, who ordained by law, that princes and chief commanders should be committed unto the fire, though the common sort had the common grave interment. So Starkatterus, that old hero, was burnt, and Ringo royally burnt the body of Harold the king slain by him.

What time this custom generally expired in that nation, we discern no assured period; whether it ceased before Christianity, or upon their conversion, by Ausgurius the Gaul, in the time of Ludovicus Pius, the son of Charles the Great, according to good computes; or whether it might not be used by some persons, while for an hundred and eighty years Paganism and Christianity were promiscuously embraced among them, there is no assured conclusion. About which times the Danes were busy in England, and particularly infested this country; where many castles and strongholds were built by them, or against them, and great number of names and families still derived from them. But since this custom was probably disused before their invasion or conquest, and the Romans confessedly practised the same since their possession of this island, the most assured account will fall upon the Romans, or Britons Romanized.

However, certain it is, that urns conceived of no Roman original, are often digged up both in Norway and Denmark, handsomely described, and graphically represented by the learned physician Wormius. And in some parts of Denmark in no ordinary number, as stands delivered by authors exactly describing those countries. And they contained not only bones, but many other substances in them, as knives, pieces of iron, brass, and wood, and one of Norway a brass gilded jew's-harp.

Nor were they confused or careless in disposing the noblest sort, while they placed large stones in circle about the urns or bodies which they interred: somewhat answerable unto the monument of

Rollrich stones in England, or sepulchral monument probably erected by Rollo, who after conquered Normandy; where 'tis not improbable somewhat might be discovered. Meanwhile to what nation or person belonged that large urn found at Ashbury,* containing mighty bones, and a buckler; what those large urns found at Little Massingham;† or why the Anglesea urns are placed with their mouths downward, remains yet undiscovered.

CHAPTER III.

PLAISTERED and whited sepulchres were anciently affected in cadaverous and corrupted burials; and the rigid Jews were wont to garnish the sepulchres of the righteous.‡ Ulysses, in Hecuba, cared not how meanly he lived, so he might find a noble tomb after death.§ Great princes affected great monuments; and the fair and larger urns contained no vulgar ashes, which makes that disparity in those which time discovereth among us. The present urns were not of one capacity, the largest containing above a gallon, some not much above half that measure; nor all of one figure, wherein there is no strict conformity in the same or different countries; observable from those represented by Casalius, Bosio, and others, though all found in Italy; while many have handles, ears, and long necks, but most imitate a circular figure, in a spherical and round composure; whether from any mystery, best duration or capacity, were but a conjecture. But the common form with necks was a proper figure, making our last bed like our first; nor much unlike the urns of our nativity while we lay in the nether part of the earth,|| and inward vault of our microcosm. Many urns are red, these but of a black colour somewhat smooth, and dully sounding, which begat some doubt, whether they were burnt, or only baked in oven or sun, according to the ancient way, in many bricks, tiles, pots, and testaceous works; and, as the word *testa* is properly to be taken, when

---

* In Cheshire.
† In Norfolk.
‡ St Matt. xxiii.
§ *Euripides.*
|| Psal. lxiii.

occurring without addition and chiefly intended by Pliny, when he commendeth bricks and tiles of two years old, and to make them in the spring. Nor only these concealed pieces, but the open magnificence of antiquity, ran much in the artifice of clay. Hereof the house of Mausolus was built, thus old Jupiter stood in the Capitol, and the statua of Hercules, made in the reign of Tarquinius Priscus, was extant in Pliny's days. And such as declined burning or funeral urns, affected coffins of clay, according to the mode of Pythagoras, a way preferred by Varro. But the spirit of great ones was above these circumscriptions, affecting copper, silver, gold, and porphyry urns, wherein Severus lay, after a serious view and sentence on that which should contain him.* Some of these urns were thought to have been silvered over, from sparklings in several pots, with small tinsel parcels; uncertain whether from the earth, or the first mixture in them.

Among these urns we could obtain no good account of their coverings; only one seemed arched over with some kind of brickwork. Of those found at Buxton, some were covered with flints, some, in other parts, with tiles; those at Yarmouth Caster were closed with Roman bricks, and some have proper earthen covers adapted and fitted to them. But in the Homerical urn of Patroclus, whatever was the solid tegument, we find the immediate covering to be a purple piece of silk: and such as had no covers might have the earth closely pressed into them, after which disposure were probably some of these, wherein we found the bones and ashes half mortared unto the sand and sides of the urn, and some long roots of quich, or dog's-grass, wreathed about the bones.

No Lamps, included liquors, lacrymatories, or tear bottles, attended these rural urns, either as sacred unto the *manes*, or passionate expressions of their surviving friends. While with rich flames, and hired tears, they solemnized their obsequies, and in the most lamented monuments made one part of their inscriptions.† Some find sepulchral vessels containing liquors, which time hath incrassated into jellies. For, besides these lacrymatories, notable

---

* *"choreseis ton anthropon on e oikoumene ouk echoresen."*—*Dion.*
† " Cum lacrymis posuere."

lamps, with vessels of oils, and aromatical liquors, attended noble ossuaries; and some yet retaining a vinosity and spirit in them, which, if any have tasted, they have far exceeded the palates of antiquity. Liquors not to be computed by years of annual magistrates, but by great conjunctions and the fatal periods of kingdoms.* The draughts of consulary date were but crude unto these, and Opimian wine but in the must unto them.†

In sundry graves and sepulchres we meet with rings, coins, and chalices. Ancient frugality was so severe, that they allowed no gold to attend the corpse, but only that they allowed no gold to attend the corpse, but only that which served to fasten their teeth. Whether the Opaline stone in this were burnt upon the finger of the dead, or cast into the fire by some affectionate friend, it will consist with either custom. But other incinerable substances were found so fresh, that they could feel no singe from fire. These, upon view, were judged to be wood; but, sinking in water, and tried by the fire, we found them to be bone or ivory. In their hardness and yellow colour they most resembled box, which, in old expressions, found the epithet of eternal, and perhaps in such conservatories might have passed uncorrupted.

That bay leaves were found green in the tomb of S. Humbert, after an hundred and fifty years, was looked upon as miraculous. Remarkable it was unto old spectators, that the cypress of the temple of Diana lasted so many hundred years. The wood of the ark, and olive-rod of Aaron, were older at the captivity; but the cypress of the ark of Noah was the greatest vegetable of antiquity, if Josephus were not deceived by some fragments of it in his days: to omit the moor logs and fir trees found underground in many parts of England; the undated ruins of winds, floods, or earthquakes, and which in Flanders still show from what quarter they fell, as generally lying in a north-east position.

But though we found not these pieces to be wood, according to first apprehensions, yet we missed not altogether of some woody substance; for the bones were not so clearly picked but some coals were found amongst them; a way to make wood perpetual, and a fit

---

* About five hundred years.
† "Vinum Opimianum annorum centum." —*Petron.*

associate for metal, whereon was laid the foundation of the great Ephesian temple, and which were made the lasting tests of old boundaries and landmarks. Whilst we look on these, we admire not observations of coals found fresh after four hundred years. In a long-deserted habitation even egg-shells have been found fresh, not tending to corruption.

In the monument of King Childerick the iron relicks were found all rusty and crumbling into pieces; but our little iron pins, which fastened the ivory works, held well together, and lost not their mag-netical quality, though wanting a tenacious moisture for the firmer union of parts; although it be hardly drawn into fusion, yet that metal soon submitteth unto rust and dissolution. In the brazen pieces we admired not the duration, but the freedom from rust, and ill savour, upon the hardest attrition; but now exposed unto the piercing atoms of air, in the space of a few months, they begin to spot and betray their green entrails. We conceive not these urns to have descended thus naked as they appear, or to have entered their graves without the old habit of flowers. The urn of Philopoemen was so laden with flowers and ribbons, that it afforded no sight of itself. The rigid Lycurgus allowed olive and myrtle. The Athenians might fairly except against the practice of Democritus, to be buried up in honey, as fearing to embezzle a great commodity of their country, and the best of that kind in Europe. But Plato seemed too frugally politick, who allowed no larger monument than would contain four heroick verses, and designed the most barren ground for sepulture: though we cannot commend the goodness of that sepulchral ground which was set at no higher rate than the mean salary of Judas. Though the earth had confounded the ashes of these ossuaries, yet the bones were so smartly burnt, that some thin plates of brass were found half melted among them. Whereby we apprehend they were not of the meanest caresses, perfunctorily fired, as sometimes in military, and commonly in pestilence, burn-ings; or after the manner of abject corpses, huddled forth and care-lessly burnt, without the Esquiline Port at Rome; which was an affront continued upon Tiberius, while they but half burnt his body, and in the amphitheatre, according to the custom in notable malefactors;* whereas Nero seemed not so much to fear his death as that his head should be cut off and his body not burnt entire.

Some, finding many fragments of skulls in these urns, suspected a mixture of bones; in none we searched was there cause of such conjecture, though sometimes they declined not that practice.—The ashes of Domitian were mingled with those of Julia; of Achilles with those of Patroclus. All urns contained not single ashes; without confused burnings they affectionately compounded their bones; passionately endeavouring to continue their living unions. And when distance of death denied such conjunctions, unsatisfied affections conceived some satisfaction to be neighbours in the grave, to lie urn by urn, and touch but in their manes. And many were so curious to continue their living relations, that they contrived large and family urns, wherein the ashes of their nearest friends and kindred might successively be received, at least some parcels thereof, while their collateral memorials lay in minor vessels about them.

Antiquity held too light thoughts from objects of mortality, while some drew provocatives of mirth from anatomies,† and jugglers showed tricks with skeletons. When fiddlers made not so pleasant mirth as fencers, and men could sit with quiet stomachs, while hanging was played before them.‡ Old considerations made few mementos by skulls and bones upon their monuments. In the Egyptian obelisks and hieroglyphical figures it is not easy to meet with bones. The sepulchral lamps speak nothing less than sepulture, and in their literal draughts prove often obscene and antick pieces. Where we find D. M.§ it is obvious to meet with sacrificing *pateras* and vessels of libation upon old sepulchral monuments. In the Jewish hypogæum and subterranean cell at Rome, was little observable beside the variety of lamps and frequent draughts of Anthony and Jerome we meet with thigh-bones and death's-heads; but the cemeterial cells of ancient Christians and martyrs were filled with draughts of Scripture stories; not declining the flourishes of cypress,

---

* "In amphitheatro semiustulandum." —*Suetonius Vit. Tib.*

† " Sic erimus cuncti, ... ergo dum vivimus vivamus."

‡ *Agonon paizein.* A barbarous pastime at feasts, when men stood upon a rolling globe, with their necks in a rope and a knife in their hands, ready to cut it when the stone was rolled away, wherein, if they failed, they lost their lives, to the laughter of their spectators.

§ Diis Manibus.

palms, and olive, and the mystical figures of peacocks, doves, and cocks; but iterately affecting the portraits of Enoch, Lazarus, Jonas, and the vision of Ezekiel, as hopeful draughts, and hinting imagery of the resurrection, which is the life of the grave, and sweetens our habitations in the land of moles and pismires.

Gentle inscriptions precisely delivered the extent of men's lives, seldom the manner of their deaths, which history itself so often leaves obscure in the records of memorable persons. There is scarce any philosopher but dies twice or thrice in Lærtius; nor almost any life without two or three deaths in Plutarch; which makes the tragical ends of noble persons more favourably resented by compassionate readers who find some relief in the election of such differences.

The certainty of death is attended with uncertainties, in time, manner, places. The variety of monuments hath often obscured true graves; and cenotaphs confounded sepulchres. For beside their real tombs, many have found honorary and empty sepulchres. The variety of Homer's monuments made him of various countries. Euripides had his tomb in Africa, but his sepulture in Macedonia. And Severus found his real sepulchre in Rome, but his empty grave in Gallia.

He that lay in a golden urn eminently above the earth, was not like to find the quiet of his bones. Many of these urns were broke by a vulgar discoverer in hope of enclosed treasure. The ashes of Marcellus were lost above ground, upon the like account. Where profit hath prompted, no age hath wanted such miners. For which the most barbarous expilators found the most civil rhetorick. Gold once out of the earth is no more due unto it; what was unreasonably committed to the ground, is reasonably resumed from it; let monuments and rich fabricks, not riches, adorn men's ashes. The commerce of the living is not to be transferred unto the dead; it is not injustice to take that which none complains to lose, and no man is wronged where no man is possessor.

What virtue yet sleeps in this *terra damnata* and aged cinders, were petty magic to experiment. These crumbling relicks and long fired particles superannuate such expectations; bones, hairs, nails, and teeth of the dead, were the treasures of old sorcerers. In vain we revive such practices; present superstition too visibly perpetuates the folly of our forefathers, wherein unto old observation this island was so complete, that it might have instructed Persia.

Plato's historian of the other world lies twelve days incorrupted, while his soul was viewing the large stations of the dead. How to keep the corpse seven days from corruption by anointing and washing, without extenteration, were an hazardable piece of art, in our choicest practice. How they made distinct separation of bones and ashes from fiery admixture, hath found no historical solution; though they seemed to make a distinct collection and overlooked not Pyrrhus his toe. Some provision they might make by fictile vessels, coverings, tiles, or flat stones, upon and about the body (and in the same field, not far from these urns, many stones were found underground), as also by careful separation of extraneous matter composing and raking up the burnt bones with forks, observable in that notable lamp of Galvanus Martianus, who had the sight of the *vas ustrinum* or vessel wherein they burnt the dead, found in the Esquiline field at Rome, might have afforded clearer solution. But their insatisfaction herein begat that remarkable invention in the funeral pyres of some princes, by incombustible sheets made with a texture of asbestos, incremable flax, or salamander's wool, which preserved their bones and ashes incommixed.

How the bulk of a man should sink into so few pounds of bones and ashes, may seem strange unto any who considers not its constitution, and how slender a mass will remain upon an open and urging fire of the carnal composition. Even bones themselves, reduced into ashes, do abate a notable proportion. And consisting much of a volatile salt, when that is fired out, make a light kind of cinders. Although their bulk be disproportionable to their weight, when the heavy principle of salt is fired out, and the earth almost only remaineth; observable in sallow, which makes more ashes than oak, and discovers the common fraud of selling ashes by measure, and not by ponderation.

Some bones make best skeletons, some bodies quick and speediest ashes. Who would expect a quick flame from hydropical Heraclitus? The poisoned soldier when his belly brake, put out two pyres in Plutarch. But in the plague of Athens, one private pyre served two or three intruders; and the Saracens burnt in large heaps, by the king of Castile, showed how little fuel sufficeth. Though the funeral pyre of Patroclus took up an hundred foot,* a piece of an old boat burnt Pompey; and if the burthen of Isaac were sufficient for an holocaust, a man may carry his own pyre.

From animals are drawn good burning lights, and good medicines against burning. Though the seminal humour seems of a contrary nature to fire, yet the body completed proves a combustible lump, wherein fire finds flame even from bones, and some fuel almost from all parts; though the metropolis of humidity† seems least disposed unto it, which might render the skulls of these urns less burned than other bones. But all flies or sinks before fire almost in all bodies: when the common ligament is dissolved, the attenuable parts ascend, the rest subside in coal, calx, or ashes.

To burn the bones of the king of Edom for lime,‡ seems no irrational ferity; but to drink of the ashes of dead relations,§ a passionate prodigality. He that hath the ashes of his friend, hath an everlasting treasure; where fire taketh leave, corruption slowly enters. In bones well burnt, fire makes a wall against itself; experimented in Copels,[3] and tests of metals, which consist of such ingredients. What the sun compoundeth, fire analyzeth, not transmuteth. That devouring agent leaves almost always a morsel for the earth, whereof all things are but a colony; and which, if time permits, the mother element will have in their primitive mass again.

He that looks for urns and old sepulchral relicks, must not seek them in the ruins of temples, where no religion anciently placed them. These were found in a field, according to ancient custom, in noble or private burial; the old practice of the Canaanites, the family of Abraham, and the burying-place of Joshua, in the borders of his possessions; and also agreeable unto Roman practice to bury by highways, whereby their monuments were under eye:—memorials

---

* *"Ekatompedon entha e entha."*
† The Brain. *Hippocrates.*
‡ Amos ii. 1.
§ As Artemisia of her husband Mausolus.

of themselves, and mementoes of mortality unto living passengers; whom the epitaphs of great ones were fain to beg to stay and look upon them,—a language though sometimes used, not so proper in church inscriptions.* The sensible rhetorick of the dead, to exemplarity of good life, first admitted to the bones of pious men and martyrs within church walls, which in succeeding ages crept into promiscuous practice: while Constantine was peculiarly favoured to be admitted into the church porch, and the first thus buried in England, was in the days of Cuthred.

Christians dispute how their bodies should lie in the grave. In urnal interment they clearly escaped this controversy. Though we decline the religious consideration, yet in cemeterial and narrower burying-places, to avoid confusion and cross-position, a certain posture were to be admitted: which even Pagan civility observed. The Persians lay north and south; the Megarians and Phoenicians placed their heads to the east; the Athenians, some think, towards the west, which Christians still retain. And Beda will have it to be the posture of our Saviour. That he was crucified with his face toward the west, we will not contend with tradition and probable account; but we applaud not the hand of the painter, in exalting his cross so high above those on either side: since hereof we find no authentic account in history, and even the crosses found by Helena, pretend no such distinction from longitude or dimension.

To be knav'd out of our graves, to have our skulls made drinking-bowls, and our bones turned into pipes, to delight and sport our enemies, are tragical abominations escaped in burning burials.

Urnal interments and burnt relicks lie not in fear of worms, or to be an heritage for serpents. In carnal sepulture, corruptions seem peculiar unto parts; and some speak of snakes out of the spinal marrow. But while we suppose common worms in graves, 'tis not easy to find any there; few in churchyards above a foot deep, fewer or none in churches though in fresh-decayed bodies. Teeth, bones, and hair, give the most lasting defiance to corruption. In an hydropical body, ten years buried in the churchyard, we met with a fat concretion, where the nitre of the earth, and the salt and lixivious liquor

---

* Siste, viator.

of the body, had coagulated large lumps of fat into the consistence of the hardest Castile soap, whereof part remaineth with us.[4] After a battle with the Persians, the Roman corpses decayed in few days, while the Persian bodies remained dry and uncorrupted. Bodies in the same ground do not uniformly dissolve, nor bones equally moulder; whereof in the opprobrious disease, we expect no long duration. The body of the Marquis of Dorset* seemed sound and handsomely cereclothed, that after seventy-eight years was found uncorrupted. Common tombs preserve not beyond powder: a firmer consistence and compage of parts might be expected from arefaction, deep burial, or charcoal. The greatest antiquities of mortal bodies may remain in putrefied bones, whereof, though we take not in the pillar of Lot's wife, or metamorphosis of Ortelius, some may be older than pyramids, in the putrefied relicks of the general inundation. When Alexander opened the tomb of Cyrus, the remaining bones discovered his proportion, whereof urnal fragments afford but a bad conjecture, and have this disadvantage of grave interments, that they leave us ignorant of most personal discoveries. For since bones afford not only rectitude and stability but figure unto the body, it is no impossible physiognomy to conjecture at fleshy appendencies, and after what shape the muscles and carnous parts might hang in their full consistencies. A full-spread *cariola* shows a well-shaped horse behind; handsome formed skulls give some analogy of fleshy resemblance. A critical view of bones makes a good distinction of sexes. Even colour is not beyond conjecture, since it is hard to be deceived in the distinction of the Negroes' skulls.[5] Dante's† characters are to be found in skulls as well as faces. Hercules is not only known by his foot. Other parts make out their comproportions and inferences upon whole or parts. And since the dimensions of the head measure the whole body, and the figure thereof gives conjecture of the principal faculties: physiognomy outlives ourselves, and ends not in our graves.

Severe contemplators, observing these lasting relicks, may think

* Who was buried in 1530, and dug up in 1608, and found perfect like an ordinary corpse newly interred.

† Purgat. xxiii. 31.

them good monuments of persons past, little advantage to future beings; and, considering that power which subdueth all things unto itself, that can resume the scattered atoms, or identify out of anything, conceive it superfluous to expect a resurrection out of relicks: but the soul subsisting, other matter, clothed with due accidents, may salve the individuality. Yet the saints, we observe, arose from graves and monuments about the holy city. Some think the ancient patriarchs so earnestly desired to lay their bones in Canaan, as hoping to make a part of that resurrection; and, though thirty miles from Mount Calvary, at least to lie in that region which should produce the first-fruits of the dead. And if, according to learned conjecture, the bodies of men shall rise where their greatest relicks remain, many are not like to err in the topography of their resurrection, though their bones or bodies be after translated by angels into the field of Ezekiel's vision, or as some will order it, into the valley of judgment, or Jehosaphat.

CHAPTER IV.

CHRISTIANS have handsomely glossed the deformity of death by careful consideration of the body, and civil rites which take off brutal terminations: and though they conceived all reparable by a resurrection, cast not off all care of interment. And since the ashes of sacrifices burnt upon the altar of God were carefully carried out by the priests, and deposed in a clean field; since they acknowledged their bodies to be the lodging of Christ, and temples of the Holy Ghost, they devolved not all upon the sufficiency of soul-existence; and therefore with long services and full solemnities, concluded their last exequies, wherein to all distinctions the Greek devotion seems most pathetically ceremonious.

Christian invention hath chiefly driven at rites, which speak hopes of another life, and hints of a resurrection. And if the ancient Gentiles held not the immortality of their better part, and some subsistence after death, in several rites, customs, actions, and expressions, they contradicted their own opinions: wherein Democritus went high, even to the thought of a resurrection, as scoffingly recorded by Pliny.* What can be more express than the expression of Phocylides?† Or who would expect from Lucretius‡ a sentence of Ecclesiastes? Before Plato could speak, the soul had wings in Homer, which fell not, but flew out of the body into the mansions of the dead; who also observed that handsome distinction of Demas and Soma, for the body conjoined to the soul, and body separated from it. Lucian spoke much truth in jest, when he said that part of Hercules which proceeded from Alcmena perished, that from Jupiter remained immortal. Thus Socrates was content that his friends should bury his body, so they would not think they buried Socrates; and, regarding only his immortal part, was indifferent to be burnt or buried. From such considerations, Diogenes might contemn sepulture, and, being satisfied that the soul could not perish, grow careless of corporal interment. The Stoicks, who thought the souls of wise men had their habitation about the moon, might make slight account of subterraneous deposition; whereas the Pythagoreans and transcorporating philosophers, who were to be often buried, held great care of their interment. And the Platonicks rejected not a due care of the grave, though they put their ashes to unreasonable expectations, in their tedious term of return and long set revolution.

Men have lost their reason in nothing so much as their religion, wherein stones and clouts make martyrs; and, since the religion of one seems madness unto another, to afford an account or rational of old rites requires no rigid reader. That they kindled the pyre aversely, or turning their face from it, was an handsome symbol of unwilling ministration. That they washed their bones with wine and milk; that the mother wrapped them in linen, and dried them in her bosom, the first fostering part and place of their nourishment; that they opened their eyes toward heaven before they kindled the fire, as the place of their hopes or original, were no improper ceremonies. Their last valediction,§ thrice uttered by the attendants, was also very solemn, and somewhat answered by Christians, who thought it too

---

* *"Similis****reviviscendi promissa Democrito vanitas, qui non revixit ipse. Quæ (malum) ista dementia est iterari vitam morte?"* —Plin. I. vii. c. 55.

† *"Kai tacha d ek gaies elpizomen es phaos elthein leipsan."*

‡ "Cedit item retro de terra quod fuit ante in terras."—*Luc.* , lib. ii. 998.

§ "Vale, vale, nos to ordine quo natura permittet sequamur."

little, if they threw not the earth thrice upon the interred body. That, in strewing their tombs, the Romans affected the rose; the Greeks amaranthus and myrtle: that the funeral pyre consisted of sweet fuel, cypress, fir, larix, yew, and trees perpetually verdant, lay silent expressions of their surviving hopes. Wherein Christians, who deck their coffins with bays, have found a more elegant emblem; for that it, seeming dead, will restore itself from the root, and its dry and exsuccous leaves resume their verdure again; which, if we mistake not, we have also observed in furze. Whether the planting of yew in churchyards hold not its original from ancient funeral rites, or as an emblem of resurrection, from its perpetual verdure, may also admit conjecture.

They made use of musick to excite or quiet the affections of their friends, according to different harmonies. But the secret and symbolical hint was the harmonical nature of the soul; which, delivered from the body, went again to enjoy the primitive harmony of heaven, from whence it first descended; which, according to its progress traced by antiquity, came down by Cancer, and ascended by Capricornus.

They burnt not children before their teeth appeared, as apprehending their bodies too tender a morsel for fire, and that their gristly bones would scarce leave separable relicks after the pyral combustion. That they kindled not fire in their houses for some days after was a strict memorial of the late afflicting fire. And mourning without hope, they had an happy fraud against excessive lamentation, by a common opinion that deep sorrows disturb their ghosts.*

That they buried their dead on their backs, or in a supine position, seems agreeable unto profound sleep, and common posture of dying; contrary to the most natural way of birth; nor unlike our pendulous posture, in the doubtful state of the womb. Diogenes was singular, who preferred a prone situation in the grave; and some Christians† like neither, who decline the figure of rest, and make choice of an erect posture.

That they carried them out of the world with their feet forward,

---

* "Tu manes ne loede meos."
† The Russians. &c.

not inconsonant unto reason, as contrary unto the native posture of man, and his production first into it; and also agreeable unto their opinions, while they bid adieu unto the world, not to look again upon it; whereas Mahometans who think to return to a delightful life again, are carried forth with their heads forward, and looking toward their houses.

They closed their eyes, as parts which first die, or first discover the sad effects of death. But their iterated clamations to excitate their dying or dead friends, or revoke them unto life again, was a vanity of affection; as not presumably ignorant of the critical tests of death, by apposition of feathers, glasses, and reflection of figures, which dead eyes represent not: which, however not strictly verifiable in fresh and warm *cadavers*, could hardly elude the test, in corpses of four or five days.

That they sucked in the last breath of their expiring friends, was surely a practice of no medical institution, but a loose opinion that the soul passed out that way, and a fondness of affection, from some Pythagorical foundation, that the spirit of one body passed into another, which they wished might be their own.

That they poured oil upon the pyre, was a tolerable practice, while the intention rested in facilitating the ascension. But to place good omens in the quick and speedy burning, to sacrifice unto the winds for a despatch in this office, was a low form of superstition.

The archimime, or jester, attending the funeral train, and imitating the speeches, gesture, and manners of the deceased, was too light for such solemnities, contradicting their funeral orations and doleful rites of the grave.

That they buried a piece of money with them as a fee of the Elysian ferryman, was a practice full of folly. But the ancient custom of placing coins in considerable urns, and the present practice of burying medals in the noble foundations of Europe, are laudable ways of historical discoveries, in actions, persons, chronologies; and posterity will applaud them.

We examine not the old laws of sepulture, exempting certain persons from burial or burning. But hereby we apprehend that these were not the bones of persons planet-struck or burnt with fire from heaven; no relicks of traitors to their country, self-killers, or sacrilegious malefactors; persons in old apprehension unworthy of the earth; condemned unto the Tartarus of hell, and bottomless pit of Pluto, from whence there was no redemption.

Nor were only many customs questionable in order to their obsequies, but also sundry practices, fictions, and conceptions, discordant or obscure, of their state and future beings. Whether unto eight or ten bodies of men to add one of a woman, as being more inflammable and unctuously constituted for the better pyral combustion, were any rational practice; or whether the complaint of Periander's wife be tolerable, that wanting her funeral burning, she suffered intolerable cold in hell, according to the constitution of the infernal house of Pluto, wherein cold makes a great part of their tortures; it cannot pass without some question.

Why the female ghosts appear unto Ulysses, before the heroes and masculine spirits,—why the Psyche or soul of Tiresias is of the masculine gender, who, being blind on earth, sees more than all the rest in hell; why the funeral suppers consisted of eggs, beans, smallage, and lettuce, since the dead are made to eat asphodels about the Elysian meadows:—why, since there is no sacrifice acceptable, nor any propitiation for the covenant of the grave, men set up the deity of Morta, and fruitlessly adored divinities without ears, it cannot escape some doubt.

The dead seem all alive in the human Hades of Homer, yet cannot well speak, prophecy, or know the living, except they drink blood, wherein is the life of man. And therefore the souls of Penelope's paramours, conducted by Mercury, chirped like bats, and those which followed Hercules, made a noise but like a flock of birds.

The departed spirits know things past and to come; yet are ignorant of things present. Agamemnon foretells what should happen unto Ulysses; yet ignorantly inquires what is become of his own son. The ghosts are afraid of swords in Homer; yet Sibylla tells Æneas in Virgil, the thin habit of spirits was beyond the force of weapons. The spirits put off their malice with their bodies, and Cæsar and Pompey accord in Latin hell; yet Ajax, in Homer, endures not a conference with Ulysses; and Deiphobus appears all mangled in Virgil's ghosts, yet we meet with perfect shadows among the wounded ghosts of Homer.

Since Charon in Lucian applauds his condition among the dead, whether it be handsomely said of Achilles, that living contemner of death, that he had rather be a ploughman's servant, than emperor of the dead? How Hercules his soul is in hell, and yet in heaven; and Julius his soul in a star, yet seen by Æneas in hell?— except the ghosts were but images and shadows of the soul, received in higher mansions, according to the ancient division of body, soul, and image, or *simulachrum* of them both. The particulars of future beings must needs be dark unto ancient theories, which Christian philosophy yet determines but in a cloud of opinions. A dialogue between two infants in the womb concerning the state of this world, might handsomely illustrate our ignorance of the next, whereof methinks we yet discourse in Pluto's den, and are but embryo philosophers.

Pythagoras escapes in the fabulous hell of Dante,* among that swarm of philosophers, wherein, whilst we meet with Plato and Socrates, Cato is to be found in no lower place than purgatory. Among all the set, Epicurus is most considerable, whom men make honest without an Elysium, who contemned life without encouragement of immortality, and making nothing after death, yet made nothing of the king of terrors.

Were the happiness of the next world as closely apprehended as the felicities of this, it were a martyrdom to live; and unto such as consider none hereafter, it must be more than death to die, which makes us amazed at those audacities that durst be nothing and return into their chaos again. Certainly such spirits as could contemn death, when they expected no better being after, would have scorned to live, had they known any. And therefore we applaud not the judgment of Machiavel, that Christianity makes men cowards, or that with the confidence of but half-dying, the despised virtues of patience and humility have abased the spirits of men, which Pagan principles exalted; but rather regulated the wildness of audacities in the attempts, grounds, and eternal sequels of death; wherein men of

---

* *Del Inferno* , cant. 4.

the boldest spirits are often prodigiously temerarious. Nor can we extenuate the valour of ancient martyrs, who contemned death in the uncomfortable scene of their lives, and in their decrepit martyrdoms did probably lose not many months of their days, or parted with life when it was scarce worth the living. For (beside that long time past holds no consideration unto a slender time to come) they had no small disadvantage from the constitution of old age, which naturally makes men fearful, and complexionally superannuated from the bold and courageous thoughts of youth and fervent years. But the contempt of death from corporal animosity, promoteth not our felicity. They may sit in the orchestra, and noblest seats of heaven, who have held up shaking hands in the fire, and humanly contended for glory.

Meanwhile Epicurus lies deep in Dante's hell, wherein we meet with tombs enclosing souls which denied their immortalities. But whether the virtuous heathen, who lived better than he spake, or erring in the principles of himself, yet lived above philosophers of more specious maxims, lie so deep as he is placed, at least so low as not to rise against Christians, who believing or knowing that truth, have lastingly denied it in their practice and conversation—were a query too sad to insist on.

But all or most apprehensions rested in opinions of some future being, which, ignorantly or coldly believed, begat those perverted conceptions, ceremonies, sayings, which Christians pity or laugh at. Happy are they which live not in that disadvantage of time, when men could say little for futurity, but from reason: whereby the noblest minds fell often upon doubtful deaths, and melancholy dissolutions. With these hopes, Socrates warmed his doubtful spirits against that cold potion; and Cato, before he durst give the fatal stroke, spent part of the night in reading the Immortality of Plato, thereby confirming his wavering hand unto the animosity of that attempt.

It is the heaviest stone that melancholy can throw at a man, to tell him he is at the end of his nature; or that there is no further state to come, unto which this seems progressional, and otherwise made in vain. Without this accomplishment, the natural expectation and

desire of such a state, were but a fallacy in nature; unsatisfied con-
siderators would quarrel the justice of their constitutions, and rest
content that Adam had fallen lower; whereby, by knowing no other
original, and deeper ignorance of themselves, they might have
enjoyed the happiness of inferior creatures, who in tranquillity pos-
sess their constitutions, as having not the apprehension to deplore
their own natures, and, being framed below the circumference of
these hopes, or cognition of better being, the wisdom of God hath
necessitated their contentment: but the superior ingredient and
obscured part of ourselves, whereto all present felicities afford no
resting contentment, will be able at last to tell us, we are more than
our present selves, and evacuate such hopes in the fruition of their
own accomplishments.

CHAPTER V.

NOW since these dead bones have already outlasted the living ones
of Methuselah, and in a yard underground, and thin walls of clay,
outworn all the strong and specious buildings above it; and quietly
rested under the drums and tramplings of three conquests: what
prince can promise such diuturnity unto his relicks, or might not
gladly say, *Sic ego componi versus in ossa velim?**

Time, which antiquates antiquities, and hath an art to make dust
of all things, hath yet spared these minor monuments.

In vain we hope to be known by open and visible conservatories,
when to be unknown was the means of their continuation, and
obscurity their protection. If they died by violent hands, and were
thrust into their urns, these bones become considerable, and some
old philosophers would honour them, whose souls they conceived
most pure, which were thus snatched from their bodies, and to
retain a stronger propension unto them; whereas they weariedly left
a languishing corpse and with faint desires of re-union. If they fell
by long and aged decay, yet wrapt up in the bundle of time, they fall
into indistinction, and make but one blot with infants. If we begin
to die when we live, and long life be but a prolongation of death,

---

* *Tibullus* , lib. iii. el. 2, 26.

our life is a sad composition; we live with death, and die not in a moment. How many pulses made up the life of Methuselah, were work for Archimedes: common counters sum up the life of Moses his man. Our days become considerable, like petty sums, by minute accumulations: where numerous fractions make up but small round numbers; and our days of a span long, make not one little finger.*

If the nearness of our last necessity brought a nearer conformity into it, there were a happiness in hoary hairs, and no calamity in half-senses. But the long habit of living indisposeth us for dying; when avarice makes us the sport of death, when even David grew politickly cruel, and Solomon could hardly be said to be the wisest of men. But many are too early old, and before the date of age. Adversity stretcheth our days, misery makes Alcmena's nights,† and time hath no wings unto it. But the most tedious being is that which can unwish itself, content to be nothing, or never to have been, which was beyond the malcontent of Job, who cursed not the day of his life, but his nativity; content to have so far been, as to have a title to future being, although he had lived here but in an hidden state of life, and as it were an abortion.

What song the Syrens sang, or what name Achilles assumed when he hid himself among women, though puzzling questions,‡ are not beyond all conjecture. What time the persons of these ossuaries entered the famous nations of the dead, and slept with princes and counsellors, might admit a wide solution. But who were the proprietaries of these bones, or what bodies these ashes made up, were a question above antiquarism; not to be resolved by man, nor easily perhaps by spirits, except we consult the provincial guardians, or tutelary observators. Had they made as good provision for their names, as they have done for their relicks, they had not so grossly erred in the art of perpetuation. But to subsist in bones, and be but pyramidally extant, is a fallacy in duration. Vain ashes which in the oblivion of names, persons, times, and sexes, have found unto themselves a fruitless continuation, and only arise unto late pos-

---

* According to the ancient arithmetick of the hand, wherein the little finger of the right hand contracted, signified an hundred.—*Pierius in Hieroglyph.*

† One night as long as three.

‡ The puzzling questions of Tiberius unto grammarians.— *Marcel. Donatus in Suet.*

terity, as emblems of mortal vanities, antidotes against pride, vain-glory, and madding vices. Pagan vain-glories which thought the world might last for ever, had encouragement for ambition; and, finding no *atropos* unto the immortality of their names, were never dampt with the necessity of oblivion. Even old ambitions had the advantage of ours, in the attempts of their vain-glories, who acting early, and before the probable meridian of time, have by this time found great accomplishment of their designs, whereby the ancient heroes have already outlasted their monuments and mechanical preservations. But in this latter scene of time, we cannot expect such mummies unto our memories, when ambition may fear the prophecy of Elias,* and Charles the Fifth can never hope to live within two Methuselahs of Hector.†

And therefore, restless inquietude for the diuturnity of our memories unto the present considerations seems a vanity almost out of date, and superannuated piece of folly. We cannot hope to live so long in our names, as some have done in their persons. One face of Janus holds no proportion unto the other. 'Tis too late to be ambitious. The great mutations of the world are acted, or time may be too short for our designs. To extend our memories by monuments, whose death we daily pray for, and whose duration we cannot hope, without injury to our expectations in the advent of the last day, were a contradiction to our beliefs. We whose generations are ordained in this setting part of time, are providentially taken off from such imaginations; and, being necessitated to eye the remaining particle of futurity, are naturally constituted unto thoughts of the next world, and cannot excusably decline the consideration of that duration, which maketh pyramids pillars of snow, and all that's past a moment.

Circles and right lines limit and close all bodies, and the mortal right-lined circle* must conclude and shut up all. There is no antidote against the opium of time, which temporally considereth all things: our fathers find their graves in our short memories, and

---

* That the world may last but six thousand years.

† Hector's fame outlasting above two lives of Methuselah before that famous prince was extant.

‡ The character of death.

sadly tell us how we may be buried in our survivors. Gravestones tell truth scarce forty years. Generations pass while some trees stand, and old families last not three oaks. To be read by bare inscriptions like many in Gruter, to hope for eternity by enigmatical epithets or first letters of our names, to be studied by antiquaries, who we were, and have new names given us like many of the mummies, are cold consolations unto the students of perpetuity, even by everlasting languages.

To be content that times to come should only know there was such a man, not caring whether they knew more of him, was a frigid ambition in Cardan;+ disparaging his horoscopal inclination and judgment of himself. Who cares to subsist like Hippocrates's patients, or Achilles's horses in Homer, under naked nominations, without deserts and noble acts, which are the balsam of our memories, the *entelechia* and soul of our subsistences? To be nameless in worthy deeds, exceeds an infamous history. The Canaanitish woman lives more happily without a name, than Herodias with one. And who had not rather have been the good thief, than Pilate?

But the iniquity of oblivion blindly scattereth her poppy, and deals with the memory of men without distinction to merit of perpetuity. Who can but pity the founder of the pyramids? Herostratus lives that burnt the temple of Diana, he is almost lost that built it. Time hath spared the epitaph of Adrian's horse, confounded that of himself. In vain we compute our felicities by the advantage of our good names, since bad have equal durations, and Thersites is like to live as long as Agamemnon without the favour of the everlasting register. Who knows whether the best of men be known, or whether there be not more remarkable persons forgot, than any that stand remembered in the known account of time? The first man had been as unknown as the last, and Methuselah's long life had been his only chronicle.

Oblivion is not to be hired. The greater part must be content to be as though they had not been, to be found in the register of God, not in the record of man. Twenty-seven names make up the first story and the recorded names ever since contain not one living cen-

---

* "Cuperem notum esse quod sim non opto ut sciatur qualis sim."

tury. The number of the dead long exceedeth all that shall live. The night of time far surpasseth the day, and who knows when was the equinox? Every hour adds unto that current arithmetick, which scarce stands one moment. And since death must be the *Lucina* of life, and even Pagans[6] could doubt, whether thus to live were to die; since our longest sun sets at right descensions, and makes but winter arches, and therefore it cannot be long before we lie down in darkness, and have our light in ashes; since the brother of death daily haunts us with dying mementoes, and time that grows old in itself, bids us hope no long duration;—diuturnity is a dream and folly of expectation.

Darkness and light divide the course of time, and oblivion shares with memory a great part even of our living beings; we slightly remember our felicities, and the smartest strokes of affliction leave but short smart upon us. Sense endureth no extremities, and sorrows destroy us or themselves. To weep into stones are fables. Afflictions induce callosities; miseries are slippery, or fall like snow upon us, which notwithstanding is no unhappy stupidity. To be ignorant of evils to come, and forgetful of evils past, is a merciful provision in nature, whereby we digest the mixture of our few and evil days, and, our delivered senses not relapsing into cutting remembrances, our sorrows are not kept raw by the edge of repetitions. A great part of antiquity contented their hopes of subsistency with a transmigration of their souls,—a good way to continue their memories, while having the advantage of plural successions, they could not but act something remarkable in such variety of beings, and enjoying the fame of their passed selves, make accumulation of glory unto their last durations. Others, rather than be lost in the uncomfortable night of nothing, were content to recede into the common being, and make one particle of the public soul of all things, which was no more than to return into their unknown and divine original again. Egyptian ingenuity was more unsatisfied, contriving their bodies in sweet consistences, to attend the return of their souls. But all is vanity, feeding the wind, and folly. Egyptian mummies, which Cambyses or time hath spared, avarice now consumeth. Mummy is become merchandise, Mizraim, cures wounds, and Pharaoh is sold for balsams.

In vain do individuals hope for immortality, or any patent from oblivion, in preservations below the moon; men have been deceived even in their flatteries, above the sun, and studied conceits to perpetuate their names in heaven. The various cosmography of that part hath already varied the names of contrived constellations; Nimrod is lost in Orion, and Osyris in the Dog-star. While we look for incorruption in the heavens, we find that they are but like the earth;—durable in their main bodies, alterable in their parts; whereof, beside comets and new stars, perspectives begin to tell tales, and the spots that wander about the sun, with Phæton's favour, would make clear conviction.

There is nothing strictly immortal, but immortality. Whatever hath no beginning, may be confident of no end;—all others have a dependent being and within the reach of destruction;—which is the peculiar of that necessary essence that cannot destroy itself;—and the highest strain of omnipotency, to be so powerfully constituted as not to suffer even from the power of itself. But the sufficiency of Christian immortality frustrates all earthly glory, and the quality of either state after death, makes a folly of posthumous memory. God who can only destroy our souls, and hath assured our resurrection, either of our bodies or names hath directly promised no duration. Wherein there is so much of chance, that the boldest expectants have found unhappy frustration; and to hold long subsistence, seems but a scape in oblivion. But man is a noble animal, splendid in ashes, and pompous in the grave, solemnizing nativities and deaths with equal lustre, nor omitting ceremonies of bravery in the infamy of his nature.

Life is a pure flame, and we live by an invisible sun within us. A small fire sufficeth for life, great flames seemed too little after death, while men vainly affected precious pyres, and to burn like Sardanapalus; but the wisdom of funeral laws found the folly of prodigal blazes and reduced undoing fires unto the rule of sober obsequies, wherein few could be so mean as not to provide wood, pitch, a mourner, and an urn.

Five languages[7] secured not the epitaph of Gordianus. The man of God lives longer without a tomb than any by one, invisibly interred by angels, and adjudged to obscurity, though not without some marks directing human discovery. Enoch and Elias, without either tomb or burial, in an anomalous state of being, are the great examples of perpetuity, in their long and living memory, in strict account being still on this side death, and having a late part yet to act upon this stage of earth. If in the decretory term of the world we shall not all die but be changed, according to received translation, the last day will make but few graves; at least quick resurrections will anticipate lasting sepultures. Some graves will be opened before they be quite closed, and Lazarus be no wonder. When many that feared to die, shall groan that they can die but once, the dismal state is the second and living death, when life puts despair on the damned; when men shall wish the coverings of mountains, not of monuments, and annihilations shall be courted.

While some have studied monuments, others have studiously declined them, and some have been so vainly boisterous, that they durst not acknowledge their graves; wherein Alaricus seems most subtle, who had a river turned to hide his bones at the bottom. Even Sylla, that thought himself safe in his urn, could not prevent revenging tongues, and stones thrown at his monument. Happy are they whom privacy makes innocent, who deal so with men in this world, that they are not afraid to meet them in the next; who, when they die, make no commotion among the dead, and are not touched with that poetical taunt of Isaiah.*

Pyramids, arches, obelisks, were but the irregularities of vainglory, and wild enormities of ancient magnanimity. But the most magnanimous resolution rests in the Christian religion, which trampleth upon pride and sits on the neck of ambition, humbly pursuing that infallible perpetuity, unto which all others must diminish their diameters, and be poorly seen in angles of contingency.†

Pious spirits who passed their days in raptures of futurity, made little more of this world, than the world that was before it, while they lay obscure in the chaos of pre-ordination, and night of their fore-beings. And if any have been so happy as truly to understand

---

* Isa. xiv. 16,
† The least of the angels.

Christian annihilation, ecstasies, exolution, liquefaction, transformation, the kiss of the spouse, gustation of God, and ingression into the divine shadow, they have already had an handsome anticipation of heaven; the glory of the world is surely over, and the earth in ashes unto them.

To subsist in lasting monuments, to live in their productions, to exist in their names and predicament of chimeras, was large satisfaction unto old expectations, and made one part of their Elysiums. But all this is nothing in the metaphysicks of true belief. To live indeed, is to be again ourselves, which being not only an hope, but an evidence in noble believers, 'tis all one to lie in St Innocent's* churchyard as in the sands of Egypt. Ready to be anything, in the ecstasy of being ever, and as content with six foot as the *moles* of Adrianus.†

    —"*Tabesne cadavera solvat, An rogus, haud refert.*" —LUCAN. viii. 809.

---

    * In Paris, where bodies soon consume.
    † A stately mausoleum or sepulchral pile, built by Adrianus in Rome, where now standeth the castle of St Angelo.

Endnotes

CHAPTER 1

1. David Firestone and Robert D. McFadden, "Scores of Bodies Strewn at Site of Cemetery," *New York Times*, February 17, 2002.

2. Carl Terry, in discussion with the author, February 25, 2002.

3. Ibid.

4. Joe Vargo and Sandy Stokes, "Man Accused of Selling Body Parts: Lake Elsinore: The Sales Earned the Funeral Home Owner Thousands, Authorities Allege," *Press Enterprise*, February 15, 2002.

5. New Haven Police Department press release, June 27, 2001.

6. Ibid.

7. Ibid.

8. Carl Terry, in discussion with the author.

9. "Historical Cremation Data—United States Versus Canada," Cremation Association of North America, http://www.cremationassociation. org/docs/WebHistData.pdf.

10. Duane D. Stanford, "Crematory Probe: Lawmaker Seeks to Close Loophole He Helped Open Snow Pushed for No Inspections for Marsh in 1992," *Atlanta Journal-Constitution*, February 21, 2002.

11. Ibid.

12. Carl Terry, in discussion with the author.

13. "Explosions Are a Growing Hazard at Crematoriums," Reuters, February 21, 2003.

14. "Dignity for the Body—Peace for the Soul," The Shema Israel Torah Network International Burial Society, http://www.shemayisrael.co.il/burial/dignity.htm.

CHAPTER 2

1. Chris Brown, "'The Mesolithic Is Often Portrayed as the "Dark Age" of Prehistory in Europe'—Is This View Really Justified . . . Part Two?" New Archaeology, http://www.newarchaeology.com/articles/mesolithic2.htm#_ftnref9.

2. Linda Larcombe, Virginia Petch, and Brian Schwimmer, "Eastern Plano, 6000 BC–4000 BC," Manitoba Archaeological Society, University of Manitoba, http://www.umanitoba.ca/anthropology/manarchnet/chronology/paleoindian/eastern.html.

3. Mount Hope Cemetery, http://www.mthopebgr.com/cremation.html.

4. Thomas Browne, chap. 3 in Hydriotaphia, Urn-burial; or, a Discourse of the Sepulchral Urns Lately Found in Norfolk (1658).

5. Revelation 21–22.

6. James Tabor, "Apocalypticism Explained: The Book of Revelation," PBS/WGBH, http://www.pbs.org/wgbh/pages/frontline/shows/apocalypse/explanation/brevelation.html.

7. Ibid.

8. Charles G. Herbermann and Georg Grupp, "Constantine the Great," Catholic Encyclopedia, http://www.newadvent.org/cathen/04295c.htm.

9. "History of Cremation," Mount Hope Cemetery, http://www.mthopebgr.com/cremation.html.

10. Cremation Association of North America, http://www.cremationassociation.org/html/history.html.

11. Alexander S. Golubov, "Cremation: An Option for the Orthodox?" St. Tikhon's Orthodox Theological Seminary Library, http://www.stots.edu/library/cremation.html.

12. "Cremation After Death: Christian?" King's House, http://www.kingshouse.org/cremation.htm.

CHAPTER 3

1. "Sir Thomas Browne," PoetHunter.com, http://poemhunter.com/sir-thomas-browne/resources/poet-21413/page-1/.

2. Thomas Browne, *Hydriotaphia, Urn-burial; or, a Discourse of the Sepulchral Urns Lately Found in Norfolk* (1658).

3. "History of Modern Cremation in Great Britain from 1874: The First Hundred Years," Cremation Society of Great Britain, http://www.srgw.demon.co.uk/CremSoc/History/HistSocy.html.

4. "Cremation," LoveToKnow 1911 Encyclopedia, http://85.1911encyclopedia.org/C/CR/CREMATION.htm.

5. Ibid.

6. Ibid.

7. "The History of Cremation," TABO Incinerator AB, http://www.tabo.com/History_E.html.

8. Dr. Richardson, "Cremation," Isle of Man, http://www.isle-of-man.com/manxnotebook/iomnhas/lm1p107.htm.

9. Henry Thompson, "Cremation: The Treatment of the Body After Death," *Contemporary Review* (January 1874).

10. "Interest Aroused in England," Cremation Society of Great Britain, http://www.srgw.demon.co.uk/CremSoc/History/HistSocy.html#England.

11. "Modern Cremation in Great Britain from 1874," Cremation Society of Great Britain, http://www.srgw.demon.co.uk/CremSoc/History/HistSocy.html. All other information in this chapter comes from this source.

CHAPTER 4

1. Stephen Prothero, *Purified by Fire: A History of Cremation in America* (Berkeley: University of California Press, 2000), p. 15.

2. Henry Thompson, "Cremation: The Treatment of the Body After Death," *Contemporary Review* (January 1874).

3. Ibid.

4. "Frothingham, Octavius Brooks," Columbia Encyclopedia, http://www.bartleby.com/65/fr/Frothing.html.

5. Fred Rosen, *The Historical Atlas of American Crime* (New York: Facts On File, 2004).

6. Prothero, *Purified by Fire*, p. 18.

7. Ibid.

8. "DePalm's Incineration," *New York Times*, December 6, 1876, p. 5.

9. Prothero, *Purified by Fire*, p. 28.

10. "Blavatsky's Life—A Brief Account of Her Career in This Country," Blavatsky Study Center, http://www.blavatskyarchives.com/philinquirer.htm.

11. Prothero, *Purified by Fire*, p. 25.

12. Ibid., p. 26.

13. Ibid., p. 28.

14. Ibid., p. 30.

15. "DePalm's Incineration." All other information in this chapter comes from this source.

CHAPTER 5

1. "DePalm's Incineration," *New York Times*, December 6, 1876, p. 5.

2. "Baron DePalm Cremated," *New York World*, December 7, 1876.

3. Stephen Prothero, *Purified by Fire: A History of Cremation in America* (Berkeley: University of California Press, 2000), p. 35.

4. A. Otterson, "Cremation of the Dead," Report of the Board of Health of the City of Brooklyn (1875–1876).

5. George Tiemann & Co., *American Armamentarium Chirurgicum* (Los Angeles: UCLA Biomedical Library, 1889).

6. Prothero, *Purified by Fire*, p. 42.

7. *New York Times*, November 20, 1877.

8. Ibid.

9. Prothero, *Purified by Fire*, p. 42.

10. "An Unceremonious Right," *New York Times*, February 16, 1878.

11. "De Palm's Incineration," p. 5.

12. Thomas Jefferson, "Letter to Marquis de Lafayette," May 4, 1817.

13. Prothero, *Purified by Fire*, p. 44.

14. Hugo Erichsen, *Roses and Ashes and Other Writings* (Detroit: American Printing Company, 1917).

15. Editorial, *Philadelphia Inquirer*, October 18, 1879.

16. Ibid.

17. Ibid.

18. "Historical Cremation Data—United States Versus Canada," Cremation Association of North America (CANA), http://www.cremationassociation.org/docs/WebHistData.pdf.

19. ChrisTina Leimer, The Tombstone Traveller's Guide, http://www.tombstonetravel.com.

20. Jessica Mitford, *The American Way of Death Revisited* (New York: Simon & Schuster, 1998), p. 113.

21. "Report on Cremation," *Journal of the American Medical Association* 6, no. 22 (May 29, 1886): 606–607.

22. Ibid.

23. "Cremation," St. Olaf Church Parish Bulletin (February 7, 1999), http://www.saintolaf.org/cremation.htm.

24. Ibid.

25. "Cremation Statistics," CANA, http://www.cremationassociation.org/html/statistics.html

26. J. O. Malsbury, MD, "Burial, Putrefaction, Disease, Death and Sorrow. Cremation, Health, Happiness and Longevity," *Journal of the American Medical Association* 32 (1899): 1102–1103.

CHAPTER 6

1. Fred Rosen, *The Historical Atlas of American Crime* (New York: Facts On File, 2004), pp. 131–35.

2. John D. Blagden Papers 46-0006, 1900 storm manuscripts, Rosenberg Library, Galveston, TX.

3. Deborah Sharp, "Deadliest Hurricane Began Century," *USA Today*, August 30, 1999.

4. "Historical Cremation Data—United States Versus Canada," Cremation Association of North America, http://www.cremationassociation.org/docs/WebHistData.pdf.

5. Ibid.

6. "Earthquake and Fire, San Francisco in Ruins," *Call-Chronicle Examiner*, April 19, 1906.

7. Tom Graham, "Sunday Interview, Gladys Hansen," *San Francisco Chronicle*, April 14, 1996.

8. William A. Proctor, *City Planner Report*, San Francisco: Department of City Planning, 1950.

9. Henry Thompson, "Cremation: The Treatment of the Body After Death," *Contemporary Review* (January 1874).

10. Robert W. Service, "The Cremation of Sam McGee," Focusing on Words, http://www.wordfocus.com/wordactcremation.html.

11. Robert W. Service, *The Spell of the Yukon and Other Verses* (New York: Barse & Hopkins, 1907).

12. Service, "Sam McGee."

13. Ibid.

14. Stephen Prothero, *Purified by Fire: A History of Cremation in America* (Berkeley: University of California Press, 2000), pp. 110–11. All other information in this chapter comes from this source.

CHAPTER 7

1. "Soldiers, 8 Civilians Killed," *New York Times*, March 10, 1916.

2. Fred Rosen, *The Historical Atlas of American Crime* (New York: Facts On File, 2004).

3. "Soldiers, 8 Civilians Killed."

4. Ibid.

5. "Historical Cremation Data—United States Versus Canada," Cremation Association of North America (CANA), http://www.cremationasso-ciation.org/docs/WebHistData.pdf.

6. Stephen Prothero, *Purified by Fire: A History of Cremation in America* (Berkeley: University of California Press, 2000), pp. 145–47.

7. "Fla. Hurricane USA's Second Deadliest," *USA Today*, September 21, 2000.

8. "Historical Cremation Data," CANA, http://www.cremationassoci-ation.org/docs/WebHistData.pdf.

9. Shelley Pinckney, "Race and Civil Rights: The 1930s & 1940s," http://faculty.washington.edu/gregoryj/cpproject/pinckney.htm.

10. Joel Connelly, "Turbulent Years Churned Out Lasting Leaders Spawned by the Great Depression, These Folks Put Life Back in the City," *Seattle Post-Intelligencer*, November 19, 1999.

11. Marion J. Castle, *Forum and the Century*, 1934.

12. Stephanie Muravchik, "American Ways of Death and Buying: A History of Memorial Societies, 1939–2000" (colloquium, University of Virginia, October 2002).

13. Don Shay, in discussion with the author, May 22, 2003.

14. Ibid.

15. "Historical Cremation Data," CANA, http://www.cremationassoci-ation.org/docs/WebHistData.pdf.

16. Ibid.

17. Prothero, *Purified by Fire*, p. 163.
18. Ibid.
19. "Catholics and Cremation," Incarnation Catholic Church (St. Petersburgh, FL), http://www.icctampa.org/FuneralRites.htm.
20. Terrance D. Mulcare, "Ashes to Ashes, Dust to Dust—What the Church Teaches about Cremation" The Leaven (Archdiocese of Kansas in Kansas City), http://www.theleaven.com/archives/mar03.htm#ashes.
21. Canon 1176, Roman Catholic Church.
22. "Historical Cremation Data," CANA, http://www.cremationassociation.org/docs/WebHistData.pdf.
23. Committee on the Liturgy, "Indult on Cremation," United States Conference of Catholic Bishops, http://www.nccbuscc.org/liturgy/current/cremation.htm.

CHAPTER 8

1. The Green-Wood Cemetery, http://www.green-wood.com.
2. Ibid.
3. Brit Ponsit, in discussion with the author, June 20, 2003.
4. Heather Wellman, "Neighbors Fight Funeral Home," Log Online, http://www.destin.com/news/archives/oct00/neighbor.shtml.
5. "TABO and Cremation," TABO Incinerator AB, http://www.tabo.com/FRAME_TABO_E.html.

CHAPTER 9

1. "What to Do with the Ashes," Funeral Consumers Alliance of San Mateo and Santa Clara Counties.
2. "AB 1705 Assembly Bill—Chapter 614," Official California Legislation Information, http://www.leginfo.ca.gov/pub/97-98/bill/asm/ab_1701-1750/ ab_1705_bill_19980921_chaptered.html.
3. National Transportation Board, http://www.ntsb.gov/NTSB/brief.asp?ev_id=20001212X19354&key=1.
4. Ibid.
5. Ibid.
6. Ibid.
7. Cf. chap. 7, note 21, Canon 1176, Roman Catholic Church.

8. Marcelle S. Fischler, "Ashes to Ashes, Then into the Briny Deep," *Long Island Journal—New York Times*, http://query.nytimes.com/gst/abstract. html?res=F50D1EF83C5B0C7A8CDDAD0894D8404482.

9. "Attended Services," Ashes on the Sea, http://www.ashesonthesea. com/attended_services.htm.

10. "Hazardous, Restricted, and Perishable Mail," United States Postal Service, http://www.usps.com/cpim/ftp/pubs/pub52.pdf.

11. Ibid.

12. "Ashes Scattered over the Mont Blanc Mountain Area," *Association Française d'Information Funéraire*, http://www.afif.asso.fr/francais/conseils/ conseil03a.html.

13. Peter Hartlaub, "Now You Can Go Out in Style," *San Francisco Examiner*, Oct. 3, 1999.

14. Ibid.

15. Ibid.

16. Ibid.

17. "Confirmed 2001 Statistics," Cremation Association of North America, http://www.cremationassociation.org/docs/Web01Confirmed.pdf.

CHAPTER 10

1. "Confirmed 2000 Statistics," Cremation Association of North America, http://www.cremationassociation.org/docs/Web00Confirmed.pdf.

2. Dean VandenBiesen, in discussion with the author, May 22, 2003.

3. Ibid.

4. Ibid.

5. "Alternatives to Cremation Ash Scattering," Eternal Reefs Memorials, http://www.eternalreefs.com/cremation-ash-scattering.htm.

6. Ibid.

7. Ibid.

8. Ibid.

9. George Frankel, in discussion with the author, June 24, 2003.

CHAPTER 11

1. Fred Rosen, "The Dead Wives Club" (unpublished movie treatment, 1997).

2. "Welcome to the Home Office," HM Government, http://www.homeoffice.gov.uk.

3. Ibid.

4. Donald Rumbelow, *The Complete Jack the Ripper* (New York: New American Library, 1976), p. 84.

5. "Modern Cremation in Great Britain from 1874," Cremation Society of Great Britain, http://www.srgw.demon.co.uk/CremSoc/History/Hist-Socy.html.

6. Billy Wilder and Raymond Chandler. *Double Indemnity*. Screenplay. 1944.

7. Rosen, "The Dead Wives Club."

CHAPTER 12

1. Norman Arey, "Marsh Wants Taxpayers to Pick Up Legal Tab," *Atlanta Journal Constitution*, November 17, 2003.

2. Georgia General Assembly, *Desecration of a Dead Body*, HB 1481.

3. David Randolph Smith & Associates Law Offices, brief prepared for Circuit Court for Hamilton County, Tennessee, Eleventh Judicial District, No. 02C-414, http://www.drslawfirm.com/tsc/classbrief.pdf.

4. Ibid.

5. Brief filed for class-action suit.

6. Eric Beavers, "Defense Attorneys Find Remains at Crematory," *Walker County Messenger*, June 20, 2002.

7. Ibid.

8. Staff Reports, "DA Will Not Seek Marsh Indictment until at Least May," *Walker County Messenger*, April 1, 2003.

9. Statement from Georgia Bureau of Investigation.

10. Georgia Bureau of Investigation, http://www.state.ga.us/gbi/crematory/crematory.html.

11. Charles Hand, "Judge Refuses to Dismiss Charges," *North County Times*, July 13, 2002.

12. "Attorney Says Grand Jury Ill-Informed in Bodies Case," *Press Enterprise*, March 15, 2003.

13. Jack Springer, press release dated February 2002, Cremation Association of North America, http://www.cremationassociation.org/html/press_tristate.html.

14. Senate Subcommittee on Children and Families, *Statement of Senator Chris Dodd, Chairman*, April 26, 2002.

15. Christopher Dodd, "Statement of Senator Chris Dodd, Chairman," Hearing before the Senate Subcommittee on Children and Families (April 26, 2002).

16. Ibid.

17. Ibid.

18. Federal Trade Commission, *Funeral Rule-16 CFR*, Part 453, http://www.ftc.gov/bcp/rulemaking/funeral/16cfr453.pdf.

19. Ibid.

20. Christopher Dodd, "Statement of Senator Chris Dodd, Chairman."

21. HR 5743; SB S3168.

22. Ibid.

23. "Standing Rules of the Senate—Index," Senate, http://rules.senate.gov/senaterules/menu.htm.

24. Carolyn J. Hayek e-mail to Fred Rosen, November 27, 1903.

CHAPTER 13

1. "Ted Williams Statistics, "Baseball-Reference.com, http://www.baseball-reference.com/w/willite01.shtml; AllSports.com, http://www.all-sports.com/mlb/redsox/.

2. Bill Redeker, "Desecrated and Destroyed," *ABC News*, September 3, 2003.

3. "What Happened to Ted?" SportsIllustrated.com, http://sportsillustrated.cnn.com/baseball/news/2003/08/12/williams_si/.

4. "Military Won't Cremate Infected Corpses," *UPI*, March 13, 2003.

5. Pamela Hess, "Military Won't Cremate Infected Corpses," United Press International Pentagon, March 13, 2003.

6. Isaac Parker, in private discussion with the author.

7. "Basic Information about SARS," Centers for Disease Control (CDC), http://www.cdc.gov/ncidod/sars/factsheet.htm.

8. "No sign of SARS Letup in Hong Kong," Associated Press, April 9, 2003.

9. "Basic Information," CDC, http://www.cdc.gov/ncidod/sars/factsheet.htm.

10. Ibid.

11. John Seewer, "Eight Decomposing Bodies Found in Ohio Funeral Home," Associated Press, June 20, 2003.

12. Ibid.

Appendix A

1. The Internet Movie Database, http://www.imdb.com.
2. Find a Grave, http://www.findagrave.com.

Appendix B

1. Find a Grave, http://www.findagrave.com.

Appendix C
1. United States Postal Service, http://www.usps.com/cpim/ftp/pubs/pub52.pdf.

About
the Author

$\mathscr{F}$red Rosen is a former columnist for the *New York Times*. One of the leading true crime writers in the country, he is probably best known for *Lobster Boy*, the book that Paul Dinas, former editor in chief of Kensington Books, describes as "a true crime classic." Rosen can be seen as the on-air commentator on the *E!: True Hollywood Story* episode of *Lobster Boy*. He has written articles for *Reader's Digest*, *Penthouse*, the *Saturday Evening Post*, and many other magazines.

Rosen studied at the legendary film school of the University of Southern California, where he earned his MFA in cinema. His film credits include association producer on *Pitch People*, an award-winning documentary that played many of the country's major film festivals. He currently teaches criminal justice and film at Ulster County Community College in Stone Ridge, New York.

Index